Touching the Dragon

Touching the Dragon

And Other Techniques
for Surviving Life's Wars

JAMES HATCH
and Christian D'Andrea

ALFRED A. KNOPF   New York
2018

THIS IS A BORZOI BOOK
PUBLISHED BY ALFRED A. KNOPF

www.aaknopf.com

Knopf, Borzoi Books, and the colophon are registered trademarks
of Penguin Random House LLC.

Grateful acknowledgment is made to The Permissions Company, Inc.
on behalf of City Lights Books for permission to reprint "It Means Shadows"
from *Neruda: Selected Poems,* edited by Mark Eisner, translated by Stephen
Kessler, copyright © 2004 by Stephen Kessler. Reprinted with the permission
of The Permissions Company, Inc. on behalf of City Lights Books,
www.citylights.com.

Library of Congress Cataloging-in-Publication Data
Names: Hatch, James, author. | D'Andrea, Christian, author.
Title: Touching the dragon : and other techniques for surviving life's wars /
by James Hatch and Christian D'Andrea.
Description: First edition. | New York : Alfred A. Knopf, 2018.
Identifiers: LCCN 2017045474 (print) | LCCN 2017060201 (ebook) |
ISBN 9780451494696 (ebook) | ISBN 9780451494689 (hardback)
Subjects: LCSH: Hatch, James, author. | United States. Navy.
SEALS—Biography. | United States. Navy—Commando troops—Biography. |
United States. Naval Special Warfare Development Group—Biography. |
Afghan War, 2001—Personal narratives, American. | Afghan War,
2001—Veterans—Rehabilitation—United States—Biography. | Disabled
veterans—Rehabilitation—United States—Biography. | Amputees—
United States—Biography. | Conduct of life. | BISAC: BIOGRAPHY &
AUTOBIOGRAPHY / Military. | BIOGRAPHY & AUTOBIOGRAPHY /
Personal Memoirs. | SELF-HELP / Personal Growth / General.
Classification: LCC DS371.413 (ebook) | LCC DS371.413 .H38 2018 (print) |
DDC 362.4092 [B] —dc23
LC record available at https://lccn.loc.gov/2017045474

Front-of-jacket photograph courtesy of the author
Jacket design by John Vorhees

Manufactured in the United States of America
First Edition

Touching the Dragon

Introduction:
An Emperor in My Pocket

Capture/kill raids often meant going to the target site on a dark helicopter, and leaving on that same dark helicopter. The benefit of a dark helicopter running no lights and flying just a few feet off the ground is that it's hard for the bad guys to see. The downside to a dark helicopter running no lights is that it makes it hard for passengers like me to get in much quality personal reading. So, on deployments, I solved the problem by carrying small editions of Neruda, Epictetus, or Marcus Aurelius's *Meditations* in my pocket, and when I was coming back from work in the blacked-out helo at night, I'd read the books by ChemLite.

The helo would often be full of me and my buddies, and our captives. All you heard was rotor drone, and all you smelled was ripe bodies—the captives' bodies tending to be a tad riper than ours. The loudness, the wind through the open doors, and the assembled company all made for a nice little cocktail of ambience that I found conducive to reading. I used these brief respites to gather some perspective.

Within minutes of being involved in violence, when I felt the full weight of the human ugliness I'd just seen, I reached for these writers. Their words were a balm. They helped me not lose hope in the rest of humanity. They also mitigated my self-indictment and helped me deal with my own moral flaw: I liked the violence. I liked going out to kill people who wanted to harm innocents, and I was saddened by this fact. Saddened and a bit shocked at the appetite I had for it. Reading those books made me feel less like a monster.

I started out by reading Epictetus. He said each of us is merely a tiny soul propping up a corpse. I appreciated those uplifting words. It helped me realize that I didn't need to worry too much about the fate of my corpse, which was a relief, because it was in jeopardy a lot of the time. Aurelius followed naturally in my syllabus, as he was a fan of Epictetus. He relayed the comforting insight that death is merely part of nature, so don't fear or fight it. All you can do is greet it with equanimity when it comes and, in the meantime, live cheerfully and with purpose. Some have paraphrased this as "death smiles on all of us, and all we can do is smile back." I thought about that on a few occasions. I honestly didn't believe that there was anything better or more meaningful than what I was doing. So, for me, death was never a terror. If I died in a gunfight, it would be doing something I loved. And besides, courtesy of Epictetus, I was less worried about the fate of my corpse.

For much of my adult life, my identity was almost entirely defined by being on what I call the Speeding Train—being with the crew that was essentially my family. It was intense. Fulfilling. Addictive. There was an enemy out there who wanted to hurt people, so we'd hurt them first. We were good at what we did. Surrounded by a lot of violence, we experienced clean, shining edges of time, where skill, brotherhood, trust, and purpose all melded into something that I can only describe with the word "pure." Gunfights in the darkness, on enemy turf, were where we were happy. As guys in my unit liked to say, we were "good at playing away games."

I guess, in some ways, being on the Speeding Train, at full throttle, was one long exercise in us smiling back.

That said, there were horrors, plenty of them, where the only one smiling was death. Horrors like the moments when innocent folks near the bad ones got caught up. Horrors like the Operation Red Wings disaster, where sixteen Special Operations personnel on their way to rescue an ambushed recon team were all killed by one rocket-propelled grenade to a helicopter. I was part of a group of Rangers and Navy guys sent into Afghanistan's Kunar Province to find and retrieve their charred and dismembered corpses. I remember coming home a few weeks after I'd been a part of that recovery effort. All of those body bags and the nastiness of the violence were fresh in my mind, and I had to go with my wife, Kelley, to run a few errands. One of them involved a trip to a consumer electronics store, where I was overwhelmed. The folks in the store were all looking at the same thing: fifty huge TV screens featuring *American Idol*. Totally engrossed. And it made me realize that a long-held suspicion of mine was true. In the normal world, I was an alien.

It's in moments like those that I was glad for the books. Aurelius reminds us of the importance of remaining true to our nature, and to our fellow man, in spite of the extremities and alienation of war. Remembering that despite all of the negatives and violence involved, you are fortunate to be exposed to moments where you see true human greatness in your crew. I sure did. I saw valor and cunning and unsurpassed focus. I was lucky to be part of a group that was thrust into moments where we were all removed from our normal meandering human selfishness and catapulted to a higher plane. A place where your idea of failure really had nothing to do with you. Failure was not being there in the moment to take care of your crew.

Curiously, the moments in my life where I've felt the most peace were in gunfights. Without a word being spoken, you knew what the people with you were thinking, and you knew that they had your back. You felt a seriously clear peace.

At home, those peaceful, clear moments were rare for me. So I retreated to war. To my crew. To constant deployments. This was unkind to Kelley.

I felt so at home in the one world, and so much like an alien in the other, that I started to think that the civilian world back home would never understand me, and that it held nothing for me.

This was a dangerous psychological division, but I cultivated it, even though Aurelius had tried to warn me. He made the point that even an emperor struggles. You may think you can exist in a heightened state forever, but humility comes eventually. I don't care who you are.

At some point, you will be forced to reckon with your actions and deal with harsh realities. It's true for emperors. It's true for everyone. And it would turn out to be especially true for me.

When I was shot in Afghanistan during a mission to rescue Sergeant Bowe Bergdahl, one war ended for me and another began. I'd served as a member of Naval Special Warfare for most of my twenty-five years and eleven months in the Navy. Because of our training and skill sets, and because of atypical psychological hard-wiring, people in my particular unit are comfortable and clear-headed in situations where panic is probably the more natural response. I'd always felt my ability to work and focus was enhanced, not diminished, by things going sideways suddenly. But when that lucky shot from the panicking enemy hit me, things went sideways in a new way, a way I was less well equipped to handle. I was forced to stop operating with my unit and reintegrate into a society that I had spent two decades defending, but in which I didn't feel I had a place.

Stepping off the Speeding Train caused me to lose my mind. I had almost always been an asset—to my team and my country. Now, all I could think about was the fact that I was a liability. I no longer had a sense of purpose. I wrestled—poorly—with a tough question: *What do you do when you're suddenly divorced from your calling?* In need of help, but unable to ask for it, I despaired, abused alcohol, and became suicidal. At one point, I even unfairly involved my wife in some pathetic gunplay.

It took a courageous, no-bullshit group of people who inserted and sometimes forced themselves into my life to get me to the point where I was equipped to receive help, and also to help myself. These people make up a chain that I credit with saving my life and my mind—a chain that starts with the friends in the firefight who risked their lives to save me on the battlefield, and runs all the way through the field hospital doctors, stateside surgeons, volunteers, fellow veterans, psychologists, and family that are still there for me today.

How they saved me—at war, and at home—is quite a story. People will rightly assume that I saw amazing things as a warfighter. But I saw equally amazing things as a recovering person.

In gunfights, what made us potent was not the gear, guns, and macho nonsense that movies and video games sensationalize. It was drive, professionalism, and love for each other—the same traits I saw in the segment of society that saved my life and repaired my spirit after I was shot. The difference is, the heroes of my second war will never get medals for the work they did.

So let this be their tribute.

PART I

The First War

In the Mix . . . and Then Out of It

A RASH DECISION

"That's it," I said. "Cut it off. Just cut it off."

I didn't want my leg anymore. It was held together by the metal beams and lattice work of the external fixators—mini-girders and stabilizing rods that poked into my leg from every direction. It looked like an acupuncturist had gone wild with big pins of heavy-gauge steel, and then decided to immortalize her work by locking it all in place. The apparatus was designed to hamper movement and help me heal. But all it did was help create the picture of a very damaged part of my body—a failing effort at recovery that only reminded me of my recent, epic failure in life.

This sad picture had a sad little soundtrack: the incessant whirring of the wound vacuum. When bone gets shattered, swelling typically equals healing. But heavy trauma to a limb causes your body to go into overdrive producing fluid to fight infection, and when there's nowhere for the fluid to go, your limb swells up excessively. Because this swelling can be problematic—potentially causing you to lose the limb—I had to listen to the infernal humming of that fluid-sucking vacuum all day long. The constant noise didn't stop me from frequently asking, "Hey, is this thing still working, or what?" because my leg would get so swollen that the skin couldn't be brought together, and the tracts of reddish second skin used to fill the gaps would often appear to be on the verge of bursting their flesh seams. At one point, they had to cut a twelve-inch gash in my shin to relieve pressure from all the swelling. It hurt.

The whole scenario looked hopeless, and I concluded that it would be better to just remove the limb, rather than waste more time and effort trying to save it.

And that's why I started casually mentioning to the staff at the Bethesda Naval Medical Center that I'd made my decision: I wanted it amputated.

POTATO CHIPS AND LOLLIPOPS

One week earlier.

It was July 2009. We'd been told that the deserter's name was Sergeant Bowe Bergdahl. He'd walked off his base in Afghanistan, gone into a nearby town, asked some people if they spoke English, and gotten himself captured. Now, Al-Qaida and Taliban militants were attempting to smuggle him to a part of the world where Americans couldn't go after him.

My unit was tasked with getting him back before that happened.

At the very first briefing on the Bergdahl matter, I remember telling one of the guys in my crew, "Somebody's going to get hurt or killed trying to rescue this kid." As it turned out, I was one of those somebodies.

Initially, after Bergdahl walked off, we didn't know where he was, so we had to wait for the right opportunity to present itself. It came a few days later. We were in our compound within a larger base, preparing for an entirely separate mission. When we operate, it's always an away game. We go to the enemy's neighborhood. To compensate, we like to have certain atmospheric conditions that are helpful. For starters, we work using the cycle of darkness, capitalizing on the sensory deprivation of nighttime as our functioning environment. This night, the target that we'd initially been tasked with (not Bergdahl) was beginning to rapidly lose fidelity, due to unfavorable environmental conditions, and due to the fact that it was already late, and we hadn't taken off yet. We were losing time. On top of that, the target was in a rather populated area. Typically, when negative conditions start to pile up like this, we begin asking ourselves if the juice is worth the squeeze.

It wasn't. When we hit our drop-dead time for the mission—either go or don't—we didn't. Too many negative variables. Too little time. It didn't make sense to go in.

We'd begun closing down shop for the night when a couple of our team leaders and one of our key planners, a friend and sniper I call the Fly Fisherman, were summoned to base HQ. They had a lead on Bergdahl's location. The fresh intel suggested there was a high probability that he was being held in a rural part of Afghanistan, in a village with scattered homes and buildings that looked like Scrabble pieces in the satellite imagery. It was very likely a staging point, from which the militants would courier him over the border. And then he'd be out of reach.

It was actionable information, but it came with some pretty big red flags. We'd already cancelled our other mission for the night due to time pressure and poor conditions. And our new window of opportunity was even smaller, given that Bergdahl was apparently being spirited over a border that was effectively a point of no return for us.

Nonetheless, it was pretty clear: this was our best chance to get him. There really wasn't much to discuss. We were going, no matter the conditions.

We started to spin back up, quickly. As everyone put on their gear, there was a fair amount of bitching directed at Bergdahl. We all knew that because of his bad decision to walk off base, we were being forced to attempt a rescue in a bad part of the world with conditions very much against us.

But here's the interesting thing: as we bitched about getting him, we prepared to do exactly that. Once we got the prerequisite and low-wattage griping out of our system, it stopped. Completely. Not one guy opted out of the mission or even questioned it. That kind of thing never happened in this crew. Regardless of whether any of us felt that a human like Bergdahl actually deserved to be rescued, everyone was 100 percent committed to doing it.

There was only one thing on everyone's mind: let's get this guy.

And how we'd go about doing that was largely the responsibility of the Fly Fisherman. He and the helo pilots had about ten or fifteen minutes to look at the imagery and generate a game plan. The time-frame was extremely compact. All of the work we'd previously done for the evening had been scrapped; they had to start the planning afresh. Because ours was a surgical unit that specialized in getting in and out fast, the Fly Fisherman was dirt-diving in his head, running through scenarios, analyzing the merits of primary and secondary landing zones (LZs), comparing possible routes to the target, and thinking of best ways to move.

The Fly Fisherman often played this role of lead planner for our crew, in part because he was good at it, and in part because, as a sniper, he tended to have a valuable understanding of the geography and lay-out of things. He was also a primary navigator, usually walking door-kickers like me to the objective building and getting into the mix with us, before he took up a nearby position or moved to long-range over-watch. Accustomed to (and fond of) being led into fights by him, I knew exactly how he walked, and if you tried to hide him in a mass of pedestrians, I'd still be able to get low, look at the sea of legs, and pick out his gait.

The drop-dead point came, and this time we were a go.

It was roughly a thirty-five-minute flight to the target. The Fly Fish-erman and I were on different birds. He was in his usual position, sitting on the open back ramp, plugged in to the pilot's comms, so that he could conduct further planning with senior leadership en route. The Fly Fisherman often points out that our unit had two primary strengths: tactics and communication. When we perform in those two departments, things work. And while that was absolutely true on the ground, it was different in the helo. Shooters like me weren't always part of the communications in the helicopters, and that was the case this night. We weren't plugged into comms, and we couldn't hear much of anything over the rotor drone. That meant we could spend the time in our heads, getting ready.

As our helicopters approached the target set, I had a small matter that needed resolving before I could go into the mission clearheaded. I was still angry at Bergdahl, because it was a genuinely bad night for a gunfight. The atmospheric conditions were extraordinarily poor, far from what we would typically choose to use. This kid was putting all of us—my buddies and the helo crews—at risk.

But I also didn't want Bergdahl's mom to see the YouTube video that Daniel Pearl's mom had to see. That gave me clarity, as did thinking about the bigger picture. I'd been told that Bergdahl had done something foolish, yes, but I also knew it was better to get ahold of him, rather than have the other side torture and decapitate him, or keep him alive and use him as a political pawn. We'd get him back, and deny the enemy those options.

But there was another reason we'd get him back, another reason our hearts were in sync with what we were about to do. We'd go fight and possibly get hurt trying to retrieve Bergdahl, because we're Americans, and we get you. Even when you do something extremely stupid.

The intel had a pretty good fix on the location. But what the intel couldn't tell us was the kind of resistance we'd experience when we got there. I presumed they'd be heavy-hitters, because they had just captured an American soldier, and he'd be worth quite a bit in terms of political leverage, and as a symbol. So I figured the people guarding him would not be ragtag, amateur-hour jihadis.

They weren't.

As we got close, listening to the time hacks—two minutes out, one minute out—the Fly Fisherman took a position beside the door gunners on their mini-guns, and stuck his head out the window to get a visual on the primary LZ. What he saw wasn't good. Both helicopters were starting to flare, and even though we were being delivered by the best helicopter pilots on the planet, there's nothing you can do to prevent that moment from being essentially the most dangerous on any mission. It's a baked-in, guaranteed, worst-case scenario. You slow down. You kick up a dust cloud. You present unmissable visual and sound signatures. All of which makes you get noticed.

And we certainly were, that night. As the Fly Fisherman navigated and helped steer both helicopters in, he saw men on the ground get off a rocket-propelled grenade (RPG), which sailed past his inbound helo and detonated in the field beyond. He also saw incoming tracer fire from small mud hut structures. One of the mud huts, in particular, seemed to be doing a bang-up job of pouring tracer fire right into the open back ramp of the other helo, sort of like roman candle sparks being sent back inside the tube.

I was on that other helo. I didn't know about the near-miss RPG that the Fly Fisherman had tracked. We weren't on the ground yet, so it was too loud for me inside the aircraft to hear the RPG's detonation nearby. But I did see the tracer fire through the open back. Although from the Fly Fisherman's point of view this fire appeared to be funneling itself into our helicopter, it actually wasn't. These folks on the ground, despite being in the upper echelon of enemy combatants, generally sucked at shooting.

Our helos touched down. After disembarking, and while the rest of us were still getting off the helos, the first thing the Fly Fisherman did was move with a group of guys toward that one particularly troublesome hut, which had a single small window and a couple of guys shooting out the doorway on its backside. Now that we, as targets, were no longer airborne, their aim was improving. This small unit of enemy combatants had a perfect bead on our aircraft, which had landed a couple hundred meters away from the Fly Fisherman's, and they were energetically pouring tracer fire into it, and us.

They weren't the only ones. From the moment we got off the helicopters, we were under heavy belt-fed machine-gun fire and RPG attacks from scattered pockets of fighters, all less than one hundred meters away. Streams of tracer bullets that looked like flaming beer cans whizzed by my head—emerging suddenly, and at all angles, from the swirling brown dust clouds. It was pretty clear to me that these guys were the best the other side had (proving the point about what a high-value catch Bergdahl was).

We had zero element of surprise. Most of us guessed that an early warning network, laced throughout nearby villages, had heard us approach, giving these combatants probably five or ten minutes to set up and prep their weapons, which were turning out to be formidable.

The first thing I wanted to do was move south, but we were hemmed in by a proximate line of fire. My tactical boss was with the Fly Fisherman's group, so I held up and waited while he dealt with the hut and its welcoming committee.

The upside to a hostile, located enemy is that objectives become clear. There's no need for the fuzziness of diplomacy. The Fly Fisherman's group was not preparing the terms of a peace treaty, just the angles of an assault. Having rushed up to the hut, while staying in what he hoped was their blind spot, one of the guys got on the window and dealt the men inside a serious blow.

The fire from the hut stopped.

But the rest of it from everywhere else didn't. Over the noise of the helos, which were still roaring, I could hear that our guys were getting busy, engaging the enemy close. It had been maybe fifteen seconds since we landed, and I was impatient. Up to that point, I'd been functioning according to two useful precepts that applied in these kinds of fights: (A) If you are hemmed in by a solid line of withering fire, don't run through it, especially if dudes somewhere else are handling it, and (B) while those dudes are handling it, you take it on faith that they've got it covered, because if they don't they will call for you.

Nobody had called. And I'd heard the hut's guns go quiet. So I broke the silence and reached out on the radio, asking if we were clear. We were. The Fly Fisherman's guys mopped up the hut and its environs.

Because people in the area were scattered and running, some in pairs or small groups, and some individually, we needed to split our forces and spread out to cover as much of the circus as possible. The occupants of my helo separated into two groups right away. Shortly afterward, I'd end up splitting my smaller group a second time, in order to deal with the chaos. This is the cell division of firefights; it's how we multiply.

As we seeped into the farmland dotted with structures, the Fly Fisherman's group moved in a very different direction from the handful of guys I was with.

Our first objectives were to move and get separation between ourselves and the helos, and then start searching the buildings. Because we didn't know where they were keeping Bergdahl, we had to clear them all. One by one. The buildings were single-story, made of mud packed with hay—very old and very strong. They'd been around for hundreds of years. And from the moment the gunfight had begun, a lot of people were streaming out of them—mostly women and children looking for a safe place to hide. The enemy used this to their advantage, shielding themselves among the noncombatants as they tried to flee. It was clear from the reckless way the enemy sprayed their fire that they had no regard for the safety of the innocents.

For about twenty minutes, our forces were split up and engaged in several different firefights spread out over a swath of dusty and agrarian terrain about 1,500 meters wide. It was mostly flat, despite the fact that we were at a fairly high altitude, and it included parts of the village itself, plus some of the surrounding fields where they grew poppies for heroin.

Because it was midsummer, the big, half-inch-thick poppy stalks were no longer green and no longer crowned with seed pods. That presented a problem. It meant the thigh-high stalks were dry. So as we maneuvered through them during various phases of the fight, our footsteps made loud crunching sounds. Like walking on potato chips.

That made it easier for the enemy to hear us.

It was also dusty. In Afghanistan, it was always dusty. Even with the helicopters gone, there was still a nice cloud of fine particles hanging in the air, kicked up by the scattershot melees happening all over this strange tract of sporadically inhabited farmland.

Luckily, we had some good techno on our guns, which helped us see bodies through the dust . . . and through other visual impairments. In short order, the Fly Fisherman and another guy found themselves chasing two enemy combatants who were trying to escape on a motorcycle into a field dotted with haystacks. They were able to drop the passenger, who was shooting at them wildly, off the back of the bike, but the driver disappeared, after scuttling the cycle. Closing in on where the bike had gone down, the Fly Fisherman was still receiving fire, and he couldn't figure out its source, until he deciphered some environmental clues that revealed where the driver was hiding, amid the clumps of hay.

That episode pulled the Fly Fisherman pretty far from where I was, compounding the spreading effect that was turning this into a battle of widely dispersed pockets.

Having split the second time into our smaller cell, my team now consisted of a dog handler and senior chief master-at-arms that I've nicknamed the Texan, his dog, Remco, plus a shooter we called Mr. Clean, because his gear and domiciles were always shipshape.

At one point, as we moved in on new clusters of enemy fighters, I could see there were people in a ditch ahead to my right as I ran. I couldn't tell who they were. All I could see were dark shapes. We had been getting engaged a fair amount from covered positions, so the assumption was that this could very well be more of the same.

Continuing to move forward, without breaking stride, the Texan sent the dog, Remco, ahead to reconnoiter. Remco rushed the figures, but then did something he didn't normally do: he stopped short. He was right next to the bodies in the ditch, but he wouldn't attack. Instead of the intense engagement the dog was known for, Remco just nipped the shoulder of one of the figures.

That nip was significant.

As I approached the figures, I saw that there were three scared children—a little boy, a little girl, and a teenage girl, who was the one the dog had nipped on the shoulder. Remco had known not to hurt her. It was something I'd seen many times—dogs distinguishing between military-age males (MAMs) and children.

These children looked at us like we were aliens. They were so frightened. Their own people had been shooting wildly. They'd heard helicopters and seen the adults scramble. And now they were on their own in this little pocket of what must have been insanity to them.

I needed to get them to where they wouldn't be hit—by their own wildly spraying people, or by the more focused fire of ours. I quickly bundled the children together and scooted them away into a nearby field, and then employed a technique that allowed the kids to be seen from the sky by the aircraft circling above. Basically, what I did identified the children as friendlies, so that our air support would know to leave these bodies alone, and know that they were not a threat.

My life was getting ready to change in a significant way. Five minutes later, I'd be lying on the ground, shot through the leg. And my own mistakes, plus the accumulation of death and ugliness I'd been a part of, would, over the coming years, almost overwhelm me.

But in that moment, where I was wrapping those kids in my arms and putting them in an improvised cocoon that said "Don't touch," I experienced a quick, small flash of redemption—the kind we felt when innocents were spared.

With the kids safely sequestered, my attention turned to a group of unknown people moving in another field, a long way off. The figures were shadowy, blurring into some taller reeds and brush that were mixed in with the poppy stalks. Even so, I could make out some traits that suggested these people were not standard villagers. They were toting bulky objects that looked like heavy equipment, and they were walking, while most everyone else in the vicinity was running. They became my focus.

Then they disappeared.

Was one of those figures Bergdahl? In order to find out, we had two options: either wait for them to re-emerge and approach us, or close on them. And the first option—waiting—was not something I was typically interested in, because when you let the other side make the decision, you give them power over you.

In my mind, there's a basic rule of conduct in this kind of gunfight: Be aggressive. Hostage-rescue missions are extremely tough. You can't just hold back and shoot from a hundred yards away when there's a hostage. You have to get in there, but at the same time, you have to figure out "who's who in the zoo" before you start shooting. Above all, you have to be fast, because that's what wins it. Aggressiveness.

That's what I was thinking as I made the decision to advance on the now-unseen specters, and bring the Texan, Mr. Clean, and the dog with me. Some folks might debate whether rushing at them was the right call, but I was clear in my mind. We couldn't mess around. If we did, they might kill the kid, Bergdahl.

I turned to my small team and said, "Let's go."

I knew Mr. Clean was ready, without having to look at him. But I did take a few seconds to scan the new members in our small band— the Texan and Remco, who were close together, on my left. This was the Texan's first gunfight, and it happened to be a heavy one. On top of that, the unlucky fellow found himself buddied up with one of the guys in the unit known for being aggressive (me), and I was inviting him to participate in something that must have seemed less than palatable: a quick advance over open ground toward unknowns in a dark zone flecked with gunfire.

Still, he nodded. Not enthusiastically, but enough for me to know where his heart was. Good.

I turned to Remco. This was also his first gunfight, and so far, he'd been extremely amped up. But the moment I said "Let's go," he changed. Now he was calm, breathing placidly, and staring with a level gaze at the Texan. This gaze was eerie for a number of reasons, the main one being that I recognized it. I'd seen that same look before, in other working dogs—an attempt to intuitively transmit meaning through the eyes, just prior to something big. I think Remco sensed what was about to happen.

We took off.

Remco trotted out in front of us, quickly stretching his lead to fifteen feet. As I moved, I watched the dog because I couldn't see the equipment-toting humans at all anymore, and I knew that Remco's body language would announce their location as we came closer. His four-legged frame quickly homed in on something, and he started moving with a purpose and vector that told us the tale: the shadow people were close, lying low in a ditch, in an area where the crunchy poppy stalks amplified every footfall of both the approaching dog and me.

The soles of my leather personnel carriers were betraying me. I was certain that the concealed men could hear us. Another reason to move and act fast.

We kept charging, even though I still couldn't see anyone. Remco picked up speed and focused his charge on a certain part of the dark ditch. The Texan, Mr. Clean, and I picked up speed, too, rushing after Remco.

In these situations, the dog buys you a few seconds of advantage, which can be game-changing when you're getting ready to engage people. Especially these kinds of people. Like other heavy-duty guys we'd encountered, these guys were wearing quick-rig suicide vests. On the sides, in pouches, they had grenades with the pins pulled, so all they had to do was ease them out of the pouch and they'd detonate.

This time, the few seconds that the dog might buy us would be critical, because even as we got within forty feet, we still couldn't see the men.

We only saw them when we closed within twenty feet and one of them shot Remco in the face.

Etched on my hard drive is the sight of the two rounds going into Remco, and the shocks of the bullets lifting him a bit, and pushing him back and then straight down. His trajectory backward was bizarre—a kinetics-defying right angle, back and down, not an arc, like you'd expect. And it was quick.

The sound and muzzle flash from the shooter's weapon revealed his location. I kept rushing him, put my laser on his face, and pumped bullets into it. In the moments after his muzzle flash outlined him, I acquired a good enough sight picture of his head to know that he wasn't an American and that he didn't have noncombatants with him, so it was OK to fill him in.

I saw the bullets hit. He was in the ditch, firing on his knees, and as my rounds impacted his face from fifteen feet away, it looked like he was unable to function, and dying. And yet he was not dropping. I wanted him to go down, but he wasn't—a by-product of the small rounds I was using. The consolation was that I don't think he got off any other shots.

As I continued running, I stepped forward on my right leg and then—wham—something went through my femur, and the leg completely collapsed on me. I'd been shot by a second man in the ditch, a panicking guy wildly firing his AK-47 under the pressure of our assault.

I went down. On my way to the ground, I felt the searing heat that my buddies who'd been shot before had described, and I was confused as to why my leg gave way. It was hard to process, like an earthquake is hard to process, because a stable earth is something we take as a given. Same with the leg. Something I'd relied on my entire life, part of my structure, just went away. Disoriented and in pain (I wasn't nearly as tough as I thought I'd be if I were ever shot), I could nonetheless tell that the guy who just shot me was now also throwing grenades, because I heard the *boom* of them going off nearby, followed by the sound of shrapnel—millimeter-sized meat-shredders—slinging through the reeds between me and the explosion.

The Texan—who was in charge of, and loved, Remco—went into a different realm after his dog was shot. In a moment of sudden and strange quiet, I could distinctly hear the crunch-crunch of the Texan walking straight toward the enemy position (about fifteen feet from where I was shot). Mr. Clean joined him. They were fearless. They finally closed to within a few feet of the entrenched enemy, and shot the surviving fighter, face-to-face. Miraculously, Mr. Clean and the Texan did not get hit, despite the fact that the enemy attacker had been unloading his AK and throwing grenades in their direction.

I could hear the gunfire and the groans of the downed enemy combatants as they circled the drain, struggling in vain to muster just that last bit of life force that would allow them to trigger their quick-rigs. But then, for me, all other sounds were quickly drowned out by a new, dominant noise: my own screaming.

And that scream signaled a major shift in the mission. The moment I got hurt, the whole dynamic of the battle space changed, because now my crew had to deal with me, and they had to move from where they were fighting to come save me. I put my crew at risk, because I got hit. I harbor a lot of guilt because of that.

Later, a friend from my unit would take me aside and say, "Hey, man, I don't want to be negative, but it was just a matter of time before you got hit, because you always just *ran at it*."

But that only makes me think, *Well, I didn't run fast enough.*

In my next war, the one with myself, the psychs made me *touch the dragon*. That's the name I gave to what the professionals call cognitive behavioral therapy. I had to identify the single thing that most violently upset me and knocked me off-kilter when it played across the screen in my mind. And what was it? It was the set of decisions I'd made that led to the moment where Remco was shot in the face and I was shot in the leg.

It got to the point where I was drowning in regret over Remco, and how I'd endangered my team by making them have to medevac me. I was so self-absorbed and fixated on that bad outcome, tangled up in thoughts of what I did versus what I should have done, that I could no longer see things rationally. That mission was, to me, a failure, and whether it was true or not, I held myself responsible. Still do.

So I had to touch the dragon. And that meant revisiting the episode and writing it down, over and over, on a pad of paper, until I realized it wasn't going to burn me, and I could start to reflect with some clarity on what the circumstances had actually been and how they affected the decisions I'd made. I'd put myself in a box, a coffin of condemnation, and this process was the first thing that started to get me outside of it.

After going over and over it, based on the information I had at the time, and based on what I'd learned in experiences with dogs in previous deployments, I knew I would do it the same way again. I'd rush the enemy with Mr. Clean, the Texan, and Remco. Because that's what worked.

Being aggressive was my operating principle, and I believe it was right. There are those who disagree with my take. Even in my own organization. I understand why. But you have to act. If you let other people decide the parameters of the bargain, then you get a bad deal. But if you initiate that transaction, then you have a little bit of an advantage. There was no way I was going to sit around waiting for those fuckers. And this turns out to have been a good policy, based on what our side discovered afterward. The enemy in the ditch was setting up to bring some hate. They were prepping rockets. The bulky shapes I'd seen them carrying were RPGs. If we hadn't struck them first, it would have been really bad for us.

I did not want any of those people to have the upper hand. Ever. And to me that meant being aggressive. Always. The way I look at it, if I'm aggressive, then everybody on my team goes home.

There is only one thing that I wish was different that night: I wish I'd been faster.

THE CUSTOMER

I think it's worth going into some detail about what happened in the minutes after I was shot. They're extraordinary minutes.

I'd been running, and the bullet hit me with so much energy from the front, above the knee, that it shoved my lower half backward, while my torso obeyed inertia and moved forward, flipping me into the beginnings of a somersault. I executed the landing poorly, and ended up facedown, on my chest.

The problem was that I couldn't move. I knew I had to tourniquet myself. But every time I moved, my femur twisted, and my femur was shattered. It was excruciating. I screamed. Responding, Mr. Clean came up to me, and I told him, "Hey, man, I can't put my tourniquet on." My tourniquet was attached to the front of my gear, which meant it was crushed between my chest and the dirt, unreachable because I couldn't move off of my chest.

Feeling stuck—and like my leg was on fire—I reverted to screaming, even though I hated myself for it. There were two reasons I didn't want to make noise. One, I didn't want to get shot at anymore, and noise is basically a target-assist for the enemy. Two, I hated making noise because it was shameful to scream.

At the time, I didn't quite realize that something profound was happening. Not just a shift in the mission. But a seismic shift in my life. It took years to figure out what it was. And here's how I see it now: at this particular point, in an instant, I went from being an Action Man to being a helpless—and, I would later realize, quite fortunate—spectator. A spectator who got to observe the human spirit, on display in others.

But all I knew at the time was that I wanted my screaming to stop as badly as I wanted the pain to stop. Maybe more. Ego is powerful. So I asked Mr. Clean to put his own tourniquet on my leg. And he did. But as he was tightening it, the pain intensified, and I intervened, saying, "That's tight enough." Mr. Clean was something special, but he was not a professional medic, and it was dark and there was gunfire and I was bleeding and screaming. The pressures he was facing were considerable. The moment I was shot, he'd just become the head guy in that tactical situation. So he had to manage the team and the operation. Plus, he had to stop my bleeding. Plus, he had to help the Texan as he dealt with his dog. Plus, he had to not get shot.

I remember telling Mr. Clean, "Hey, get a grid [GPS coordinates], and tell the good guys where we're at, so we can get a medevac in here soon, because I will bleed to death." Just one more thing he had to worry about.

Unbeknownst to me, because my screaming had been captured on the radio, two other guys from my unit were leaving other parts of the target set and sprinting toward me to help.

One was the Fly Fisherman. And I try to imagine his mindset. He was in a gunfight, with a lot of chaos enveloping him where he was, and now, adding to the pressures, he heard screaming over the radio. The screaming was not readily discernible, because I was howling out "I'M HIT" along with something more muddled—a word that most folks couldn't recognize at the time, and the identity of which I would only recall later. But when he heard "Man down" along with my call sign, which was given by someone else, he knew it was me. He assessed his own situation, judged that his team had things somewhat contained, and then told his partner, "Hey, I'm going over there to help."

"Yeah, OK," was the response.

One small problem was that he didn't know where I was. Over the radio, he asked Mr. Clean, who was next to me, to use a technique with his equipment that would allow him to see where we were, in the dark. It worked. The Fly Fisherman took off toward it. And in the years that have followed, I've often come back to this particular action. Without hesitation, the Fly Fisherman started running across a wide, violent plain of battle that was basically guaranteed to feature at least one or two of the hammers of hell.

It felt like a long run, roughly 300–400 yards. During the sprint, he turned on a force identifier (a marking device we carried) and got hold of the air platforms above, letting them know there was a friendly moving the way he was moving.

Generally speaking, you don't want those air platforms mistaking you for a running enemy.

As the Fly Fisherman was coming toward me, his crunching footfalls on those big thick reeds made quiet transit impossible. Hearing him, two fuckers lying in ambush suddenly popped up in a ditch close by. They had AK-47s, so the Fly Fisherman shot them, as he ran. Still in motion, he threw an infrared ChemLite, marking the spot in case our people wanted to get intel off those bodies later.

He showed up where I was and realized that another one of our guys had made it there, too. I'll call this other guy the Mechanic, because he could fix just about anything, including me. The Fly Fisherman had been harboring a small concern as he ran: he knew that the radios and our unit's dedicated medics were with another cell, not with me. So he was glad to see the Mechanic. Although neither of them was currently a medic by specialty, the Fly Fisherman had been pre-med in college, and in the more recent past, both he and the Mechanic had been to an advanced Army medic school—18 Delta—so they knew that they could assist each other in saving me.

Slinging their rifles over their backs, they assessed things and got to work on my leg—trying to prevent my life from draining out of me, while also trying to keep from getting killed themselves. I really wish I could transport people to that flat field in Afghanistan so they could witness what I saw: a few Americans doing their best.

I was a screaming mess, facedown in a puddle of my own blood. The enemy was still shooting at us. The medical resources that the Fly Fisherman and the Mechanic had were limited to basically the small amount of baseline equipment that we kept in our pockets. We all had some, but it was not anything an EMT would call "sufficient." Nor was the ambient light. Think about it. It was dark, and these guys had a heavy trauma wound they had to fix, without the benefit of headlamps or flashlights, which would only get us killed.

So they adapted, using other bits of ingenuity to assess and deal. The first thing the Fly Fisherman did was notice how much blood was on the ground around me. It had saturated the dirt, which he remembers as being fine, like talcum powder, not the gritty sand everyone assumes Afghanistan has. He immediately started scooping up that red coagulated dirt, using a tally of handfuls to measure how much blood I'd lost—turning the dirt into a triage aid.

The verdict on blood loss was . . . a lot. But the volume of clotted, increasingly O-positive mud was not enough to suggest that the main artery in my leg, right next to the exploded bones, had been severed. That was good. He then scanned my leg and saw that blood was still pulsing out of the wound, but not profusely. He also saw that the tourniquet was slipping down over the wound site. That was bad. It was supposed to be above it. He scanned the enemy all around us and judged that the fire we were receiving was residual spray and not concentrated on us. At the same time, he got on comms and explained he was working on me. He could tell I was in extreme pain, and he knew I wouldn't like what he was about to say next. "Hey, Jimmy, it's me," he said. "I gotta tighten this tourniquet."

"No," I replied.

The Fly Fisherman remembers thinking it was a lucky thing that he'd put on a few tourniquets before in his life. It's one of the most painful remedies, especially with broken bones, because the cardinal rule of tourniquets is that they have to be tight. Overruling my "no," he put his weight on me, in my back, pinning me to the ground so that I wouldn't move around. The extra measure of pain that was about to happen would cause me to jerk and strain, and if I moved too much, the severed, sharp bones still in my leg would shift and likely cut the artery, which, to this point, had remained miraculously intact.

Before he could up-torque the tourniquet, he had to make sure it was in the right place. He studied the wound itself, palpating the back of my leg, starting at the hip, pressing and twisting as he went down. You can imagine my glee. He was listening for crepitus, the sound of Rice Krispies crunching, which indicates the location of fractured bone and cartilage. As he neared the open gash of the exit wound site, I started losing my mind. Mapping by feel, his hands discerned the scope of the wound beneath the pulp, and he slid the tourniquet about two inches above what he had decided was the top limit of the Rice Krispies symphony.

He shifted more weight on top of me, and cinched up on the tourniquet, preparing to twist. He knew that stopping circulation in my leg was all that mattered, nothing else. Not pain management. Not stitching flesh back together. Not being nice. But he was still not relishing the prospect of doing what he was about to do to a friend. He knew it was going to hurt, and he knew there was considerable risk attached, too. A lot of times, when you move or tighten a loose tourniquet, guys bleed out, because it blows the clots that have formed, like a faucet building up pressure.

No choice.

He cranked down on the tourniquet. I screamed. He punched me in the side and said, "Shut up, man. There are bad guys all around us."

With the tourniquet reset in the right place, and tightened, the Fly Fisherman and the Mechanic moved into the next phase of care, which required supplies. All we had on us were our "blow-out kits," the small set of personal medical supplies that each of us carried. There was a rule: If you're helping someone, you always use the other guy's kit, instead of your own, because you, the healthy one, are still in the fight, and might need it later. Heeding that protocol, the Fly Fisherman and the Mechanic began by clearing away the pieces of bone that had been blown out the back of my thigh, and then they unceremoniously raided my blow-out kit. They jammed gauze and other things into the hole in the back of my leg, pushing it through my shredded pants into the flesh, to stop the bleeding. I was still facedown, screaming. They told me to shut up. I replied, politely, "Hey, you can't talk to me like that. I've been shot."

After that half-hearted attempt to keep the mood light, I shifted back to my prior modality—screaming like a madman, while being told not to. I also took up a new pet project, begging for a fentanyl lollipop. And there was a good reason why I wanted the lollipop: so that I'd stop screaming like a bitch. I was supposed to have one on me, but I never carried one, for two reasons. First, there was a lot of accountability associated with carrying one. You had to sign for it, and if you lost it, it was a huge deal, because they're a controlled item. Why bother. I had radios and guns and equipment already, so forgoing the lolly just meant one less thing I had to sign for and manage. The second reason I didn't carry one was because I never thought I'd get shot. I was vain, and an idiot. You might also say I took Epictetus too literally.

The Fly Fisherman did have a lollipop, but he said, no, I couldn't have his. "You still have one good leg and a gun, and I need you to be able to fight." What a bastard. On top of cruelly denying me the fentanyl, he had the gall to be right, too. The target wasn't even close to secure, and he knew we could be there for another hour fighting, depending on how Mr. Clean was doing wrangling the helos.

The truth is, when he said he needed me to have my gun online, that put me back in the right frame of mind, momentarily. Mission is a pretty good palliative for stupefying pain.

That said, I still wanted the lollipop.

During the fentanyl debate, the Fly Fisherman was also checking my back, to make sure no rounds had hit me through gaps in my side plates. He was shoving his hand around under my armor, which he didn't want to remove. Once he'd scanned my torso and rechecked the back of my leg, he felt he'd stabilized me enough to do what was really required: roll me over.

He remembers looking at me, as I lay there on my belly, and thinking that I had struck the exact pose of the police chalk outlines you see on TV, the ones that look like the murdered Egyptian hieroglyph. "Jimmy, we have to move you," he said. "We have to roll you over." I said, "No." Being moved was a horrible prospect, because every time I'd moved in that last minute, it was excruciating. But he explained that they had to. He and the Mechanic couldn't tell if I was bleeding out the front. They couldn't see it, but they knew there was a hole, so they had to flip me over. And that's what they did.

I screamed heartily. I still had my gun, my night-vision goggles, my helmet, and all my other equipment on. They left it on me, ripped my pants open, and went to work on the four-inch-diameter hole in the front of my leg. They rammed it full of Kerlix to stop the bleeding as best they could. Then they wrapped my leg in two bandages and finished it off with an Ace wrap over the top, all of which was incredibly painful because it compressed the tissue around the jagged bone that was floating around inside my thigh. They were doing this in the dark, with enemy maneuvering around us, and with me making noise that was basically the equivalent of standing in a field with a megaphone telling everyone in the neighborhood to come kill us.

We needed those helos.

Luckily, Mr. Clean had done a good job orchestrating the medevac, given the chaos all around. The helos now had basic grid coordinates and they were three to five minutes out, flying back in from a nearby support base where they were staged during the fight, a place that was also the location of our mobile medical-surgical unit. The Fly

Fisherman jumped on the horn, too, helping clarify exactly where and how the LZ would be marked when the pilots came in, and making sure they understood how much they were going to get shot at in the process.

The Fly Fisherman let the Mechanic and Mr. Clean look after me for a second, while he checked out Remco. The Fly Fisherman cared deeply about dogs like Remco. They'd saved his life on previous occasions, and it stung that he could only now turn his attention to the dog, having had to focus on me initially. Assessing things as best he could, he could see that Remco was missing his lower jaw, but couldn't tell where else Remco had been shot in the head, because he was working without lights. For now, all the Fly Fisherman knew was that Remco wasn't breathing and had blood in the back of his mouth. The fluid was obstructing his airway, but the Fly Fisherman couldn't tell why exactly, so he criked the dog—performing a quick cricothyrotomy by making a vertical and transverse cut in the throat, and then putting a tube down it. He instructed the Texan, who was probably in shock, to wrap his lips around the plastic cylinder and keep blowing on that tube.

The procedure, which was the quickest way to get a secure airway, was new to the Texan, but it was not new to the Fly Fisherman. Later, when I asked him if he'd ever criked anyone before Remco, he said, "Yeah, in Fallujah. A Marine got blown up and his face was torn apart. So I criked him." That Marine lived. And so did a handful of others, thanks to the Fly Fisherman. In Fallujah, during the worst of it, when the Marines were getting chewed up badly, the Fly Fisherman came in as a medic and sniper, and ended up involved in some very violent actions, during which he saved a lot of lives.

On our bloody patch of talcum in Afghanistan, he was trying to do the same.

The quiet, except for the occasional sound of shooting, made it easy to hear the approaching helicopters. Knowing they were close, the Fly Fisherman contacted the pilots, confirmed the location, and marked the hot LZ.

———

Big helicopters like the one that came to medevac me have been shot out of the sky in Afghanistan on several occasions. The crews of those helos are an unusual breed. They call us "the customer." We want something, and they provide it. We want them to fly their school bus with jet engines into a shit-show to pick up a dog that got shot in the head, and me, and they don't ask any questions. They don't say, "We'd rather not." They go. They heard someone got tagged, and they were on their way back, risking their lives again. For me. The Customer. And here's a measure of how good those guys are: I never had a sliver of a doubt that they'd come. How many people have a resource like that? When you're getting ready to die, to know that someone will plunge into a horrible firestorm and pull you out?

This returning air crew knew what they were facing. They were going back into a place where they'd just done a hot insert and received fire. And yet there wasn't a moment's hesitation. In fact, the opposite was true. They got as close as they could. There are rules about how close to troops you can land a helicopter. But those guys didn't give a fuck, because they knew I was a mess. They were shooting and receiving fire as they came in, and they still landed within thirty feet of me. Close. I didn't see it, but I heard it. The Fly Fisherman and the Mechanic propped me up and started carrying me. The Texan followed us, carrying Remco.

Hopping toward the ramp with my arm around the Fly Fisherman, I said, "Listen, you gotta go with me, because I don't know who's on the helo." I was worried that they might not have a medic of his caliber on board. He agreed to go, and got on the horn with the head shed, telling them that "three plus one" would be leaving the battlefield (the Texan, Remco, himself, and me).

The Mechanic peeled off and re-engaged in the fight.

The rest of us boarded the helo and took off for the four-minute flight back to the nearby support base, which actually had a fairly robust medical facility, staffed with some pretty amazing doctors attached to our unit. As soon as we got airspeed, the pilots kicked on the little green interior lights which allow you to see. After the Fly Fisherman checked all my bandages to see if I was still bleeding, he took a quick moment to formally lift the moratorium on lollipops. Hearing this, the

Texan quickly gave me his, even though he probably still had a gun-fight to go back into.

It took me years to forgive myself for screaming that night. I wish I would've been tougher. But I also have a hard time forgiving myself for taking another guy's fentanyl. I feel like a tool, because not only was I a liability—in so much hurt that I wanted the pain remedy—but I also robbed someone else of his. Here's a lesson for all of you reading this that have the insane desire to do this kind of work: Carry your own fucking lollipop. Don't make your buddies give up theirs because you're an ass.

Once the Fly Fisherman had authorized the lollipop, he grabbed my camera and snapped a pic. I struck the most appropriate portrait pose I could think of in my fuzzy frame of mind. For some reason, it seemed to me that blood-soaked pants and a cheek bulging with lollipop would

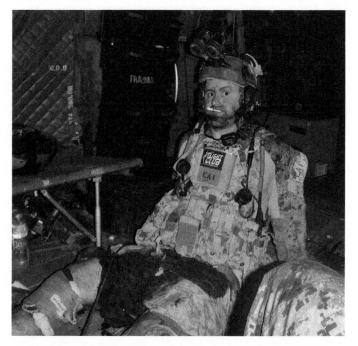

July 9, 2009   The Fly Fisherman took this photo about twelve minutes after I'd been wounded, while we were on the helicopter that had pulled us out of the fight. Right after this, he taped that fentanyl lolly to my right thumb.

somehow communicate what I was trying to convey. Reflecting on that episode now, all I can say is: what arrogance. *Hey, I'm shot . . . Let's make sure we get a good picture of me.*

After the impromptu photo shoot, the Fly Fisherman taped the lollipop to my thumb, a measure designed to mitigate the potential fallout from the fentanyl. The National Institutes of Health doesn't mince words in its warnings about the stuff: "Fentanyl may cause serious breathing problems or death if it is used by people who are not being treated with other narcotic medications." None of us were using other narcotics. So there was always that risk, I guess. And it was the reason my thumb was taped, as a safety measure. If I were to pass out from the potent opioid, my falling arm would yank the lolly out of my mouth, preventing death by choking.

The Fly Fisherman moved to check on the dog—this time with some light on the subject—and ensure that the Texan was OK. The Texan was not. He was traumatized by the condition of his dog, whose wounds we could now assess. Remco had been hit in the face from about six inches by two 7.62x39 bullets shot out of an AK-47. The missing jaw was one obvious result, but now, with the light, the Fly Fisherman also found a bullet entry point by Remco's left eye, with no corollary exit wound. Taking into consideration the severity of these wounds, along with the total lack of breathing, the Fly Fisherman could only say, "Hey, there's not much more I can do for the dog. Sorry, man."

Despite this grim prognosis, I watched the Texan continue to minister to Remco, who was quite still. Refusing to relent, the Texan yanked out the crike tube and put his mouth over the gaping wound where the dog's jaw had been shorn away. And he breathed into it. Occasionally, he'd take a break from this mouth-to-wound resuscitation and come over and check on me. Then he went back to his dog, trying again to revive him, although he was pretty obviously dead.

Remco had saved our lives, but his was over.

I don't remember the helo landing. Or the short ambulance ride from the helos to the clinic area. The next thing I do remember was hopping on my left leg and feeling really light-headed, with the Fly Fisherman's arm around me. We were moving toward what looked like a tent. This was the field hospital, where the heavy-duty work of saving my life was about to commence. Because I'd lost a lot of blood, I began to feel really dizzy, and I collapsed, at which point the Fly Fisherman said, "You can't pass out on me. I can't carry your fat ass." So somehow I mustered up the gumption to hop the next however-many paces, through a door that got pushed open, and into a blinding white light. Inside, as my eyes adjusted, I made out two guys with medical scissors, standing there like sheep shearers at the pearly gates, and looking at me as I stood on my left leg. With great efficiency, they proceeded to cut every stitch of clothing and gear off of me, leaving me naked. Next, they grabbed me and put me on a stainless steel table. I lay back on the table, and then so many people swarmed me as they prepped me that the Fly Fisherman recalls not being able to see me through the crowd.

It was loud from the rotor noise of the helos still running nearby, and all I could think of, as I lay there naked with people cleaning and inserting catheters into me, was how cold it was in that room. So I dropped my arm, eagerly trying to signal to the Fly Fisherman. There was something I needed to tell him. He saw my arm emerge from the buzzing swarm of medics, doctors, and nurses, motioning him over. He squeezed in next to me. Making sure he and everyone nearby could hear, I offered up a disclaimer: "Hey, nobody laugh at my junk; it's fucking freezing in here."

I could hear the voices of doctors telling the Texan that his dog was gone, giving formal sign-off to a reality that we were all denying.

Then they put the mask over my face, and I remember the Texan coming over to check on me as I started to fade. He was one of the fellows that I'd asked not to laugh at my cold-sensitive manhood. He gave me a smile. Then I lost consciousness, and I don't remember much after that.

Having seen me safely into surgery, the Fly Fisherman now wanted to rush over to our unit's HQ, which also happened to be on that small base for this deployment. But the medics and nurses accosted him and wouldn't let him leave. He was covered in a bunch of my blood, so they extended him the same courtesy they'd shown me: they started stripping him down. Protesting, he listed enough medical credentials and articulated enough capacity for self-analysis that they agreed to stop when they got to his T-shirt and shorts. They just wanted to make sure he wasn't hit. Sometimes you can take a frag and not even know it.

Cleared, and with his gear back on, the Fly Fisherman made his way over to the HQ, where he gave our senior people an update and learned more about the three other potential locations for Bergdahl that were being hit by other crews simultaneously. Because Bergdahl would not actually return to America for years, as it turned out, all we can do is guess about his whereabouts that night. But here's what I believe: Based on the amount of resistance we ran into right from the get-go that evening, Bergdahl was very close. The people we were shooting at, and who were shooting at us, were heavily loaded with very good equipment. So I have to presume we were close.

And because we believed we were, do you know what the Texan and the Fly Fisherman did when the brief was completed? They went out to the tarmac, got back on the bird, and went back to the fight. Minus one lollipop.

They were still fighting when the sun came up that morning.

The Fly Fisherman was an extraordinary medic. Had he and the Mechanic not gone to that Army Special Operations medical school, I'd be dead.

The Fly Fisherman was also an extraordinary sniper. Some time before the Bergdahl event, in Ramadi, a lot of American troops were getting picked off by an elusive sniper that nobody could trace or find. The Fly Fisherman went into the town, set up, and took the time needed to ascertain the assailant's technique, and then use his understanding of that technique to know where to look for him. Shortly thereafter, the Fly Fisherman killed the sniper.

But he never discussed it. I learned about this feat of his in Ramadi—and the other ones in Fallujah—from mutual friends. When I hear people talk about the epic records being set by snipers and other folks, I smile. What the Fly Fisherman has done, the world will never hear about. Unless I recount at least some small part of it. He does not want me to, but I'm stubborn.

I had to pull teeth for permission to relay even that skeletal Ramadi sniper story. And having pulled incisors, I had to start yanking molars to get him to let me talk about his role in saving my life overseas, and again later, back home. I'm glad he acquiesced. My memory of what happened after I got shot is foggy in places, and many of the details I'm able to share come from difficult conversations I've had with friends like him, long after their life-saving actions.

It's worth pointing out that the Fly Fisherman's exploits in Ramadi and on the night he saved me—as amazing as they are—are not the most extraordinary events of his career. Not by a long shot. Regarding those he wants to remain mum. He's done many incredible things that are just simply hard to fathom, but he is not inclined to talk about them, and he would certainly never tally them.

At some point, I believe there must have been a cage match in the soul of the Fly Fisherman, between self-interest and selflessness. Self-interest lost, badly.

It was a privilege to serve in a crew that had men like him. The extent of my love for the crew is in direct, inverse proportion to the depth of my despair when I was forced out of it. And because of my respect for its members—guys who are quiet about the very things that make them extraordinary—I've struggled with whether I should speak about my time among them. But I think it's important to touch on the mettle of people like the Fly Fisherman. Ironically, it lands me in this curious, uncomfortable position: speaking about the folks who refuse to.

So be it. The public needs to know about him, and others. And why most of us would probably agree that the absolute worst thing about being in our crew was the moment when you realized you would one day be leaving it. Either in a body bag or of your own accord, you'd be leaving it. What surprised me, and nearly broke me, is that for many years after getting shot, I felt strongly that the body bag would have been the better option.

Beginnings

I guess you could say that life on the Speeding Train was something I'd hungered for since I was fourteen years old.

As a kid, I didn't have a good outlook on life. I failed in my early familial relationships. I didn't feel like I fit in, or that I ever would. Dwelling on this situation seems too much like whining, and cultivating excuses. So, instead, I'll just quickly summarize . . .

The last I saw of my natural mother was when I was eighteen months old, when she put me up for adoption. After some false starts with new families, and a brief stint as a ward of the state, a kindly attorney hooked me up with a couple that took me in. My adoptive mother had problems with me, and with her husband. They divorced when I was eight. After that, for various unpleasant reasons, I began running away a lot, either riding my bike or stealing money and riding the bus. Eventually, about the time I was eleven or twelve, I was able to stop splitting time between my parents and opt to go live with my long-suffering dad, who had remarried. He was a very good man. Though he worked hard, I'm fairly certain he never felt appreciated. This hurts to think about, because I added to his woes. I was not respectful. I got in a lot of trouble, including vandalism and petty theft. I barely made it to seventeen, but when I did, he was the one I asked to sign the papers permitting me to join the military, where I felt I'd find what I hungered for.

My whole young life I'd seen people around me tell others they loved them, and it was mostly a lie. Words were cheap. So I wanted something that was real. And you know how you find something real? You make sure people have skin in the game, yourself included. Something in my gut told me, from a young age, that when you're out in a hellhole, in a gunfight, where you can die, that's when you'd know it was real. I was optimistic about what the military could provide. I needed it.

I'd gravitated to books about Vietnam-era Green Berets, and it seemed that in the Special Operations world, things were tougher and harder. From what I could tell, the folks who earned the right to be in that family had demonstrated the ability to commit to something and make it happen, and the reward was that they were exposed to greatness and true brotherhood and raw human goodness.

I wanted to belong to a group like that, where no part of it can be faked. I was looking for love in an atmosphere where agendas and emotional subterfuge could not exist, an atmosphere that I felt would prevail in war. It seemed to me that it would be impossible to fake helping your brother out in a gunfight, where such things are verified by death. I imagined that when people risk their lives to save yours, they do not need to say *I love you*.

Those are all things I believed instinctively, and I wanted to prove that they were true by living them. But there was one other thing I wanted. I wanted to be part of the group that got called upon when it was time to punish the enemies of decency. I wanted to be right there, eye-to-eye with the enemy, not somewhere else and only hear about it later. I envisioned this just as vividly as a young future ballplayer envisions hitting a 100-mile-an-hour fastball in the majors. How does he know he wants to face that pitch one day? He's never experienced it. And yet he knows. That's how I felt. The only difference is that I wanted to hit the enemies of decency, not fastballs. I wanted this deep down, in my bones, in my heart, or whatever organ is the seat of true desire. I knew this about myself at seventeen, and it was still true at forty.

PORN AND SMOKE

Many of the people close to me didn't mince words when it came to sharing their outlook on how I'd do in the military. They told me I'd never make it. As a result, when I enlisted in the Army National Guard at seventeen, I didn't go in with high confidence levels, or what could be called an "optimal platform for success."

I took advantage of an Army program where you could do boot camp between your junior and senior year of high school. In boot camp, I came to understand that there were people in the military who were great Americans and patriots, but they were doing the military route in order to gain skills they could use later on as civilians, in their "real" life. I was different. I wanted to be close to the enemy.

After boot camp, I progressed quickly to jump school at Fort Benning. I was the youngest guy in my company, and I was the guidon bearer, meaning I carried the flag when we ran as a company—you've seen them, the flags with forked notches on the end denoting the regiment or unit. I grew up in the mountains of Utah, so I could run. And so could our company commander, who was a Ranger, a guy who just seemed to have been born fit. He and I often ended up out front, running together, which was a curious pairing, given that I was seventeen and he was someone that I considered to be a bit like a god. One day, he said, "You know, Hatch, occasionally we get guys who go through here who are from the Navy, and they're kinda crazy, they're a little off, they're from Naval Special Warfare. Have you thought about that?" And I said, "No, I haven't." To which he replied, "Maybe you should."

I didn't know Naval Special Warfare teams existed. Having grown up reading Vietnam combat books that focused on the Army, I thought the only thing to be was a Green Beret.

But a company commander's nudging is not easily ignored when you're a teenager, so I figured I'd try to make it into Naval Special Warfare, and I joined the Navy at eighteen. I started off in medic school, training to be a corpsman, but I got in trouble for allegedly stealing a pair of hospital scrubs. OK, not allegedly. Actually. I thought they'd make great pajamas. A few of us had been involved in that sartorial heist, and we got kicked out of school for our troubles and fined half a month's pay for two months, which was no small thing. As further punishment, I was sent to a ship, a frigate, where I was part of deck division, basically the lowest form of life on the ship. It was not technical. It was not skilled. I scraped paint, and I painted—a never-ending cycle aboard an oceangoing vessel that's constantly bathed in saltwater.

My wife has a thoughtful and nuanced way of describing that particular phase of my life: "You were a deck ape."

And then, amazingly, I got accepted into the training for the Navy's Sea, Air and Land Forces. I'd sent a request, and I'd bided my time. Candidates need to have been trouble free for a while, so I'd spent a long time on that ship letting my pajama heist recede into the darkness of history.

I don't know why they accepted me, but I was fortunate that they did, and so I went.

Less than an hour into Hell Week, the physical toll was already noticeable. It sounds strange, but it was true. We'd been sitting in the surf for just under fifteen minutes (although it felt like days), with waves crashing over us. It was chilly. And "chilly" might not sound like much, but this was a punishing kind of chilly. There was a guy in our class of candidates who had done the Iron Man, and he was an athletic prodigy. He could do virtually anything. He could swim, run, crush pull-ups, you name it. His muscles looked like someone had abandoned the enterprise of making a huge pretzel and then haphazardly balled all the huge ropes of dough into clumps. He was big. A specimen. But with Hell Week not yet sixty minutes old, and with this malicious kind of chilliness laying siege to our bones, he got up and quit. And when he did, I said to myself, "Self, if that guy won't make it, there's no way you'll make it. If that guy is outta here, you're screwed." It turns out that about ten other guys in my class shared that precise sentiment at that precise moment, and we all got up and rang the bell and quit, en masse.

An hour after I'd quit, I realized what I'd done. I'd made a mistake. As a result, the next chapter of my life was essentially a penalty lap. It was clear I needed to develop some character. I knew it. The Navy knew it. So I received a massive promotion . . . right back to deck division on another ship. I spent the next three years on that ship. It was out of hand. Life on a ship is unpleasant at times; everyone knows that. But I'll provide one quick measure of just how unpleasant. We all slept in crowded berths packed with bunks. Those rooms were always full of two things: porn and smoke. Each night, as you'd be trying to go to sleep, with the lights on, you were sucking down many cubic meters of smoke, while being lullabied by the sights and sounds of ungroomed '70s porn stars and starlets.

On that ship, I had a lot of time to reflect on my failure at BUD/S. But there was one facet of it that I would only come to understand years later, when a veteran Navy operator noticed I was still viewing my ability to run as a badge of honor. He said, "You know, Hatch, a good athlete does not necessarily make a good member of Special Warfare." And that helped me understand the Iron Man. He couldn't suffer in the kind of conditions we were suffering in. The truth is, his motivations were likely different from mine. His motivations were perhaps to get the Naval Special Warfare emblem pin, or tell friends, or prove something.

Not me. I wanted love—to be part of a human bond that had no lie as part of the attachment. And I wanted to punish people who were cruel.

I reapplied to Naval Special Warfare training two and a half years into my penalty lap, and after precisely three and a half years on board that ship, they took me back. I considered myself pretty lucky.

This time, as the waves were hitting us, an hour into Hell Week, I thought, *There is no fucking way I am going back to deck division.* At one point, I was climbing a rope as part of training, and as I got to the top of the climb, I crested a bar and could see my old ship in the distance, taunting me with the prospect of deck division. And I remember thinking, *Screw that.* I knew where I'd go if I failed, so I didn't fail.

In general, I didn't really suffer as well as I wanted to, just like when I got shot later in my career. But for some reason, I made it. I graduated in 1990. Barely. By the skin of my teeth.

After I'd been in Naval Special Warfare for a few years, I got into a position where I was able to try out for one of the highly specialized units. I felt it would be a good fit because of the nature of the work, the quality of the leadership, and the level of commitment one has to make in order to be involved in a unit like that—where time-sensitive missions are always available, and can happen at any time. But another key reason I wanted to join this particular unit was because it was the hardest. It was a challenge way beyond what I'd already undertaken.

I'd say I chose wisely, although I wouldn't necessarily say they did. I was fairly lucky to get in, having earned mostly average performance marks in the evaluation phase. My unspectacular scores did not make my résumé particularly glossy, but they did make clear how fortunate I was to be joining the ranks of this crew. Its members were something. And not just the shooters and the EOD techs. Every single person was vetted. The support staff, everyone.

For those who passed and made it through, there was no graduation ceremony. We took our gear upstairs, and immediately commenced a year of probation, during which, at any time, they could have said, "It's not working out, buddy."

Physical exertion was part of the proficiency they sought, but rating a slot had more to do with being able to make quick judgments in severe circumstances. You can practice with your gun all you want, but the skill in aiming while standing still isn't really the issue. The main skill is understanding what motivates you to use the weapon. Can you get to a point where it's natural to very quickly weigh the Knowns against the Unknowns and determine if it's a scenario that merits action? Once the shooting starts, a big risk in taking down a structure is running into each other. There is a small window of time during which you can recognize a hostile or a friendly, or distinguish a combatant from a non-, and you have to hope that you're quicker in that moment than they are in getting you.

So we did a lot of close quarters shooting, on buses, in boats, on trains, in buildings—focusing always on shooting and moving and communicating. As much training as we did, I feel we could have done even more. Unfortunately, our preparation for war was frequently interrupted by bureaucratic fluff—mandatory seminars designed by those in the military who are not focused on war and fighting, but rather on covering their hindquarters. These time-sucks included lessons on the inappropriateness of grabbing a woman's breasts in public and other stunning revelations about the social code. Luckily, in addition to the structured training, we could get a gun out of our cage any time and go to the 7-meter range. At 3 a.m., if you wanted to. And a lot of guys did. Every week, each of us would shoot at least 1,000 rounds of 9mm and 2,500 rounds of 5.56.

Close-quarters battle is extremely difficult, and making a person a discriminating shooter is a never-ending process. That process continued every day, for the fifteen years I was in that unit, after I was selected to formally join it in 1994. The idea was that we'd train so hard, so long, so frequently—despite the seminars—that when it came time for us to use our guns in a real gunfight, it would be automatic. We'd react the way we'd trained. No matter how bizarre or chaotic the conditions (and they'd be bizarre and chaotic in ways that were impossible to predict in our training scenarios), we'd know we could rely on our set of tools, and each other. Those things would be constants, while the conflicts fluxed around us.

For the mechanics of war—the gunfights—we were prepared. But for the other facets of war, we were not. I think training for Naval Special Warfare is as hard as people think it is, but I think war is harder. Actually, I think war is a lot harder.

SHOELACES AND THE UNDERSIDE OF MINES

My first exposure to war and its pungent quality was in Bosnia in 1996.

The formal cessation of hostilities in the Bosnian War was date-stamped December 1995, so a large part of our mission in that country was providing security for the IFOR (Implementation Force) delegations who were there to manage the peace, per the Dayton Accords. It sounds august, but our work essentially amounted to being eye-candy protection for bigwigs, driving them around, and doing advance scouting of the locales they visited.

At one point, I found myself standing at the edge of a dusty swale, looking down into a mass grave. It was a big pit, excavated in accordance with the curious procedural priorities of a crime scene investigation: the covering layers of dirt had been carefully removed, but the bodies were mostly left where they were. At my feet lay a tangle of women and children with bullet holes in their foreheads. Nearby, U.N.

forensics teams scoured the area, analyzing what was clearly evidence of Serbian crimes against humanity and slowly putting bodies into bags.

Up to this point, I'd been ignorant as to the actual smells and sights involved with mass killing. I'd seen the news reports, but it's impossible to grasp what it's like unless you're actually there. My mind struggled to take it all in. I found my attention drawn to one particular woman in my vicinity. She wore a floral print dress and brown leather shoes, and she still had her scarf on. What struck me and held my attention was not the glaring fact that something had smashed her forehead in, but a much subtler detail: her shoelaces were missing. *Where are her shoelaces?* I kept asking myself. I was obsessing about the tiny detail because my mind needed a safe place to go. As tough as I thought I was, and as much training as I'd had, my psyche couldn't process what I was seeing. All the bodies being piled up. All the death. So I fixated on the shoelaces. I looked and looked for them. And finally I found them.

They'd been used to tie the woman's hands.

Shoelaces. They were the signature of precisely the kind of person I longed to meet face-to-face. The enemies of decency.

But those shoelaces were also evidence of a different struggle inherent in war—the struggle to make sense of things, and process them. In Bosnia, breathing the air at the edge of that mass grave, polluted as it was with the smell of rotting flesh, I realized you can't short-stroke the realities of this world. You can't just create and live by platitudes like *We're good, and that other faith is nothing but evil*—which is essentially what I'd been doing.

That woman with the shoelaces . . . she was a Muslim.

As a teenager, I'd hoped to find a family in Special Operations, and that hope was fulfilled. My idea of what kind of family I'd find on the Speeding Train was pretty accurate.

But my idea of what war would be like was less so.

Before ever deploying, I'd held it as an article of faith that war was mostly a clean transaction. It was willing participants volunteering in the destruction of other volunteers. But it turns out it's not that way at all. When combatants involve the innocent—or prey on them—war is not the clean thing you were hoping it would be. It becomes dirty.

The woman in the pit was my first introduction to the realities of how dirty war is. And during my time in Sarajevo, the lessons about conflict didn't end with her, even though the bullets weren't flying anymore.

Warped by war, almost everything in Sarajevo was now strange, even the normally innocuous little details of our travel, like pocket change and hotels. The petty cash I'd been given was not petty at all—three money belts filled with $37,000 in cash. That was more money than I'd ever seen in my life. And for my accommodations, I was billeted in the Holiday Inn on Sniper Alley, which did not make you feel like you were either on holiday or at an inn.

Sniper Alley was the city's main thoroughfare, running east to west the length of the city, from the industrial sector to historic Old Town. It was a street that seemed prone to dramatic nomenclature. Its proper name had been Dragon of Bosnia Street, named after a Slavic Bosniak hero who wrested a brief moment of independence from the Ottomans and created a fleeting multicultural haven back in the early nineteenth century. During the Bosnian War, it was nicknamed Sniper Alley because it was where Serbian snipers shot a lot of Bosnian civilians.

Wide, heavily traveled, and with the tram running along it, Sniper Alley was basically the main artery for foot and automobile traffic through the city. Which is why the Serbs targeted it, both from positions in nearby buildings and from the hills to the south, which they controlled.

At one point, Sniper Alley ran alongside the river Miljacka, the same river near which Franz Ferdinand was shot. That river is obviously a strife magnet, a place for wars to start. And this propensity for conflict was one of the many reasons Sarajevo was puzzling. The city's dynamics were discordant. It featured the trappings and urban buzz of a Western, European city. It had opera singers, cafes, pizza . . . and snipers murdering people as they waited in line for water.

The whole face of the Holiday Inn adjacent to Sniper Alley was damn near completely destroyed, a good indicator of just how much chaos that infamous road had seen. There were blood trails on the hotel's carpet, and I followed a lot of them, trying to piece together the events that had caused them. One clearly told the story of a person who had been in a room facing Sniper Alley, gotten shot, and had tried to crawl away to safety, down the hall.

While there, I met an eighteen-year-old local kid who was a cook, and he and I became friends. Recently, he'd been revisiting the home where he grew up—a house on an outlying hill. My young friend remembered when the Serbs had seized it as part of the encirclement of Sarajevo and used it as a spot from which they could overlook the city and shell it indiscriminately with mortar fire. None of the homes in his neighborhood had roofs any longer, because after the Serbs had used the residences for their purposes, they had a habit of turning on the gas and lighting a candle as they left.

But roofless neighborhoods weren't the Serbs' only parting gift. My friend talked a fair amount about the land mines that still littered his former property, and it made me start to wonder just how heavily mined a single residential home could possibly be. So I asked if I could see it, and he brought me there.

The first thing that blew my mind was the sheer number of big, dangerous 2.2-kilo mines that he had stacked in the basement of his former home. These were anti-tank mines. "Who put these here in the basement?" I asked.

"I did," he replied.

It dawned on me that this eighteen-year-old kid had been personally de-mining his old, abandoned home.

I did the only reasonable thing, which was to ask if he could teach me how to do it. "With pleasure," he said. Or at least he said something to that effect, in his native tongue, because the look on his face was the universal look of a guy with a skill he's eager to share.

He dove right into a live demonstration of his de-mining techniques, which apparently the neighborhood kids had taught each other. And I spent a pleasant afternoon learning, and using, the peculiar de-mining techniques required in a suburban yard outside Sarajevo. We were on hands and knees, feeling for the bombs, and then digging them up.

The Serbs had modified the mines. They were pressure mines, like in the Bugs Bunny cartoons, with the spring-loaded button on top. But they'd been specially rigged so that if you lifted one, it would also go off, because they'd added a second, pressure-sensitive button on the bottom. The mine-layers had put those second buttons there to kill the folks who were trying to disarm them. Foiling their plans, my friend had devised an ingenious technique whereby he ran a wire around the whole mine while it was still in the earth, so that he could feel the nub of the reverse pressure sensor on the underside, if there was one. He'd learned that trick as a young teenager.

So why'd he do it? Why was he risking his life to clear sophisticated double-armed mines from the yard of a destroyed home? In a nutshell, he was trying to reclaim his property. Fool's errand or not. All his happy memories were associated with that home.

I wondered about his family. He explained that his father and mother now lived in an apartment complex near the airport, and after we hung out a few more times, he said he wanted me to meet his mother.

I accepted the offer of local hospitality, and went to their home. There were plastic tarps, provided by the U.N., covering the gaping holes that bombs had ripped in their walls.

For the early part of the evening, it was just me, my friend, and his mother. But then eventually a wraithlike figure shuffled out from a back room. It was his dad. The father was a heartbreaking portrait of a broken man. And I mean "broken" in a non-figurative way. He looked like a sheaf of twigs that had been snapped in a number of different places. I shook his hand. It was lifeless and limp.

The boy later explained that he and a bunch of kids from his neighborhood had found their fathers, including his own, in a makeshift Serbian prison camp and broken them out of it. It was this prison camp that had drained the life force from his father.

The broken man's wife put a small bowl of nuts out on a table. We all sat on a ratty, chewed-up couch, and I did everything I could to act very obviously nonchalant, like I was unaware or uncaring of the rattiness. But it wasn't my posturing that made us relax. It was the mother's innate graciousness, a way she had that lent a kind of natural dignity to the proceedings, despite the shabby furnishings. She was trying to maintain an air of solid ownership over this home and these circumstances, as broken as they were.

She had poise, but it started to break down the longer the visit went on.

Even innate, internal pride is vulnerable to the relentless siege of shame. She had lived in a nice, clean home before the troubles started, and now, not so much. The mother suddenly got up and went away. The boy went after her, and then he came back out, saying, "She's ashamed that we live this way . . . she's afraid you will think that we live like refugees . . . eating this little bit, on a salvaged couch, with tarps for walls."

I reflected, then and there, on my own ignorance. I'd never grasped that this madness goes on. These Bosnians lived in a city, with highways and an airport. The Olympics had been held there in 1984. They were sophisticated European people, with the habits and demeanor of advanced Westerners. And yet they had brutalized each other. Over the course of a few short months, that city had turned into the capital of carnage on the globe. In the hills to the south, I visited the Olympic bobsled run that still snaked down through the beautiful trees, and I could see the gun portholes that the Serbs had bored into its sloping walls. That bobsled track began as an icon of human accomplishment and harmony, but within a few years, it had been converted into a cement bunker.

It was impossible for me to understand that, until I touched it.

The switch can get flipped quick. Sarajevo had seemed relatively harmonic, right until it wasn't. The heavy-duty Sarajevo police team is a good example. The team had been made up of all three main ethnic groups—Croat, Serb, and Muslim—just like the multicultural city it was tasked with protecting. But when things went sideways, the officers from that team who went to the Serb side kept their police radios . . . and they used those same radios to call their former confederates and say, "Hey, we're coming to get you tonight."

You could say—and the U.N. does say—that all the ethnic groups were committing war crimes. Serbs, Croats, and Muslims were all beating up and raping each other.

But I never did see a mass grave with Serbs in it.

CROWDED SKIES

It was five years later, and I was standing on the open back ramp of a C-130 with seven other guys. We knew we had to get out of the plane low, due to the other aircraft in the area—primarily helicopters and one curious dirigible.

I was scared, which was strange, because it was a day jump, and those are typically safer than night jumps. The terrain beneath us was urban, thickly populated, but also dotted with some hills and scrub brush. The fact that we had to get out so low added to the complexity of the jump, for obvious reasons. It meant less time to fly your body, aim, and position yourself. It also meant the ground was closer.

We left the back of the C-130 as a group. Once we got out, we identified the landing area and set up to fly into it. And although we had a primary objective—hitting the targeted landing spot—I had another personal objective of my own that rated pretty high in relative importance: to not fly through the rotors of one of those helos in our airspace. Or hit the array of aerial wires and cables spanning the basin between the ridges surrounding our target.

It was tricky.

I could see where I didn't want to go, and I knew where I needed to land. So I steered my chute and started to see the landing area come into clearer focus. It was a limited patch of earth, smaller than I'd anticipated.

Adding to the fun, just before we'd left the plane, we'd been given a last-minute refinement to our orders. There would be a certain part of the drop zone that we absolutely had to avoid . . .

The infield. Because they'd just raked it and didn't want it mussed. I landed, and as my parachute billowed gently to the ground around me, eventually coming to rest on the cultivated grass of the outfield, I noticed that it was eerily quiet. The first person I recognized was Jackie Robinson. His picture adorned the center field wall. My fear had been drowning out most of the environmental noise, but now it was abating. It felt a bit like a fog clearing. And once it had, I heard the screams of the 53,154 people around me.

It was opening day at Dodger Stadium in Chavez Ravine, Los Angeles. April 2001.

I stood there, frozen in place for a moment, until a buddy yelled, "Hey, jackass, pick up your chute and let's get going." He was right. We were the Navy's skydiving team, and we were there to swoop in, land dramatically in front of the crowd, and then clear out.

In the years after Sarajevo, there hadn't been much in the way of combat happening, so I had volunteered—and tried out—for the Navy demonstration parachute team. We traveled widely, doing exhibitions at air shows, racetracks, and stadiums. And like our other events, this Dodgers game was on a tight timeline. We had to get off the field. So we gathered our gear and dropped it in a designated holding location. We were then shown up to the owner's box, where we were promptly served the finest meats and cheeses (to borrow a phrase from one of my favorite sports analysts, Kenny Mayne). I was grateful to be there. I was also ruined for life, as far as my standards for attending a baseball game go. This was the first time I'd ever been to one.

From the lofty vantage point of this skybox, I saw a curious thing.

There was a prominent member of the Dodgers who was being derided in the press, Gary Sheffield. Apparently Sheffield was upset with the team because he'd caught wind of winter trade rumors and because he hadn't been granted the contract extension he felt he deserved. In an effort to show just how serious he was, he'd put his $3 million Los Angeles home on the market. To this, the team's management and fans had reacted negatively.

On that opening day, I saw Sheffield booed before each at bat. *Sorry, Gary,* the crowd seemed to say, *we are a relentless band of stalwarts who cannot be moved to pity when it comes to ingrates such as yourself. You gainsaid our team, and that's that.* This remorseless attitude was a monument of unwavering conviction . . . right until the moment Sheffield thwacked a 440-foot missile strike to center field in the sixth. Everyone cheered. And just like that, the villain was a hero again, it seemed. The fact that he'd been holding out for a better contract was forgotten.

I don't mention that to chide anyone's fickleness. Those fans were human, that's all. I mention it because the emotions of hero-ordination are volatile. Remember that.

TBI #1

This career phase—being on the Navy skydiving team—landed me in a number of places, none of which were war zones. Still, in a lot of ways, it was quite exciting. The skydiving skill level of the guys in that group was astonishing.

One of the best examples of their skill and how fiercely dedicated they were to getting things right is, curiously, an occasion where something went wrong. During a training session in San Diego, another guy and I inadvertently hit the ground at a high rate of speed, probably 25–30 mph. Without the benefit of our chutes.

This was not one of our designated stunts.

As demonstration jumpers, our job was to leave planes and do impressive things under canopy that showed the proficiency of the U.S. Navy. Showing this naval proficiency required practice. The stunt we were trying to practice that day was called a corkscrew.

I was learning the stunt, and the seasoned team member teaching me was the best. The two of us were using special parachutes designed to do "canopy relative work." Meaning they run into each other.

It was my first time doing it, but for my partner, it was old hat. He was quite experienced. The early stages of this corkscrew proceeded according to plan. I flew my parachute canopy into the lower torso of the more experienced jumper, at which point he compressed the formation, meaning he slid down the lines of my parachute system with his feet and hooked them into my risers, two inches above my head. From his perch, he handed me a piece of what we called "protection," which is a strap with carabiners at either end and a three-ring cutaway system in the center. Once that was connected, I let the experienced jumper know, and then the mechanics got a bit more interesting. We both turned our canopies in opposite directions, creating diametric spin, each of us rotating around an axis in opposite directions, attached to each other, while "corkscrewing" toward the ground. We basically looked like a rotating baton, with humans in the center and parachutes at both ends.

As we descended, there was a designated altitude at which we were supposed to break the protection between us and cut away from each other and safely land. This time, the cutaway system failed. We tried to get it to work. No joy. We were still attached, and our parachutes were pointed straight at the ground. Our canopies were designed to use forward motion to generate lift and speed, sort of like airfoils. And like airfoils, they're typically supposed to be pointed in a horizontal direction. Here they were accelerating us downward.

The last thing I remember is looking at the approaching, whirling ground, thinking, *We are dead.* After that, I don't remember much. I learned afterwards that the more experienced jumper had grabbed his rear risers and slowed our descent. I had basically frozen up. He had not.

We hit the ground. Imagine that big human baton landing with a thud. I woke up a week later with three broken vertebrae—L1, L2, and L5—and a severe head injury. Fortunately, it had rained that day in California, so the ground was softer when we hit it. My partner, the more experienced fellow, broke all his ribs and punctured a lung. If he hadn't pulled on his rear risers, we'd be dead. Those risers changed the angle of his wing, flaring it from a vertical and pushing the back toward the center of our twirling baton, creating a mild braking effect. Mild, but enough to save our lives.

My head injury was significant. I had open bleeds in my skull, and the bulk of my initial recovery involved simply waiting for the brain to recede from its swollen state. "Diffuse axonal injury" was the actual name of what had me somewhat by the balls, neuromuscularly speaking. Part of my brain stem was affected, as well. It resulted in a slight paralysis on my right side. It also left me with some severe mental deficiencies, and it wasn't immediately clear how quickly—or if—they'd resolve themselves.

I knew my name. I knew how to talk. I knew my status in my

career. What I could not do was move very well, or perform simple mathematical tasks or other minor memory exercises. For example, when a therapist would ask me to "repeat these numbers after I'm finished . . . 6, 2, 9, 3, 1, and 7," I could maybe remember three or four digits, but beyond that, I was lost.

I had to go through a thirty-day rehab period with stroke patients, where I relearned how to do basic things like go grocery shopping. Seated at desks in a hospital classroom, we were given a piece of paper featuring a list of grocery items, along with their prices. We were then told we had $20, and the challenge was for us to figure out if we had enough money to buy what was on our list. It was hard for me.

While I worked at getting back into the swing of being able to do basic life chores, the Navy was assessing whether I should stay in the service at all. During this time, I happened to be under the medical supervision of an interesting fellow. He was a former Naval Special Warfare operator (in Vietnam) who had then decided to become a fighter pilot for the Air Force. After those passing fancies, he'd concluded that his real calling was to go to medical school and become a neurosurgeon. Dark-haired and very deliberate in his thinking, he spoke slowly and in a measured tone. He was not a BS artist. I asked him why my injury was considered so severe. I pointed out that "football players get their bell rung all the time." He said, "Football players run into other humans at full speed. You ran into a truck at full speed. There is a difference."

After extensive rehab and testing, the decision of whether or not I would stay in the Navy was pretty much in the hands of this frogman-turned-pilot-turned-doctor.

I remember the day that we learned of his decision. One feature of the day that stands out was the fact that I could not yet drive, so Kelley drove me. We sat down in the doctor's office. I remember looking at his BUD/S diploma on the wall, some pictures of the F-15s he'd flown, and a photo of his med school graduation. I remember the part of the discussion where he asked me what I wanted to do, and I said I wanted to continue being in Naval Special Warfare and finish my career. At that point, he turned his attention to Kelley and asked her, "What do you want to have happen?"

A lot was in the balance right then. But I was basically numb.

She said, "If that's what he wants, then that's what I want." And the doctor said, "Okay." Had Kelley said something other than what she did, I don't believe he would have signed the paperwork. So it's all her fault that I got shot later on.

When you look at the spine, conceptually, you recognize the spaced pieces of bone with the discs between them, and the wings coming out of those bones. The wings are what I'd damaged. A bunch of them were cracked and almost broken off. For this variety of fracture, what's primarily required is rest. I needed to be still, avoid engaging in vigorous activities, and give the vertebrae a chance to re-stitch themselves. Being still is not a favorite pastime, so this was a challenge. But after approximately eight more months of this low-key rehab, I was placed back on jump status. I could go back to work on the jump team.

In a sense, all was well. And I was jumping out of planes all day long. But two things were beginning to undermine me. The first was that while I was still in recovery from the parachute accident, September 11 had happened. I watched the news from my apartment in San Diego, prone in bed. I quickly found myself undergoing some unpleasant self-reflection. I was an idiot. I'd left a crew of hard-chargers to do a stint with the flashy parachute team, and now that we did have people to punish, I was not in a position where I could play a role. This gnawed at me.

The second factor sabotaging me was that I didn't understand an important by-product of head injuries. What I failed to realize is that when you have trauma to your frontal lobe, you can undergo some significant (and problematic) personality changes. I certainly did.

DON'T SLIP

Late in 2001, having just been cleared to jump again after my heavy injury, we were in Perris, California, and I was the aerial videographer for some of the other members of the parachute team who were going through training to get their instructor rating.

Having situated myself outside and to the rear of the plane's open door, in preparation for one of the many jumps that morning, my right hand was grasping a handle high on the exterior of the plane, and my right foot was on the exterior camera step. I was wearing wings (under-arm spider-man flaps curving from wrist to waist) and a helmet camera operated by a bite-trigger. With my left hand holding the back edge of the door frame and my left foot dangling, my right foot slipped off the step. My right hand decided to follow suit; it came off the top handle.

Wind speed, drag coefficient, and every other facet of aerodynamics did what they always do when you find yourself outside of a plane: they act on you mercilessly. I rocketed backward, and all of my body weight was quickly caught by my left shoulder, which was still solidly attached to the arm hanging on to the door frame. I couldn't climb back into the plane, and because my carelessness didn't mean that I was absolved of my obligation to get the video, I just flopped there for the time being, beside the fuselage, banging like a rag doll against the rivets and thin metal skin, waiting for the others to jump.

It was pretty clearly the kind of jolt that rips your shoulder out, but of course I had the benefit in that moment of not yet knowing how badly I'd damaged it. When the group exited, I let go and went with them. My left arm hurt a bit. But that was no surprise. What was sur-prising was that I couldn't control the limb. It was just flapping around. Happily, I discovered that operating with 75 percent of my limbs was within my power. I'd always told students that legs are more important for flying, and now that maxim was being borne out.

The pain intensified, though, and I bailed on the filming early, pull-ing at 8,000 feet instead of 3,500. Fortunately, it was the left arm that was damaged, because the right arm is the one you use to pull your chute. I could reach and throw the pilot chute, situated behind me and down to the lower right. The pilot chute inflated and commenced its multi-stage sequence—pulling open the main chute container, and then continuing to drag until it opened the main chute itself.

As I came in to land, I couldn't pull the toggles or flare or slow the wing down as much as I needed to, so I came to earth at a high rate of speed, and when I did, I rolled over on the shoulder I had just dislo-cated. It turns out I'd torn the labrum. Doctors inserted anchor pins and resecured it to a part of my shoulder. I was out for six weeks.

It was just after this recovery period that the latent brain trauma from my corkscrew mishap finally manifested itself, in the form of dramatic personality glitches that brought my opening-day visits to Dodger stadium to an end. Because I disagreed with the training regimen one day, I deemed it appropriate to tell the head enlisted fellow to fuck off in front of the entire squad. It was a trumped-up beef on my part, not really legit, and a complete non-issue (basically, I didn't like the Plan of the Day). But I put the cherry on top by leaving work in a fit of anger. The object of my ire didn't deserve to be disrespected or spoken to like that, especially in front of the group. I was completely at fault.

Now, the thing that allows me to make these remarkably level-headed and fair assessments of my behavior is, of course, hindsight. I deserved to get into more trouble than I did. The higher-ups actually took it easy on me. They convened and judged me to be of very little use to the Navy parachute team, because I was lacking the necessary qualities and comportment that would have given them confidence in my ability to perform. So, early in 2002, my leadership kicked me off the jump team and—instead of returning me to my crew—sent me to be a military free-fall instructor in Yuma, Arizona.

The people at Yuma were top-drawer, and I actually thought it was relatively slick being there, until the wars started. And then it began to feel like something else—another penalty lap. I started seeing news reports about incidents where friends of mine had been killed, and I felt like a piece of garbage for not being with them.

Ever since my shoulder incident, each time I climb out of a plane, I think, *Don't slip*. It's a good mantra. And it works well for skydiving. But with my insubordinate outburst, I had slipped in a more profound way. While it's true that I was neurochemically inclined to be negative and angry, it's no excuse. I was still the one who made the choices. And as a result of them, I found myself stuck in a place that was pretty damn far from combat.

Sad and bitter about having been blocked from going back to my friends who were fighting, I let my spirits sink. They only lifted again when my sentence was commuted, two years in, and leadership finally allowed me to return to my unit.

In Iraq, with Dogs

THE FIRST RAVEN

When I went through BUD/S, my favorite instructor was a man who'd been a Naval Special Warfare operator and dog handler in Vietnam. He'd survived consecutive, consistent combat deployments, and on a number of occasions, dogs had saved his life. And I've never forgotten what he said about dogs: With patience and commitment, you can have a relationship with an animal that will save your life, and in return, you need to protect him. After that, it was always a dream of mine to work with combat dogs.

In the '90s, I wrote a point paper recommending that we use K9s to enhance some of our missions at Naval Special Warfare. It was read by superiors and promptly put in a filing cabinet. After 9/11, some of the other Special Operations units started using dogs, and because folks remembered that I'd written that paper once upon a time, they asked if I wanted to handle a dog in our unit. I wasn't being asked to be in charge, just to be involved. I said, "Hell yes."

And so, early on in my first Iraq deployment, in 2005, I got the opportunity to stress-test the wisdom of my BUD/S instructor.

We were in a suburb of Baghdad, and our target was the leader of a cell of insurgents that was responsible for ambushing and killing Americans, using IEDs they built in-house.

In order to deal with this fellow, we were going to conduct a capture/kill raid—our stock in trade. And it might be good to provide a quick gloss on what capture/kill raids are. When we were sent to get human targets, we were supposed to capture them, if at all possible. It's axiomatic that when you go into a violent person's house at night without their permission, there's going to be a fight. And we'd step up the level of force based on the level of resistance. So if they were trying to punch us, it was a brawl, and we didn't have to shoot them. But if they attempted to hurt us or other humans in their vicinity with more than their fists, we would kill them. They had a choice. Some of them we subdued before they could make that choice. Others got to choose, and sometimes they decided to raise their hands and surrender. Most of the time, though, they wanted to get their jihad on, and that resulted in death.

On the night of this particular raid, after walking a good distance in the dark along muddy roads, we got to a palm grove, where we stopped to coordinate. Prior to arriving at the actual target, this was our last geo position where we'd have the opportunity to discuss things or account for any details that had changed in the window between the drop-off and when we hit the target.

Standing next to me in that grove was my working dog, Spike, who looked upward at something. Moving around in the trees, disturbed and making noise, were ravens. Spike looked at them, and then looked at me. Hard. He was just gazing at me. It was odd that there were ravens, and it was odd how Spike stared.

I would only see ravens, or birds of any kind, for that matter, on two occasions during my fighting career in Iraq, both times with Spike— first, at this gunfight, and then later, the night Spike died. On both occasions, Spike would first spy the birds, then eyeball me.

It's important to understand that dogs feel what you feel. That night, I was pretty uptight, and Spike could sense it. His look, I later came to believe, was meant to communicate that something was askew— maybe with the environment, maybe with me, maybe with both.

He was a Belgian Malinois. Agile body. Rippling front rack of chest muscles. Spirited face. Expressive, long ears. I'd been working with Spike for several months at this point. And although I knew his demeanor well enough to know that something was different with him now, it didn't occur to me that the night orations of the birds and the dog's gaze were bona fide ill omens. I wasn't trained in omen detection. Plus, other matters were more pressing.

Having done our quick prep in the palm grove, we then walked the several hundred meters to the building that our target called home. We didn't need to talk too much or throw a lot of chatter on the radio in order to coordinate from that point forward. When someone started shooting, we typically knew what to do. The theory behind our constant training had proven true.

We split into teams, and set up on the target. Boom. There went the front door.

Even though the breach detonation sometimes dazed folks inside and bought you a little time, on this occasion, almost immediately after the entry team went in, all hell broke loose.

While the breaching team entered at the front and woke up the folks in the house, my job was to be on the backside of the house to make sure that nobody went in or out using windows or other apertures. I was covering down on two sides of the structure, watching, along with a fellow shooter, who was looking in a window to make sure there was no movement inside. Right away, he saw a MAM with an AK-47 get up and point it in the direction of our colleagues entering the house. So my buddy started filling him in, putting a fair amount of lead into the building through the window, and his gun brass was raining down on Spike and me.

The total elapsed time from the moment of the breaching charge to the brass shower was about four seconds.

For all of those four seconds, I remember being pretty amazed that Spike was staying where I'd asked him to, despite the noise. Then, in the fifth second, I felt him tug. He was yoked to me by a three-foot leash. One end of it was affixed to his harness with a brass connector, and the other end was attached by a carabiner to my web belt, which was soaked in sweat from the fast, hard hike after the drop-off.

Because he was tethered to me, I could feel Spike's tug on my hip. His tug forced me to turn around and look down at him. His ears were up, and he was in full business mode. Following his gaze, I saw that he was looking intently at a handful of hostile men running out of a building directly behind us. None of us had heard them make their exit or run, due to the gunfire and yelling. My training had not put eyes in the back of my head (yet). But it did kick in smoothly the moment I noticed that one of the runners was leveling an AK. I started filling him in.

A lengthy gun battle ensued, involving a half dozen or so houses and a good chunk of the neighborhood, which came out to join the fray. We spent the next hour and a half moving systematically to places where we could engage all these folks who were shooting at us. Sometimes during that hour and a half, when I wanted to protect locals we were encountering, Spike was attached to me. And sometimes he wasn't.

Afterward, we walked to a safe spot, where the helos picked us up. On the helo ride back, I took the first opportunity to reflect. If Spike hadn't turned me around, I would be dead. No question. I'd neither sensed the movement of those men leaving their building, nor heard them, because I was just listening to my buddy's rifle. In that situation, Spike didn't bite anyone. He didn't find a bomb, or anything else dramatic. He just used his senses, amidst the gunfight, to detect a threat distinct from all the other commotion, and alert me to it so that I could deal with it. Yes, he'd been trained extensively in situations with guns going off, but how he knew that that particular pack of scurrying humans was keen on killing us is a bit of a mystery.

And my mind went back to the ravens. Spike had been different before we walked in on that target. I recalled how he'd looked at me. And I started to feel that Spike had known something was going to happen.

We got home. I took Spike to his kennel, made sure he had water, checked his carcass to make sure he wasn't hurt or burned, fed him, told him I loved him, took him to the bathroom, did my debrief, and went to sleep so we could do it again the next day.

As I fell asleep, I mused on a hard truth. Spike, this dog I loved, had no choice in the matter. He didn't opt to be in that gunfight, or any others that were coming up. I brought him there. I derived a touch of comfort from the belief that the work he was doing, with me, was what he was on earth to manifest, as a dog. But it's possible that I just told myself that—then and now—in order to feel less bad about involving him.

500-POUND BOMBS AND SMALLER ONES

Here in the U.S., we didn't have sendoffs or homecomings. It was *Hey, be here at such-and-such a time*, and we'd get dropped off, get on a plane, and go. And it was the same coming home. We'd walk out the gate, where our wives were waiting for us, and we'd get in cars and go home.

I spent a lot of time deployed to Iraq between 2006 and 2007. During those years, I came home four times, but never for long. My unit was part of a special missions task force supporting Operation Iraqi Freedom. Essentially, we were there to help the American-supported Iraqi regime stabilize, which, for us, meant going after those who were trying to destabilize it. There were various loosely organized networks jockeying for position as the premier enemy organization in Iraq. Some considered themselves members of the greater Al-Qaida in Iraq (AQI) movement, but many liked to simply claim the affiliation while actually resisting the idea of being under a central command. Abu Musab al-Zarqawi was the predominant Al-Qaida–affiliated leader and the figurehead of AQI, up until he was killed in mid-2006. He was the most brutal, which, unfortunately, is how potency and effectiveness are measured in Iraq. The most brutal one rises. That's how Saddam got to be in charge. But even with Zarqawi's quasi-eminence and his attempts to unify militants, what the situation really amounted to was a ramshackle assemblage of about a half-dozen different networks always popping their heads up and trying to make a name for themselves by killing Americans and members of the new Iraqi government. Sometimes they were in cahoots with each other, and sometimes not.

I met many AQI people. In my opinion, they were basically gangs of thugs hell-bent on mayhem. A death cult that preyed on people who were easily scared.

Our job was to disrupt them.

From my vantage point, this violent insurgent free-for-all was not surprising. It's what happens when you invade a country, overthrow a regime, and then fire the tens of thousands of men who were in the army. What are those men going to do? What do they know how to do? They're fighters. It's pretty straightforward. So despite what you may read in administration policy papers about the value and necessity of releasing those tens of thousands of soldiers as part of a purge intended to clean out the remnants of Hussein's Baathist regime, I can tell you what actually happened on the ground: I ended up facing a goodly number of them in gunfights.

On one of our missions in Iraq, we were sent to a locale where one of these gangs of thugs—an unusually vicious iteration—was capturing Iraqi cops, skinning them alive, torturing them, and beheading them. Perpetuating the gory cycle, they took the uniforms of the cops they killed and used them to create subversion, which in turn allowed them to kill more Iraqi cops. Essentially, their cop masquerade involved putting on the police uniforms and going out and committing crimes. It was a tactic that did two things: (1) it meant a higher likelihood of getting away with acts of violence, because they looked like police officers, and (2) it engendered distrust between the population and the fledgling community leadership that was trying to establish itself, because as far as the population could tell, uniformed police officers were the ones running amok.

We were sent in because our side had dropped two 500-pound bombs in the area where this group was operating, but the bombs hadn't detonated. The suspicion was that they'd landed on a riverbank, where the soil was soft. Our job was to get the guys, and the bombs, so that they couldn't be used against us later on.

Generally speaking, on deployments like this one, my first job was to protect the people of the United States, and that typically meant punishing a brutal enemy. My second job was to take care of my teammates. And the dogs were my teammates, too. Very much part of our crew. In fact, the dogs that I worked with were another pure incarnation of those original things I was looking for as a seventeen-year-old. Commitment, and true love. Dogs don't lie about their love. And dogs don't project fraudulent versions of themselves. They are who they are.

They also have an innate ability to discern who the enemy is and put themselves in a position to create an interaction that, 95 percent of the time, ends up with his pack (i.e., us) being successful.

Dogs are capable of many things, but they cannot protect themselves from phenomena they don't understand. Their senses and athleticism are force multipliers, and they have an amazing ability up to a point, but after that, they need help. Once they get to the scent they're seeking, they don't have the ability to reason out whether the device at their feet is an explosive or not. And once they smell a particular human and get to him, they don't know whether they'll get beaten with a gun or shot. I felt bad that I couldn't inform them what it was they were running into. Another reason why it was my job as a human to protect them.

But often it wasn't just the dogs who didn't know what they were running into. In addition to *Protect the dogs, and they'll protect you,* the Vietnam-veteran dog handler and special warfare instructor had harped on another lesson, which I thought I'd internalized, but which, it turns out, I had to learn more than once. He'd warned us about the likelihood that when we got into the mix, we'd almost certainly think we knew more than we actually did.

He was right. And that night in Iraq, hunting for bombs on the riverbank, Spike helped prove his point.

I was pretty sure I knew what we were looking for: two 500-pound bombs that had been dropped twelve hours earlier. The urgency was a bit heightened at this point because the bad guys had been demonstrating that they were quite smart when it came to repurposing unexploded heavy ordnance and using it against us. Their typical MO involved baiting coalition troops into buildings and then clacking the bombs off. A few days earlier, a group of good guys had followed some clues regarding the whereabouts of a target to a house in suburban Baghdad, and when they entered that house, it blew up, killing them. The fellow who'd slipped them the bogus clues was part of an insurgent group that had gotten its hands on a JDAM (Joint Direct Attack Munition) that had failed to detonate.

As we landed at the site, our helos took scattered fire from random men in an adjacent neighborhood, far enough away that we didn't need to engage them. On foot, we moved toward our primary target—the building that served as the base of operations for the cop-killing gang. We knew we were basically racing to get to the bombs before the bad guys found them and showed up with shovels, but we also knew we had to clear the building first, before we could do any scavenging for missing munitions.

As our shoes sank a bit in the soft earth, Spike, who was lighter on his feet, moved ahead, toward something that was nestled near the building, at the base of some thin rushes. Spike had a good nose for explosives, but I knew that whatever he was sniffing, it wasn't our 500-pounders. And therefore it wasn't the priority. The building itself was. So I discouraged him, wanting him to focus.

What he'd found was two grenades. I didn't know it at the time. And because I refused to acknowledge his body language, we were in a position where those grenades could have hurt us.

We kept approaching the building, and I was giving Spike commands to drop his little side project and keep moving. But he wouldn't. We got very close to those grenades before I realized what he was telling me. Spike pointed at them with his snout, without touching them, and basically forced me to see.

He'd been right. What he did was dead-on. And he retaught me the lesson of the Vietnam-veteran instructor. There are just too many variables. The worst thing you can do is think you've considered them all. I thought I knew all the parameters in my mind, and Spike's info did not fit those parameters, so I almost missed it. I'd been unable to stay alert to the possibilities I wasn't expecting. I was concerned about enemies and 500-pound bombs, which were a real threat, yes, but not the only threat.

Thanks to Spike, we ensured the grenades were nonthreatening and then moved into the building.

Inside, we didn't find anyone, but we did find a pile of police uniforms in a room that had timbers suspended between the walls. You could tell these timbers had been used for hanging and skinning people. You could tell this because there was a good amount of blood and guts on the floor, where people's innards had drained out.

Outside, we found the 500-pound bombs we were looking for. They were embedded deep in the soft earth of the riverbank. We took a coordinate and relayed it. As we left, two jets rolled in and handled the job of bomb disposal—by placing a couple more high-velocity 500-pound bombs in their vicinity, but not in the riverbank this time. The idea was to have the new bombs trigger the old ones.

I hope the blast radius of those chain-reacting bombs included the building. The only thing that could have sanitized that place was about 8,500 units of Fahrenheit.

BEVERLY HILLS ON THE EUPHRATES

The gory remnants of the skinned humans left a stink in my nose, but memory is courteous, and it's done me the favor of forgetting that smell and replacing it with another, as the signature scent of Iraq. Honeysuckle. Whenever I smell honeysuckle, I'm transported to a different riverbank at night, just after another encounter with some ordnance. This time, it was an IED. And it did go off.

We were west of Baghdad, speeding down the Euphrates in a boat being driven by a crew of specialized boat drivers—part of that hard breed that doesn't mind war-torn commutes on behalf of the Customer. Although to us they were angels, in the eyes of the locals these drivers were probably more like Charon, because their ferry often brought a kind of darkness.

The boats were pretty nifty speedboats. It was night. We were moving across the water at a fairly good clip. As we approached the destination, we slowed down.

Pop.

That's what we heard off the starboard side of the boat. Right away, we knew it was an IED that must have been detonated remotely, and probably by wire, by a human who could see us. It was clear we were being watched. It was also clear that the IED had been poorly staged, because none of us got hurt.

After the pop, we heard the sound of objects hitting the water and the side of the boat, but there was no harm done. The smattering of dirt and metal fragments lacked both propulsive force and direction.

We'd lucked out.

Perhaps the best gauge of that IED's unimpressiveness was the genuinely disdainful look Spike gave it when he heard the explosion. Most living creatures would jump at the sound of a bomb going off. Dogs, especially. But Spike just cast a casual glance in the direction of the noise, like the event was beneath contempt.

The boat dropped us off. We hopped out into the deep, slippery mud, and started walking in toward what I considered to be the Beverly Hills west of Baghdad, due to the huge houses. And that's when I smelled the honeysuckle.

The cities in Iraq are planned out. The suburbs, for the most part, are not. There do not seem to be any zoning laws. Often, we'd see walls around the house, and it was evident that the residents were just throwing trash and debris over their walls to the outer side, where it would sit, like it had been evacuated out of an airlock on a space station into what was essentially oblivion. There was no solid infrastructure. And that's because they'd lived through over a decade of sanctions, war with the Iranians, and then our invasion. It was a small miracle that there was any sense of normalcy in their lives at all. Folks sometimes remark, "Oh, they're so tribal," as if that were a critique, and the whole story. But, to be fair, that's also how they survived. They had to help each other out. And that's why they're stuck. Because tribalism provides a kind of order, along with its oppression and backwardness.

Having waded through shore muck and then inland debris and litter, we wove through the neighborhood and passed the barrier of the outer wall of the first house that we were searching for targets. That wall was indeed like an airlock. Within its confines, the grounds were stately.

We quietly entered the house. My first thought was *This is odd*. The home had vast marble floors. Grandiose staircases. Arched doors. Cornices and wainscoting. My second thought was *Wet boots on this kind of floor are dangerous*. It was very slick. Trying to be quiet, while moving, was challenging.

The folks who lived there did not know they had visitors.

We searched that house, and three others, before we found our man. There was no security in any of the homes. How unconventional. The man we captured, without a struggle, was a local financier and leader of the AQI affiliate. He was a terror-funder who secured payments that brought suicide bombers in from other countries to carry out attacks and coordinate new explosives technologies. But from what I could tell, he treated it like it was just another day job. Apparently, he got up in the mornings, went to the office, worked a solid eight hours funding death, and then came home to his luxo pad and had a nice dinner.

While we walked him back out of the neighborhood, we made comms with the boats, which headed back to a different spot to extract. Our man was wearing the standard long-sleeved daytime robe and flip-flops. We'd put a hood on him, but we pulled the hood up so he could walk without bumping into obstacles and debris outside his walls.

I caught glimpses of his face. His expression remained tranquil.

Once on the boat, we pulled his hood back down. He didn't need to see or know too much about where he was going, or the identity of the folks whisking him away. Curiously, he wasn't the only one in the dark, being ferried by anonymous folks. I never knew the names of any of the men driving those boats—or where they slept, where they ate, how they lived. I never saw any of them again.

WHAT NO HOPE DOES

It was strange that the terror-funder's facial features were so unruffled and unscarred. There were no signs of strain. Brutal career fields typically leave their mark on faces, especially around the eyes. It made me wonder: did that man ever witness the fruits of his labor? Because I sure did.

I remember my first suicide bombing. We were moving. It was dark. And I was looking through green night vision. Then, boom, I saw limbs fly. The first time you see it, it's absolutely shocking. We always knew the threat existed, but it, too, was impossible to understand thoroughly until you'd touched it, and seen it face-to-face. The thing is, when you see it, you're moving, and you're in a fight, so you can't sit and digest. You do your job. But later, the temporal lobe starts whirring and the image returns. And then the rest of your lobes protest—"What the hell are we supposed to do with this?"—because it's an insane image to process.

Generally, when they'd blow themselves up, the hero-martyrs would be carrying vests packed with nuts, bolts, washers, and other assorted debris. What they would not be carrying is hope. And that's why, even after experiencing one up close, my reaction to willing suicide bombers is not just to condemn them as evil, which they are, but also to see them as sad. Their culture has betrayed them, and each explosion is a testament to the failings of the leaders in those places where young people see blowing themselves up as an honorable option, as a kind of heroism. They do not see a way forward, or out.

It's one thing to fight an enemy. It's another to fight a hopeless one. Hope—or the lack thereof—is a big tactical factor. Most folks understand that. Islamic State sure does; that's why their recruitment numbers have been solid. They prey on the hopeless. And those who still have a shred of it? In Syria, of late, notice the direction that the refugees have been running: west, toward the cultures that take care of each other.

PREDATORS, LOWERCASE "P"

We always had the intel on what our targets had done, but we didn't always get to see or hear live recordings of it. The night of the eleven-year-old boy, we did get to see their crimes. Well, most of them, anyway.

We'd watched it all on a Predator feed. A group of local Iraqis had machine-gunned a bus full of other local Iraqis serving in the police, along with some American instructors, killing over twenty in all. The attackers drove away from the ambush site to a house abutting a canal. Late one day, we took a helo and visited that house. When we got there, we expected a fight, because we'd already seen their tactics on DroneFlix. But, to our surprise, they put up no fight at all. We were puzzled. Our interpreter asked them why they wouldn't fight, and he started giggling when he heard the answer given by one of the men. The terp turned to us and said, "He admitted that he didn't want to fight because he is a pussy." And when the terp asked the assembled gang the broader question of why they perpetrate the mass killings, another one of them said they did it because they got paid to do it. "This is our job."

We encountered this a few times. And there were surely many factors at work. But a key one I always come back to was that big, foundational mistake we made: taking a large army and disbanding it, thereby creating widespread, dangerous disaffection among a group of people trained to fight. And because the folks who got fired had already been involved in some roughness in their lives, and were probably psychically fragmented after years of it, there's a good chance that their dismissal pushed many of them to where they just didn't care about themselves, or others, anymore. This night, the main fellow being questioned by the terp was fairly blasé, projecting an attitude I can best describe as *Take me, or kill me, I don't care.* He wasn't so far gone, yet, that he was a suicide bomber, but he was OK slaughtering a bunch of Iraqis in a bus, and doing something else pretty vile.

After we completed the "capture" component of the evening by rounding up the men, we searched the house. Spike found the guns they'd hidden, and we also found some women and an eleven-year-old boy. Through the terp, we learned some of the boy's story. He'd run away from home because his dad was beating him. So he'd come here, seeking refuge, and the men had taken him in, and then started a daily routine of raping him. We couldn't capture him (take him with us) because he was a kid. So we left him there with the women, hoping that without the lowercase predators around, things might improve for him. It made my heart a little sick. I wonder where he is today, and if he has any hope.

Also, I wish his rapists had pulled guns on us.

THE LION

Commentators have said some very interesting things about the Awakening, but here's the meat of the issue for those of us whose lives were directly impacted by it:

Iraqis had gotten to the point where they had no real love for Americans, because they saw we had no plan. But many of them had even less love for Al-Qaida, with whom they were growing increasingly disenchanted.

It was a state of affairs that created new dynamics on the ground. In particular, we started to notice a considerable shift in our ability to make functional, spontaneous alliances with the locals when we went out at night. This shift was demonstrated rather dramatically in a certain troubled city that we spent some time in, north-northeast of Baghdad.

Although situated in a zone that was typically part of the Sunni swath of the country, this city was an unusual place because Sunni and Shia were somewhat melded. During my time there, it was also unusual because of its threat level.

For many Americans, the term "Islamic State" is something they've only recently become familiar with, but as far back as 2006, Al-Qaida had been designating this city as the capital of what it was already calling its Islamic State of Iraq.

Consequently, in 2007, on my third deployment to Iraq, coalition forces were doing a lot of heavy fighting in and around this besieged town, working to kill the AQ octopus that was strangling it.

As an assist to that larger effort, we'd been sent there to capture or kill AQ affiliates who were regularly attacking American troops and Iraqi police at checkpoints, with some real success. The intel told us that the cohort doing the damage was a fairly decent-sized force, a dedicated and extremely violent crew of committed guerrillas who were also good at planting lots of IEDs in the region.

There was a relatively small operating base located at the edge of the tumultuous little town. We would commute nightly from this small base into the neighborhoods that held our specific targets. Sometimes we traveled on foot. Sometimes we went by helicopter. And sometimes we used vehicles.

One mission involved a small group of us going after these AQ guerrillas in an outlying neighborhood. We tracked their activity to a certain geographic area, and then we used additional intel to basically identify a particular house as the one most likely to have them inside of it. Were we 100 percent sure that this first house held the targets? No. But we always went in ready for anything. You could never go someplace half-assed.

After our commute to the neighborhood, we gained access to the home, and we quickly realized that we could secure things without any violence. There were a few children and several adults inside. While some of us checked the house and made sure there were no weapons, others rounded everybody up and began a bit of questioning, using our terp.

The father of the family had not needed a lot of explanation in order to figure out what we were up to, and he volunteered, "I know who you're looking for."

"Can you lead us to him?" we asked, cutting to the chase.

"Yes," he replied, matter-of-factly.

We went outside, and the father agreed that he'd walk with us and point us in the right direction. It was late at night. Nobody was out. Just us. But the risk this father was taking was still considerable. In fact, he was making a very serious wager. He was bringing us to the bad folks we were after, assuming we would deal with them or at least remove them, right then and there. Because if we didn't neutralize them on this little stroll, then he'd likely have to deal with them later. And they were a vicious, vengeful lot. In an indirect but real way, this father was betting the lives of his family members on our ability to do our job.

He pointed to a palm grove that was far off, and explained that the people we wanted were "in there."

That simple gesture—pointing to a palm grove—was a key reason the Awakening was a significant movement in the Iraq war, from our perspective. This had never happened before, in our experience. Previously, nobody in Iraq had wanted to be a snitch. But now, this father of multiple children, all of whom we'd just met under less than positive circumstances, was eager to help us.

A year earlier, if this man's neighbors had seen him walking through the Iraqi night with a half-dozen scruffy Americans loaded out to hunt down a violent enemy, he would have been in trouble. But at this point, the locals had grown tired of AQ indiscriminately killing civilians and blowing up mosques and markets, so they were more willing to help us. That said, their options for fixing the problem were limited. The father and his neighbors couldn't just go walk into a U.S. base and say, "Hey, I want to collaborate, and I know where the bad guys are," because the bad guys would see them entering the base, and they'd exact retribution. So we probably did him a favor by showing up at his house that night.

As we walked, our trailblazing ally-for-the-moment took a second to enumerate some of his grievances, a key one being that these AQ in Iraq thugs charged him and his neighbors a fee to use the road in front of their own homes. "They make us pay them, and they are not even from here."

We weren't from there, either. We were invaders. But we didn't blow up mosques, and we didn't blow up markets.

Awakening or not, we kept security on him as we walked together, because, hell, this was Iraq and this was war, and there was no guarantee he wasn't leading us into an ambush, something that had happened to us a time or two previously.

It was summertime, and even at night the temperature was well above 100 degrees Fahrenheit. But this part of Iraq probably looks a bit different than most folks would imagine. It was not desert. It was composed of rolling hills that were brushy, and more green than brown. There were many palm groves. The way we saw it, palm groves provided two very important things: dates, and cover for the enemy's ambushes. The palm groves were popular spots for the AQ guys to hide out.

It's why we were quiet. There was a puff of a breeze, and the crickets were the only noise-makers as we walked a few hundred meters along the hard-packed dirt road, eventually coming to a place where a different dirt road ran into the palm grove.

Our new friend pointed, but not to any one spot, just in the direction of the other dirt road, and said, "They're up there." It was pretty clear that he didn't know *exactly* where the targets were, and it was equally clear that he would not be guiding us any further to explore, because he was afraid. But he wasn't planning on bugging out; he wanted to see what transpired. So we told him to move back and stay with the interpreter and security team.

It was time for me to let the dog start searching the area. I knew he would lead us to the people we were looking for.

The dog we took out that night was the other dog I worked with during my time in Iraq, a Belgian Malinois named the Lion. He was given that name by Iraqi locals after his encounter with a particularly hostile target a few weeks earlier. The Iraqi bystanders had told the conventional American troops in charge of the area that strangers had come the night before and captured a group of bad men . . . and that they'd had a "lion" with them.

After I unleashed him, the Lion took a few steps, and then his whole body changed—muscles, posture, attitude, everything. He became something uncanny, and we all knew what was coming. He quickly turned and ran, kind of bounding, with a violent purpose to his movement.

It was *on*.

I knew the Lion was getting ready to punish people, and he needed our help. So I ran after him, as did the other five guys. With fast but silent footfalls, the Lion ran across the packed dirt road, straight into a thicket of heavy brush. He disappeared. We followed in after him, through the screen of bushes, and when we came out the other side, we saw a wonderful thing.

The Lion was engaging five armed men lying in a ditch, where they'd been waiting to ambush us.

Having quickly assessed the quintet, the Lion had decided that the man in the middle was the one to whom he should introduce himself first. Accordingly, he was now crushing that man's left arm. The stunned fighter was trying to swing his AK-47 around with his right arm, so that he could shoot the Lion with it. But the Lion was shaking the AQ guy so violently that he couldn't get to his feet or stabilize himself sufficiently to bring his gun to bear.

The other four individuals did nothing. And it didn't take a behavioral psychologist to decode the reason why. Staring with horrified eyes at this ferocious hound fighting with their friend, it was pretty obvious they were overwhelmed by what was happening, petrified by the shock of it all.

I wasn't surprised by their reaction. It was something we'd seen time and time again . . .

They'd been hit by the Hair Missile.

That moment is etched in my mind. I wish I could paint it. It would be a sort of twisted Last Supper: four guys flanking a central tortured figure, frozen in clean states of disbelief and horror. And this disbelief and horror generated by the Lion gave us the few moments we needed to quickly engage the enemy.

It turns out there was a second row of two or three fighters farther back from this first phalanx of the Frozen Five. From what I could tell, the second row was scared to death, too, and they just started shooting wildly in our direction. In my opinion, based on their undisciplined spraying, they wouldn't have cared if they'd hit their own men.

We put them all down. The first five bad guys didn't get off a single shot. And that's a good measure of the Lion's impact. His work that night was a piece of intensely focused and exquisite violence. He sensed danger before we did. He addressed the threat before anyone even knew it was there. He waded into five full-grown men hiding in a ditch with machine guns, and with zero hesitation he crushed them.

I admire the Lion's drive. I'd be dead without him. And it's not just me who'd be dead. And not just that one time.

After the shooting, we searched the bodies for intel, looking for anything that might be of value in understanding what they were doing and who they were doing it to. It turns out this particular crew was engaged in a grim routine of murder similar to the one practiced by the gang near the 500-pound bombs. They'd been killing local Iraqi police in brutal fashion, by hanging them, beheading them, or skinning them alive. We knew this because when we searched a well building in the palm grove, we discovered video equipment and a computer they'd used to burn a pile of DVDs. The DVDs contained videos set to music glorifying the brutality—part of that weird impulse of theirs to make those twisted digital scrapbooks.

After we emerged from the bushes, back onto the road, and cleared the rest of the area, we met up again with our Iraqi friend, who had been standing a ways back. We said to the terp, "Tell him the neighborhood is a little safer now." The terp relayed the remark, and the Iraqi father nodded. He had helped us, and we had helped him. Like so many other regular Iraqis, he was just a man caught in the middle of a larger battle, struggling to maintain some semblance of civilization while AQ tore up his town and the Americans tried to tear up AQ. Tired of being perpetually under someone else's thumb, he'd decided to do something about it. I think all of us were pleasantly surprised to find ourselves on the same team that night.

Immediately after checking the bodies and chatting with our Iraqi friend, we headed back out. We had some more work to do. Luckily, it was nearby, so we didn't have to walk too far. As we hoofed it to the next engagement, I gave the Lion a bit of water. He needed it. He'd just done all that work while fully clad in fur. He was basically wearing a permanent sweater in the Middle East, in summer. And not only that, but when he rolled with us, he also wore a mesh and fabric vest, with gear pockets and patches on it.

Yup, he wore patches. The same ones I wore.

SHARDS AND ASHES

Their patches were the same, but the vests that the dogs wore were different from ours. Their vests were fabric—mostly nylon and Cordura—and even with the attached lights, zippers, straps, and a big handle that turned the dog into a bit of a furry suitcase, they were lightweight. This had advantages and downsides.

The advantage was that they kept the dogs mobile. The folks we fought overseas were shooting big AK-47 bullets, so we humans wore big, heavy ballistic vests that clocked in at a little under twenty-five pounds. The dogs would have needed a vest of almost similar size, given their long torsos, and that would have meant essentially wearing a straitjacket that was about a quarter of their total weight. That weight would have been debilitating. It would have meant they could not patrol long distances into a target and be expected to fight. With the lighter vests, though, they could, and did.

The downside to the lighter vest was that they provided the dogs no ballistic protection.

The second time I heard birds in Iraqi trees was the day before Christmas Eve, just prior to an assault. It was ravens again, and they were cawing, not chirping. The sound was harsh, not sweet. Which was appropriate.

I read somewhere that before they were referred to as flocks of ravens, they were called an "unkindness of ravens" or a "conspiracy of ravens." I cast my vote for the reinstatement of "unkindness" as the collective noun, because that's what their sound is to me now, after hearing it that second time in Iraq.

We were doing our last-minute prep a few hundred meters from the target set, kneeling in a copse where the birds were. Spike was with us. He became calm and turned his gaze from the ravens to me, ominously. It was a look that I remembered from our previous encounter with Iraqi birdsong, and I thought, *This is going to be something.* I just didn't know what it was going to be.

We'd soon find out. Not long after the ravens commenced their clamor, we commenced our assault. We were hunting a man and his crew who specialized in importing young men into Iraq from Syria and turning them into suicide bombers. The evening's exertions involved searching a set of buildings within a larger neighborhood—a sweeping series of assaults on multiple structures that were conducted simultaneously. As Spike and I approached one of the target buildings, a man darted out of a building adjacent to our initial target and took off toward another one. In his native tongue, I yelled the most important words I knew: the verbal commands to stop. He didn't. I shot two warning rounds. The man kept running. So I sent Spike after him and began running at him myself.

Spike hit him. Because it was December 23, and cold, the man was wearing multiple coats. The man was about fifty meters away, and Spike had built up a lot of speed by the time he hit those coats. He was moving so fast that he didn't get good purchase on the thick layers of cloth, and instead flipped out from under the runner and landed about three meters in front of him. The man fell down from the force of Spike's strike. When he stood back up, he was facing Spike, who had quickly gotten his bearings and was now running at him hard. Spike hit him in the upper chest. Spike was 65 pounds. The man was 210 pounds. Big, and smart enough to use his size advantage, the man deliberately fell on Spike and tried to smother and crush him. Probably lit up by endorphins, the man also bit back, chomping on Spike's chest.

That was enough. I stopped running about fifteen meters from the enemy combatant, who was smothering Spike on the ground, and I shot him several times. The enemy rolled off Spike. When he did, Spike ran out from under him and turned back toward the combatant as if he was going to re-attack. But he didn't.

On my way to the downed combatant, I said to the fellow assaulter running alongside me, "Hey, I think Spike broke his leg." My buddy said to me, with the tone folks get when they know they're admitting the truth before you are, "No, he's hurt really bad."

I covered the remaining few meters and came up to the man, who, although he'd just been pierced by bullets, had risen to a kneeling position. (Those endorphins are something.) My buddy came up alongside us and took control of the enemy, whose role in the suicide recruitment crew would be confirmed by some information we came across subsequently.

I went over to Spike and noticed two things immediately. He was wobbling, unsteady on his legs, and his breathing was wrong. It was too shallow and weak. He wasn't breathing heavily, like he'd just been in a fight. There wasn't much else I could tell, given that I was looking through night vision, and all I could see in the green glow was his harness and his face.

But from his breathing I knew all that I needed to know: when I'd shot the man, the bullet had continued through his body and hit Spike.

I picked my dog up by the handle on his vest, threw him over my shoulder, and started running back to the main objective. As I was running, I felt Spike stop breathing altogether and go limp. I rushed him to a medic, a PJ, who was situated in a building that had already been secured, at the heart of the melee, which was still going on all around us.

When I got there, it was clear that the PJ had heard me on the radio talking about what had occurred with Spike, so we promptly laid him down on the dirt floor and took his vest off. In the general darkness, the PJ used his red-lens headlamp to see what the nature of the injuries were, after which he looked up at me and said, "I'm sorry, Jimmy. I can't do anything for him. He's gone."

While the rest of the team finished the work of taking down the other buildings and locating the main fellow we were looking for, I sat on that dirt floor with Spike for a bit, until it was time to go. I then threw Spike over my shoulder and walked with the rest of the crew—and the MAMs that we were taking off target—to our extract landing zone, where we met the helicopters.

It was the worst helicopter ride of my life, much worse than the helo ride I would later take the night I was wounded. Spike sat in my lap for the duration of the flight. I say "sat" out of habit, but it's not technically accurate, since the word implies agency, and Spike was not alive.

When we reached our home base, I took him back to his kennel. The kennel, located in a little building next to where most of us lived, was the size of four very large closets, with each closet designed to hold one dog. At the time, we had two dogs, and Spike was one of them. Over the course of several months, we'd used this particular base as a launch point for about forty-five missions. And usually, when we returned from the mission, I'd open the kennel and let Spike do the thing he most wanted to do right away: drink water. It would often be the first time I was in the light with him, meaning it was the first time I could look him over and check his whole carcass after I'd gotten the gear off. From his feet to his tail, I'd check everything. And then I'd get him some food, fill his water dish, tell him I loved him, and go to the debrief. After that, I'd check on him, make sure he'd eaten his dinner, and take him out for a walk, where he could do important things like go to the bathroom. After our stroll, I'd take him back and give him a treat, generally some kind of dog biscuit. And then I'd give him a hug and go to bed, and he would, too.

Back this time, with him a corpse, I carried him inside and laid him on the floor in his kennel, dead. He just lay there. I probably looked at him for five minutes. All that fur and muscle and spirit, which I'd only known as a life force, now morbid. Motionless. It was hard for me to process.

I didn't need to do my normal spot-check of his body, in the light. The PJ had already done one that was plenty brutal and plenty final, in the glow of his red headlamp.

Now, instead of checking him or feeding him or saying I loved him,

I took out my American flag, which I always carried with me in my gear, and, because it seemed like the right thing to do, I spread it out and put it on top of Spike. Spike's feet were sticking out from under the red and white bars. Perhaps I was hoping those red and white bars would add meaning to what had happened to the dog they were covering. But I couldn't loiter any more and indulge in wondering about the Why; I had to go share the What.

At the debrief, I explained what had happened in my part of the mission—how I'd shot and killed Spike. There were forty guys there. And there was no demonstrable sadness. It was a debrief. Not the time for emotion. When we walked out of the briefing room, I realized that enough time had passed to make it now the wee hours of Christmas Eve.

Christmas was not on my mind.

I went back to the kennel, where a bunch of my crew had gathered to say their goodbyes to Spike. As I watched them, I had a sudden and unexpectedly clear thought: I knew I'd get a tattoo, as a way to keep Spike near, perhaps on my forearm or bicep.

Breaking my reverie, my buddy Frank, who was the other dog handler, approached me and said, "Hey, let's go to the vet." We put Spike in a truck and drove for a bit, as the base was fairly large. When we got to the clinic and met the lead Army veterinarian, he knew the story, because Frank had called ahead to prep him regarding the evening's events.

The doctor began by observing the obvious. There was a BB-sized wound on the right lumbar area, and a larger ½" x ¾" wound on the left side of Spike's chest wall. There was severe blood loss from the mouth. The doctor noted that "rigor is starting to set in, as I examine Spike."

"Necropsy" is typically the term used for autopsies on animals. After a short while, the lead doctor noted that "no additional necropsy was performed because we know this MWD [military working dog] died from a fatal GSW [gunshot wound]." He did not know the author of that fatal GSW. He just saw that a bullet went in and out. So I told him what had happened. Hearing it, he was still. And I was still after I said it, not so much out of respect for what was obviously a solemn moment, but more because I was just seriously numb.

After showing me the bite marks from the man on Spike's chest, the Army vet who'd done the autopsy noticed me looking agitated and asked me what I wanted to do. Having learned that they had a crematorium right there, on-site, I said I'd decided that we should cremate Spike, because I didn't want to see him in the state he was in.

Immediately, some of the staff fired it up. While the chamber warmed, they brought Spike out on a stretcher into a different room and performed a little memorial ceremony, with a doctor or two, and me and Frank, at 3:30 in the morning.

I noticed that our small group wasn't small for long. The vet, who was an Army major, woke up members of his staff, basically four kids who had worked all day, and asked them to join us. They didn't complain. They put their uniforms on and did a memorial ceremony with me for my dog.

Those folks didn't know me. But they did Spike that honor, and me that favor. It's endlessly strange how horror and self-loathing allowed me to see people do amazing things. After the ceremony, I watched them slide Spike's body into the flames. I felt it was fitting, a Viking-like end. They told me to come back later that morning, when they'd give me the ashes.

I returned to my unit's area, and set off to find two people with whom I needed to have two important discussions. First, I found my boss, the same guy who coined the phrase "you're either an asset or a liability," which is my favorite saying ever. I floated the idea of maybe burying Spike there, in Iraq. He said, "Fuck that. Fuck this place. Take him home and bury him where he belongs. Not with these savages." After that strong display of his inability to mince words, he said he was going to set some kind of commemoration in motion for later that morning.

The second overnight meeting I had was with Scrumptious, the guy in our troop known for being (visually) what his nickname implies, although it's the least of his talents. I asked him if he could paint an ammo can to put Spike's ashes in, and he did it that night. He spray-painted the can with our squadron insignia and also mounted Spike's patches on it.

A little while later, I took the ammo can back to the vet, and they gave me the plastic bag with Spike's ashes. The smooth curves of the ashes pressing against the clear plastic bag were disrupted here and there by the chunks of bone that hadn't gotten refined.

After sunup that same morning, in our little compound's courtyard, my boss had arranged for a second memorial ceremony. Everyone from my immediate strike group was there, but it was also multiservice, and the people who folded the flag and handed it to me this time were Army Rangers. There were forty people present, along with a chaplain . . . plus Spike, in a plastic bag inside a painted ammo can. I don't remember too many details of the ceremony. All I remember is that I was staring at the flag in the courtyard wondering who had put it at half mast, and that I was thinking, *I killed the dog, and now we all have to stand here and do a ceremony.* It's not that simple, but it's one way people could look at it, and I wouldn't blame them if they did.

But they didn't look at it that way, even though, in my sad, self-loathing state, I tended to. The truth was, yes, I'd shot Spike, and yes, these people were being asked to stand there and do a ceremony, but there was no substrate of bitterness. They were earnestly taking the time to make me feel good and pay honor to Spike. And that was a big deal. Those Rangers were very, very kind. The flag they handed me that morning is the one sitting on the mantel in my house right now.

It's called a "shoot-through," the way I killed Spike. The bullet I shot traveled through the bad guy, into Spike. It might be a stretch, but I think shoot-throughs can happen with things other than bullets—when objects or ideas with velocity punch through their intended target and hit something deeper, beyond.

Like with Neruda's poem "It Means Shadows." It hit me hard when I first read it. But after Spike was dead, it shot right through my probably damned and definitely scarred soul and touched something else.

That poem was already my favorite. Now it meant something more. After the ceremony with the Rangers, I went to Spike's kennel, grabbed a silver marker, and wrote the Neruda poem on the large plank of wood that spanned the space between Spike's now-empty kennel and its neighbor.

What hope to consider, what pure foreboding,
what definitive kiss to bury in the heart,
to submit to the origins of homelessness and intelligence,
smooth and sure over the eternally troubled waters?

What vital, speedy wings of a new dream angel
to install on my sleeping shoulders for perpetual security,
in such a way that the path through the stars of death
be a violent flight begun many days and months and centuries ago?

Suppose the natural weakness of suspicious, anxious creatures
all of a sudden seeks permanence in time and limits on earth,
suppose the accumulated age and fatigues implacably
spread like the lunar wave of a just-created ocean
over lands and shorelines tormentedly deserted.

Oh, let what I am keep on existing and ceasing to exist,
and let my obedience align itself with such iron conditions
that the quaking of deaths and of births doesn't shake
the deep place I want to reserve for myself eternally.

Let me, then, be what I am, wherever and in whatever weather,
rooted and certain and ardent witness,
carefully, unstoppably, destroying and saving himself
  openly engaged in his original obligation.

So I killed him. I killed my best friend. I spent a lot of time wrestling with that fact, back then, and I still do now.

In the days after Spike's death, I was pretty sad, and I don't remember too much about that period. Sensing that I was not, at that juncture, an asset, my master chief, a man I respected greatly, took me aside and pointed out that we were almost done with the deployment, so maybe I should just go home. This was as much a friendly decision as a professional one. He politely sugarcoated the message by saying there was nothing wrong with going home a few weeks early, and his recommendation was that I go take care of myself. I did. I took the ashes in the can and flew on a helicopter to the main base in Iraq, and then waited a day for a flight home.

That plastic bag has held up pretty well, all things considered, because those shards of bone are big, and they still push against the thin plastic, inside the can. Spike's ashes are in my house now, and I guess that's where he's been laid, but not really "to rest." I don't think the idea of laying-to-rest jibes with Spike. He was too much of a life force for that.

I don't trot out Spike's ashes very much. But a few years after Spike's death, a friend had an idea for a salute that felt right. CrossFit had created a series of workouts, called "hero workouts," in the name of dead service people, firefighters, and cops. The owner of a gym I attended wanted to do one for Spike, with the funds raised going to the charity I eventually created in Spike's name. The workout involved rope climbs, a bit of running, and some kettle bells. I partook. And in my backpack, which I carried for the entire workout, was that bag of shards and ashes.

A more visible tribute is my bicep tattoo band featuring Spike's name and the date I killed him. I got it in Arizona, from an artist who also did the skulls on that arm, and Remco's name, which is not as big as Spike's, because he only saved my life once and wasn't my dog. My arms end up being where I do a lot of my memorializing, whether it's a scar or ink, and both pay tribute almost entirely to the stuff that's hard for me, that I'm not proud of, that I don't want to forget.

In the military, we're given shadow boxes at the end of our careers. They're large, framed, and somewhat three-dimensional collections of our medals and ribbons. I guess they're called shadow boxes because the beveled edges of the frame compartments and the suspended ribbons and medals cast little shadows. The one I eventually got now sits at the back of a closet in my guest bedroom. I'm more interested in focusing on the painful and real shadows, not just the handsome shading behind our shiny medals. I live with those shadows, and carry them, and I can't change that. So I wear them, mostly on my arm, because I don't want them to lose their weight. It's not morose. It's just that it's dangerous to try to forget them, because that gives them more strength.

THE ROOM RULE, AND CHILDREN

One of the tattoo sets on my arm is an assemblage of skulls. Precisely why they're there is not important. What is important is the truth with which they are associated:

Killing is ugly.

We got in a gunfight one night where we shot a man, and boom, he fell down in the doorway. We went into the house and gathered the kids that were present and bustled them out another door, so they wouldn't see the dead fellow in the main doorway. Returning the way we came, so that we could get back to the front of the house, my friend Bestseller and I stopped about two feet from the dead man to take in the scene. He was crumpled on a concrete floor that was littered with granite fragments and pocked with one-inch-deep divots. His blood was pooling in an area, making red rivulets in those divots. And there was a kitten, licking up the blood and brains. Just lapping up the blood and brains. It was surreal.

On another occasion, we shot the father and uncle of a group of children, in front of those children. Yes, those men had it coming. They had guns drawn on us, and they were using their kids as shields, but we still put them down in front of their sons, daughters, nieces, and nephews. The men fell on the floor in a lump, and then relaxed in a way I sometimes wish I could. In my mind's eye, today, I can clearly see the faces of those kids. I'll always carry that.

Killing is ugly. And because it is, I have a serious problem with the glorification of violence. With the elevation of macho bullshit. And with the video-game-ification of war.

A few years ago, I was describing a particular gunfight that I was in, and some of the weapons that were being used. The gentleman I was chatting with said, "Yeah, I've done those same things and used those same guns in *Act of Valor*." *Act of Valor*. The video game. I looked at him to see if he was being serious. He was. I was completely baffled. Speechless, in fact. I didn't even have the wherewithal to say something clever like "Are you fucking kidding me?" In his mind, this fellow felt he understood the realities of war, even though all he knew was the digital fantasy.

Chest-thumping portrayals of war and the superabundance of video games propagate a false idea of what it is to fight. So do terms like "confirmed kills." Does anyone really believe that there is someone out there with a stethoscope, checking corpses for signs of life, and, finding none, asking one of the combatants in the raging firefight, *Hey, was that you who shot this bullet? If you'll just slow down for a second, can I get your name and ID number?* I never saw that. And to this day I still haven't found the office in the Pentagon that's responsible for confirming kills.

In order to help shift the focus to what matters, and away from what doesn't, this story needs to pass a standard I've applied to myself called "the Room Rule."

My rule, when I talk about what I did, involves imagining that I'm in a room, standing in front of the men with whom I served, and men from other units who were in close combat. And then I ask myself, *OK, would I say this thing in that room, in front of those people?* I would never stand up in a room and say I am any kind of superlative—the best this, the most that.

Do I probably have a couple of Mosts and Onlys? Maybe. But there are guys who have more significant ones, and many more of them, than I do. And they never mention theirs. So neither will I. (Well, actually, there is one Most and Only that I intend to reveal. But that'll come later.)

One thing that has been bothersome to me about much of the media's over-hyped dialogue concerning warfighters is that a lot of the language and sound-bite-worthy points of emphasis are the very last things I would ever use to describe the people I worked with. They are extraordinary people, but what I want you to know about them has absolutely nothing to do with body count.

One night, during Iraqi Freedom, while I was kneeling outside the door of a target, next to Spike, with every nerve alert and my body feeling like one big trigger that was being pulled, I witnessed something that I still think about frequently. I watched four of my friends rush through the front door, into the first room and a barrage of screaming people. There were kids inside. One of my colleagues, who was a left-handed shooter, used his right arm to grab two small children—the children of the people who were very upset about having uninvited visitors—and pull them behind his body to protect them. The enemy had thrown those kids down the hallway to buy themselves time. So my buddy used his body as a moving barricade, shuffling them outside to a less dangerous place.

Back inside the home, the capture/kill mission played out. That night it was a brawl, one that ended in a capture. When the mission was over, I went back to my little hut and swore that someday people would know about my friend and his protective right arm. And that wasn't the only night I saw men do such things. The risks I saw them take aren't in any playbook. You don't train to fight with children running around. There is no training scenario that prepares you to risk your life to shield and evacuate the enemy's children so that they don't get caught in the crossfire. That's just natural. It's either in you as a human or it isn't.

So forget the superlatives, and the labels. That's not what describes my experiences, or the guys I worked with. They are not the best, the most, the deadliest. They are humans who shield children with their own bodies.

HOLIDAYS

The toilet paper holders were gold-rimmed, and there were droll articles written by clever folks commenting on how wonderfully ironic it was that the American Multi-National Force (MNF) commanders in Iraq now used them.

I failed to see the humor.

The toilet paper holders, and other gilded fixtures, were features of an old Saddam palace, on a lake near the Baghdad airport, inside what became the Camp Victory compound, from which the coalition mission in Iraq was coordinated and led. I think as many as five commanding generals of the MNF slept in the bedroom of that palace, as they succeeded each other over many years. The green and gold bed that they initially slept in was Saddam's, and its headboard was apparently crowned with ornate, interlocking winged doves.

I do not know why the U.S. overthrew a dictator and then moved its commanding generals into his garish, twenty-room, Al-Ez lakeside palace. It's a powerful message, and we might want to reflect on whether it's the right one. In contrast to them, I think of General McChrystal, who, later, would be much more of a Spartan, living in a plywood hut, and sleeping on a cot, like me.

I never went into a palace in Iraq. I was never in the Green Zone at all. I didn't get my picture taken under the crossed swords. What I did do, once, was huddle in a plywood supply hut and choke back tears while another grown man read a kids' book to his daughter, who wasn't there.

We were in western Iraq, and I always had a camera with me. The wife of one of the Air Force PJs had sent him a Christmas book. When I first saw him bring it out, it seemed to be a strange care package item, as it was a children's book. But all became clear when he asked if I would film him reading it, so that he could share the video with his daughter back home. She was three.

Good. A mission. First, we needed a soundstage for this dramatic reading. We decided on a quiet spot inside a supply hut, which was really a one-room shanty with a door and bare light bulb. It was cold, and drizzling rain, as he and I walked through the tiny little outstation camp we had, en route to our shoot. He had his book tucked under his jacket to protect it from the dampness, and I was doing the same with my camera.

Once inside, he untucked the tome—an illustrated version of *The Night Before Christmas*—and started reading it. As he did, he kept pausing and turning the book to the camera, to show his daughter the pages. Here he was in this hellhole, reaching out, talking to a little girl that he clearly loved, as if she were there. And I was right in the line of fire, which was surprisingly heavy. The story of the joy that merry St. Nick brought when he snuck into homes at night made me reflect on what I brought when I went into homes at night. I had my one eye closed and the other almost glued to the viewfinder for the duration of the reading because I was tearing up badly, and it seemed like the manly move was to disguise that fact.

As the PJ got deeper into the tale, he started tearing up, too. And so, in this little war-torn slice of western Iraq, two tough guys accustomed to chockablock missions and living through crazy wildness were crying in a room with a light bulb and a Christmas book being read for a three-year-old back in the U.S.

When he finished with the narrative, we just smiled at each other. I downloaded the footage, edited it, put it on a DVD, and gave it to him, and he mailed it. We never talked about it again. In subsequent days, which were unlike the cozy Christmas scene in the poem we'd shared, I sometimes would imagine her, the little sweet girl, watching Daddy on a TV screen somewhere.

As sentimental and sugar-sweet as it is, I do sometimes wonder when we'll get our act together so we no longer have to love remotely like that.

Afghanistan

THE HAND OF THE LITTLE GIRL

A target littered with people running everywhere was typical, and somewhat expected. But there were never—not in any brief that I ever read, or in any training I ever received—lessons or SOPs or indications that such-and-such type of person would likely throw his children at you as you storm his house. Or self-detonate. Or that they'd have a kid that they're raping, on the regular, in the compound when you raid it.

In Iraq one night, our interpreter used his Arabic to ask a combatant we'd detained, "Why did you push your children toward us?" I heard that man reply, in plain English, like he was from Boston, "I will not let my family interfere with my jihad."

You had to learn things like that for yourself. And those lessons created a whole new algorithm that governed how dangerous things were. Tactically, I felt that the presence of children meant we had to understand distance even better than we did when training, be even more aggressive, and accelerate the timeframe in which our decisions were made.

When it comes to lessons learned in war, I think the ones taught by children often have the most impact.

I did my first deployment to Afghanistan in 2005. I returned there in 2008, and did two more deployments as part of Operation Enduring Freedom.

One night, as I sat on the floor of a dark helicopter, flying through the high mountains of Afghanistan, I thought about a handful of things. I thought about the men I was with and about their families. I thought about how I was lucky to have hot chow while some of the other deployed, fighting Americans were eating cruddy MREs. I thought about the number and type of assets—meaning supporting firepower—that were escorting us on this mission. I thought about the sentinel gunship overhead, tracking us to our target. I thought about my sincere hope that we had an uneventful insert into this op, because I really had to pee.

We got the "thirty seconds out" sign from the crew, and we readied ourselves. I put my goggles on because it was about to get dusty, unhooked my safety strap, and then did what we always did—looked at the door gunners for clues about the situation that would greet us when we disembarked. The gunners were a good indicator of whether or not you were going to be getting off the helicopter in a shit-storm.

Here's a quick primer on the Semiotics of Door Gunners . . .

Obviously, if they were shooting, the situation was pretty clear. Same thing applies if we were getting shot at, although detecting this wasn't as effortless. When you're in a helo, you can't hear anything above the engine noise, so we'd be looking for tracers, not listening for gunfire. But the door gunners didn't have to be exchanging fire to be giving off clues. You could also just pay attention and sense how serious they were. If they were super-focused, you knew that something was up.

On this night, they looked focused. But not *super* focused. A good sign. It meant that we'd get a moment when we landed. I felt the helo flare, and as smooth as a car pulling into a freshly paved driveway—without even feeling a bump of contact—the pilot set us down on the rocky slope of a hill in eastern Afghanistan. We unloaded quickly. In the dust, I could see our point man and the rest of the crew. We took a knee and waited for the helos to depart. When they did, we all removed our goggles, and those of us who had to relieve ourselves (it had been about an hour-long helicopter ride) did so.

Shortly thereafter, we began our walk. We walked for quite a while. Dark skies, rugged terrain, and a cool breeze wafting—that was the universe we were in that night.

As we approached the village where we would try to capture or kill our objective, we slowed down, and the leadership got together to talk about a few things. On this mission, I was a "middle manager" of sorts, in charge of about seven men, which was roughly a third of the force that night. We talked about where there had been movement. What the overhead assets could see, and what was unusual about it. One novelty was that almost all of the village's inhabitants were sleeping outside. It was late summer, and it was too hot inside the rammed-earth-and-mud houses for people to sleep comfortably. This part of the world did not have central air.

As we got close, a group of seven to ten men ran out from behind a small structure in the village and started to head the other way. Up front, the leader responsible for the other two-thirds of the crew made the call to chase after the runners and see what they were up to. For various reasons (including the fact that they were awake in the middle of the night, alert, and ready to bolt), I was betting that these runners were some of the folks we wanted.

A small firefight broke out about 150 meters from where my smaller detachment remained formed up, having stayed back. We could see the tracers and hear the enemy shooting. Our folks were shooting, too, but their guns were much quieter.

Pretty soon the enemy's guns stopped, and the silence was back.

We assessed our environs. On one side of us was a small group of buildings that we had to clear in order to make sure there were no more attackers hiding inside. On the other side of us was the clearing where, unmolested, the women and children were all sleeping outside—or, more accurately, where they had been sleeping. The gunfire had awakened them. The clearing now made for a striking visual—a disorganized tangle of mosquito nets, blankets, pillows, and groggy humans. We wanted to get them back inside as soon as possible, so that they'd be safe in case there was another flare-up, given that the bad guys tended to "spray and pray" when it came to firing their weapons.

Some of my colleagues went into the buildings. I stayed outside with a few others to watch the women and kids, sifting through them to make sure there weren't any men in their midst, trying to hide.

On my radio, I listened to the overhead assets as they reported what they were seeing and helped us coordinate. My subset of the crew was going to stay where we were, gather up all the innocents, and do a little tactical questioning, while the bulk of our force dealt with the handful of inhabitants still moving around at the other end of the village.

When I got the signal that some of the structures in our neighborhood were clear, I asked the interpreter to tell the women to gather up their children and move into those buildings. It was obvious that they were quite frightened. Understandably so. As always, I suspected we probably looked like aliens to them. On top of that, they'd just heard gunshots and the explosions of small bombs from the overhead gunship. They didn't really know what was going on, or what to expect.

In keeping with the instructions we were giving them, the women quickly gathered up the children and headed as a group into the structures next to the clearing. We kept a very close eye on this mass movement, because the commotion meant a heightened risk of men trying to sneak among the women. In the past, we'd caught them doing exactly that, and were they to get the drop on us now, we'd be in a bad way.

But everything seemed to be on the up and up, so I asked the terp to tell the moms to count heads and make certain they had all of their kids. I then surveyed the scene again. The little exodus had left the blankets, pillows, and mosquito-net tents in disarray. And it had left something else, too. I looked down to where my eye caught a bit of movement about two feet from my leg. It's important to know that looking through night vision goggles (NVGs) is like looking through toilet paper tubes, so when you caught peripheral motion, it was a very lucky catch.

The source of the motion was a tiny, young girl who was probably close to eighteen months old. She was wearing a light-colored nightgown, and she had curly hair, which was flat on one side because she'd been sleeping on it between two large pillows and a pile of blankets. Without frowning or scowling or crying, she was now sitting upright and whipping her head from side to side, coolly trying to figure out why she was suddenly unaccompanied. It was clear that her mother had yet to realize she was missing.

I scanned the rest of my crew, all of whom were busy, some watching the people filing into the cleared structures and some searching the remaining structures for weapons and bombs. And then I glanced back at the girl. She was looking up at me in a manner I found surprising, because there was warmth in it. She didn't cry or act scared at all. She reached her hands up to me, undaunted. It was hard to resist the gesture. I made room for her by shifting my gun to my right side. Then I bent over, picked her up, and seated her on my left forearm and hip. With this girl along for the ride, I began walking through the craziness toward the center of the buildings, listening to the radio and watching my buddies move about, doing their business.

And then I felt it. Like a bolt of lightning. Well . . . as strong as a bolt of lightning, but much, much softer.

I felt the girl reach up with her right arm and wrap it around the back of my neck, and I felt her tiny little hand on the skin of my neck.

It was a shock. It seriously jolted me. It made me almost stumble, it was so foreign, in that moment. I had come that night to bring nothing good to her neighborhood. I had come to capture or kill members of her family. I was dressed like a complete freak. My eyes were glowing. On my right swung a rifle, which took life. On my left was this new one. I couldn't turn my face directly at her because the NVGs would bump her head, so I looked at her by turning only my eyes.

After rubbing her sleepy little eyes with her left hand, she looked at me like I was her uncle, completely comfortable sitting on my hip being carried toward the houses. I could tell she trusted me. It made me feel dizzy.

In order to collect myself, I stood still for a second, trying to figure out why this little hand was knocking me for such a loop. And then I heard the scream. . . . It was the young girl's mother. I knew it had to be. We were close enough to the buildings that the folks inside could see me, the large alien with the glowing eyes and a gun, holding this tiny child. I saw that the terp was already telling the woman to be quiet. It wasn't working. The mother was talking animatedly to the terp as I walked up, and when I got close to her, she looked over at me in total fear. I slowly handed the curly-haired girl to her mother and watched the woman's tense, teary face relax under a wave of relief when the child was safely in her arms. I lingered there for a moment longer and let my line of sight drift to the little girl, who, though crushed to her mother's chest, was nonetheless looking back at me and holding my gaze warmly, despite the freakish apparatus strapped to my face.

She and I parted company, and I went back to work. But on the way home, on the floor of the helicopter, I found myself thinking about the little girl again, trying to decode the nature of her impact. It dawned on me that what she'd done, unwittingly, was give me a gift. She'd helped me realize that in her eyes I was still a human being—something that I didn't think would happen over there.

A little while later, I'd be hit by a bullet that would travel through me at 2,800 feet per second, without paying me the courtesy of stopping. The girl's hand knocked me at least as hard as that 7.62x39. In fact, looking back, it's difficult to determine which was more powerful.

MEETING GABBY

During one of my 2008 deployments in southern Afghanistan, we learned that we were slated to have a visit from a congressional delegation. This news cheered me not at all, because I tended to be cynical with regard to politicians.

Especially galling, for all of us, was having to get gussied up for alleged dignitaries and don uniforms that featured, of all things, name tags. It felt infantile, and tied to a world of shiny badges and passes that we didn't care for. We were briefed on the sparkling itinerary, which would involve going to a room, sitting, listening, and then maybe answering some questions about what was happening on the ground.

Name tags, for Christ's sake. Not unlike show-and-tell day for third graders.

When the House Armed Services Committee delegation came in, a young woman wearing jeans and a long-sleeve T-shirt stood out. This was Gabby Giffords. She looked like she could have been one of our intel people, a resemblance that we were not expecting. For such an august personage, she mostly had an air about her that seemed to announce how down to earth she was.

It turns out she wasn't just down to earth. She was way deep down to earth.

When she looked at our gear, what struck me was that she did so for the right reasons. Not to gee-whiz about our equipment, but to make sure we had what we needed.

She asked smart questions. She was warm and friendly. I gravitated to her, and was listening in as she told us where her district was. It occurred to me that a part of the state she represented happened to be near a corner where we sometimes trained. So, being a smart-ass, I went to one of the other shooters who had a K9 assigned to him, grabbed the leash, and used the K9 to introduce myself to Gabby. I said, "Why don't you come train with us?" She replied, "OK," and gave me her card.

That's that, I figured. Wrongly.

THE WILD WEST

Afghanistan still, 2008.

We were flying in on two helicopters, and the people who point us—the intel folks—were saying that a large house at the base of a hill was the primary objective.

Our intel guys always took great pride in gathering as much information as they could to help keep us alive and prepare us for what we were going to encounter.

Even so, once we showed up, things were often not quite as they should be. And that would be the case this night, too. As you approach a target, things happen, and things change. Assaults are dynamic. Men appear on roofs. Kids scramble across the terrain in front of you.

For my part, I always wanted to get where we could best kill the enemy. I wanted to understand as much as I could about the mindset of the people we were going after, so that I could hedge my bets on how they would react to things. What they had done. What their patterns were. Knowledge could equal proximity, which is what I wanted. As we approached, I'd try to listen in as much as possible when I was on comms, so that I could hear what was changing and where the action really was. Then, once we landed, I'd adjust and try to go there. My preference was to go out and be eye-to-eye. It didn't always work out that way. But if I could, I liked to be among the Close Ones.

It had been about seven years since the U.S. had ousted the ruling Taliban regime—the fundamentalist Muslim outfit known for being brutal to women and cozy with a certain 9/11 architect. But now, in almost every province in Afghanistan, there were still Taliban running the show, despite whatever tribal or clan administration was put forward as the local authority. The shadow governments did things like impose drafts and penalties and establish separate tax, police, and court systems.

We didn't visit your house unless you'd generated a certain amount of negative attention. And the guys we were targeting this night had. They were the local Taliban shadow government for this particular province. The heavy hitters.

Their redoubt was nestled in a fairly standard high-altitude, semi-urban area—their main high-walled compound sitting about eight meters higher up the hillside than a cluster of four or five other high-walled compounds, which were at the hill's base.

As we approached and prepped to land, I could hear, from the reports of the overhead asset, that there was a sentry outside the main target building. You didn't have to be a forensic ethnographer to know that if a man was awake and standing sentinel at 1 a.m. in this part of the world, there was a good chance he was up to no good.

For his part, he also did not need to be a world-class sentry in order to detect us. In Afghanistan, it's quiet—a kind of quiet like you've never heard. And our helos were loud. I heard on the comms that in response to our arrival, this sentry had gone back into the main building.

We flared and landed in a flat area just beneath that building, so that it was in front of us on slightly raised terrain, and the four or five other structures were behind us.

As we got off the helicopters, we saw eleven guys emerge from behind the primary building into which the sentry had gone, and start moving up the slope of the hill in patrol formation, in front of us and to our right. They were heading for the hilltop, in order to seize the high ground, which is something you never want to give away. We could tell by their movement that this wasn't the first time they'd walked together tactically. We could also tell that these fellows were not toting rakes and shovels. They were armed. They had a PKM, AKs, and an RPG.

A PKM is a belt-fed machine gun. If they were to get that thing set up at the top of the hill, it would not be good.

I knew that a bunch of our guys were heading for the main compound that the patrol had come out of, and they had it covered, so a few of us broke right and started running to cut this patrol off before they grabbed the crest of the hill. Bestseller and I were in front. We didn't say anything to each other. We just started running. He, like me, enjoyed being a Close One. And in this case, I knew there was a good chance he'd be even closer, faster, because he was very quick on his feet. As obsessed as I was with closeness, I actually didn't mind that Bestseller was in front of me, because he was easily one of the best operators I ever saw, and you could always rely on him to know exactly what to do.

Lying between us and the patrol was an orchard. I call it an orchard because there were tightly spaced trees, in an area where there generally weren't a lot of trees. We sprinted into it. The Mechanic joked afterward that he had a hard time keeping up with my fat ass.

Let me take a minute to address that insensitive remark. They called me Phat Jimmy. I don't know why. I used to be able to run pretty well, even when I had some strategically allocated glyceride reserves on my midsection—or "a gut," to use the parlance of people who have not received adequate sensitivity training.

Luckily, the hurtful references to me being "phat" were spoken, on that occasion, by the Mechanic, whom I loved.

A word about the Mechanic . . .

In the beginning, I'd picked the Mechanic to join our crew from a group of people that had recently completed the selection course. I liked him because (A) he was older, which meant he'd bring maturity, and (B) he'd survived testicular cancer and still wanted to be an Action Man.

He was one of the best picks I ever made.

Once he joined us and we started prepping to deploy, it was clear he was an asset for a number of additional reasons. Mostly his drive. And, as an added bonus, he was incredibly adept at fixing all kinds of things, as I've mentioned. My unit had lots of specialty high-speed vehicles, which required dedicated maintainers—guys who accompanied us on our deployments. On an early one, I remember a night where the Mechanic was working away in the little shack we lived in, rewiring something. The next day, he had the hood up on the trucks we used, installing his gizmo, and he ended up making the vehicles work more efficiently. I wondered where he got that skill.

The answer: before joining the service, he'd worked at an auto parts store, something he'd done since high school. Legend has it that not-unattractive ladies would come to his store, needing his help, and he'd help them. I believe he improved his love life by being a good mechanic. Luckily for us, the same skill that enriched his adolescent romances also came in handy in war. If we ever got new equipment that was technical in nature, he was all over it. He'd learn it inside and out. Instantaneously. And he'd do it without ever encroaching on the specialist maintainers, or seeking acknowledgment; he'd just find an unobtrusive way to master the machines, which always made us feel good.

At one point, we hired a civilian to help fix the nonmilitary parts of a satellite comm system, and we asked the Mechanic to be the escort for this expert. We basically just flat-out asked the Mechanic to observe him. Was the expert miffed, or uncomfortable? Who cares. It was our asses that needed those sat comms to work, not his. Lo and behold, after an hour of shadowing this highly paid guru, the Mechanic realized he was not capable, and was flubbing things. So the Mechanic just stepped in and fixed it himself.

Like I said, he was a very good choice for our squadron, because of his mechanical acumen. But he was a good choice for another reason, too: he would save my life, later on.

———

Back in the orchard, Bestseller and I had just broken free of it. We stayed at its edge, because it provided cover and afforded us a good view. Bestseller and I could see that the patrol was already at the top, and they were setting up to lay down fire on the building they'd come from, and into which our brothers were going as our primary objective. They did not see me and Bestseller.

As they prepared to unleash a lot of heat with the PKM and the RPG, I was struck by how much they seemed to be basically screwing around, chatting and puttering. I remember thinking they were far too casual, and far too cocky, given the circumstances.

Bestseller hit one of them with his laser and started filling the guy in. I put mine on his neighbor. We put two of them down right away, and the rest dropped what they were doing, ditched the RPG and the heavy weapons, grabbed AKs, and scattered, pulling off the side of the hill.

They had no unit integrity. They lost discipline completely and ran. And it again shows—just like the night I'd get hit—that this particular breed of fighter has no discipline. They live in a world where their actions are never questioned. And it's a shock when someone does.

We got to call their bluff, all the time. I lived for that.

I hate arrogance. I believe arrogance is at the root of many of the things that go wrong with humanity. So I like to punish it, face-to-face. These fighters, and their warlords, were arrogant. Their whole life was established on the premise that they have dominion over everything else around them. They only answered to each other. They molded their religion around however they wanted to treat women and children, which was like property. No, that's inaccurate. Property you might still cherish. They treated women like garbage. You've heard about the rape, abuse, and the shutting down of schools that catered to girls. Here's another quick glimpse into the Taliban psyche: at one point, their leadership had created rules that forced male physicians to only examine women if the women were fully clothed. When you consider that women were almost completely forbidden from working—

meaning the prospect of female doctors was essentially nil—you get a pretty good idea of how interested they were in the well-being of their female population.

I was more angered by the fact that they preyed on the weak and vulnerable in their own culture than by their shooting at me. It gave me more pleasure than you can imagine to take that anger out on them. To provide a little payback for the preyed-upon.

And almost invariably, when we went after them, it was like Mike Tyson said: Everyone has a plan until you hit them in the mouth. It was deeply satisfying to know that one of the only sights that ever shocked these people in their lives was the last one—the vision of us or the Hair Missile hitting them.

I'd always heard that the Taliban were superaggressive. But the truth is, they were superarrogant, and they didn't respond well the moment they got hit by a significant enemy that didn't really acknowledge their implicit superiority. It was certainly true this night. Here's the key stat: there were seven of us, plus a dog, and there were eleven of them, plus a rocket and a belt-fed machine gun. And they ran.

Critics might object: *Well, yeah, they ran, but you had night vision and they didn't.* And I would say this: If the roles were reversed, if we were under fire and armed as they were against us, we would have behaved differently. They stood up there like they were the kings of the world and they were going to kick some more American behind, because so far they had an unblemished record of doing ambushes on presence patrols, where they clacked off IEDs, sprayed them down, and then ran away before planes got there. These brave hit-and-runs made them the bee's knees, right? No. They are not the bee's knees, when someone else determines the contact point. And that's what we'd done.

The Mechanic and the rest of our team were with us now, and I knew we had to clear this situation and chase these guys down fast, because otherwise it would quickly turn into a shit sandwich. The good news was that we pretty much knew where they were going to run, based on the terrain—i.e., down the far side of the hill.

So we ran to the crest of the hill as fast as we could. Once there, I quickly capitalized on the fact that they'd violated that age-old adage of war: Don't leave a live RPG behind. I used theirs on a couple of places I figured they'd run, and lost some of the hearing in one ear for my trouble.

The rest had dispersed into the tall grass on the hillside. But the dog found them. And so did the gunship.

Throughout the gunfight, there was little to no chatter. Every message we sent to one another was sent through movement. The only person who said anything was me. On comms, I told the ground force commander and the gunship where we were, and where the bad guys were. We coordinated fire and put munitions on the running enemy, about fifty meters from us. The gunship didn't use heavy bombs, because it was a populated area. But what they used, worked. I would never for a minute doubt the precision of those gunship dudes. They were very good.

It was a loud, concussive event. But it was not the crescendo. The evening's truly bizarre vignette had yet to play itself out.

From another house, back toward the top of the hill, a man emerged and started strolling down toward us. Think about that. It was 2 a.m. Bombs had been going off, delivered by a heavy gunship, and guns had been peppering the air. And yet here was this fellow, sauntering down the hill nonchalantly. We were in tall grass. I popped up and yelled, "*Wadrega!*" Which means "stop" or "hands up," I forget which. He reached into his breast pocket and grabbed what I thought was a weapon. So we hit him. He went down, but his arm was still moving. We thought he might have a suicide vest, and he was close enough that it could be a threat. So we hit him some more.

Our EOD tech still had to check him out, because sometimes they were rigged with pressure detonators, so that when they roll (or are rolled) over, they go off. The EOD threw a hook on a string over his body, made sure the hook caught, and then rolled him over. There was no bomb. We went over and checked him.

It was the Wild West. Inside his jacket, the Downhill Stroller had a bona fide pistol scabbard—ornate, embossed, and with a leather flap. In it was a shitty, shiny pistol, which he was trying to go for when we shot him. He was the shadow governor, himself.

And it proved the point yet again. Guys like this one come up in a culture where they are unquestionably and unassailably The Man. And it goes to their head, makes them delusional. I honestly believe that this fellow thought he was going to prevail, that he figured he was going to John Wayne it—whip out his polished sidearm, provide a bit of fancy gun-slinging, and successfully disperse the marauding American savages. *They have a gunship with them? No matter. I have a shiny gun in a scabbard, and the world works my way. I am not to be questioned.* Keep this delusion in mind when you're trying to make peace with them and you're trying to gauge whether they're really going to be sound partners in well-reasoned negotiations.

The last thing we had to do was mark all the bodies with specific geo points, so that they'd be discoverable by the conventional forces that came in afterward to take control of the area. Their bodies were not too badly churned up, despite the munitions from the overhead asset, so we noticed some details. And it was strange: looking at their hands, you could see most of them hadn't been working very hard. It gave you the impression that they were a bit like royalty, the effete kind. However, there were also a few whose hands and faces made it clear that they were hard, not soft. Those were the guys we didn't get right away.

The sun was coming up as we flew out of there. The next day, we heard that locals had gathered up the bodies and posted them in front of what was essentially their city hall, right in the center of town, with placards bearing messages along the lines of "This is what happens to Taliban." Tombstone-style.

Wild West, indeed.

FOLLOW-THROUGH

We finished the 2008 deployment, went home, and promptly started up our training cycle, which involved a stint near Gabby's state. Always eager to call everyone's bluff, I referenced her business card and rang her up.

She answered the phone. I said I'd be near her district on a certain set of dates and asked if, while I was there, she'd like to skydive. She said yes and assured me that she would make it happen. We worked it out that we'd do a Saturday morning jump, beginning the day with a meet-up at a certain restaurant for breakfast, and then driving together out to the remote training site to conduct the jump.

When the Saturday morning came, I arrived early at the restaurant with Bestseller. We were anticipating a posse of uptight slicksters in button-down collars. Instead, in walked Gabby, in jeans, tennis shoes, and a sweatshirt—which seemed to be a bit of a uniform with her. She grabbed a seat, and we chatted. A political issue surfaced regarding something that was hampering our work slightly. She filed it away, and later handled it. Finishing our southwestern-style amalgams of beans, peppers, eggs and other savory a.m. options, we left and got in the car.

Bestseller drove. I rode shotgun. Gabby sat in back. As we headed to the training site, our conversation meandered. Don't Ask, Don't Tell came up. She asked our feelings on the subject. Bestseller said that, for his part, he was a staunch believer in Live and Let Live, but he did have to admit that he had mixed feelings about being in a shower with a gay fellow. It was a sentiment that had an economic fallout, he realized, because the military would be saddled with the costs of creating partitioned showers.

My turn. I said I really didn't care if there were gay fellows in my unit, or in the shower. Bestseller laughed, looking forward, as my buddies often did, to the entertainment value inherent in my rationale for things. Soberly, I turned to Gabby and explained that, as a general principle, if someone is looking at me in the shower, I'm flattered, and it doesn't matter what gender they are. I gratefully accept the attention.

We got to the training site. Some of our buddies were there, along with an air crew. Seeing them, Gabby pulled me aside and asked where the air crew was from. "I want to be able to thank them properly," she said. A short while later, when it came time for her to get her kit on, she indicated that she'd like to have "some cammies, like you guys have." Seven men immediately started ripping their clothes off and proffering their camo, in order to accommodate the congresswoman's request.

But despite the flurry of pants and shirts, she was hard pressed to find anything that fit her, because she was much smaller than the seven stripped-down gents. Fortunately, there was one compact gent whose duds came closest, although they were still oversized on her. They'd do, though. She eagerly accepted them. And now that she was more appropriately accoutered, she donned the rest of her equipment and a frap hat—a little ribbed, padded cap that was basically useless but required by the military.

During the jump, the most important thing she was going to be strapped to was me. And I let her know this fact, in no uncertain terms, during my brief. I got chided about my brief afterward, because it was extremely detailed, and some surmised that I might have pontificated a little excessively, in order to give Gabby an inflated sense of my importance in the upcoming proceedings. It was a fair critique.

When we got on the airplane, with engines running, but still earthbound, she walked around and thanked everyone. Then we sat down, affixed seat belts, and let the plane climb to altitude.

It was time to go. She got up, and all the guys gave her a little high five. She was absolutely unafraid. Not intimidated at all. I think it had to do with her rugged upbringing. She'd told me on the way up to altitude that she used to race motorcycles and jump horses. Strapped together for our tandem jump—with my front attached to her back—we approached the rear door of the C-130, which opened, revealing a beautiful view of the desert below.

We did a backflip out of the plane, and she was smiling ear to ear (I later confirmed this visually, in photographs). The free fall was good, although she hooked her legs through mine like an MMA fighter because she thought she was going to fall off of me. Embarrassingly, it wasn't her form but mine that merited censure. I think because I was slightly nervous about the high-profile jump, I forgot one of the tandem procedures—tapping her shoulder, which would have meant "bring your arms out."

I had given an overly long oration on procedures, as a display of my mastery of them, only to forget one of the most important ones.

At the appropriate altitude, I got things sorted out, and it was time to deploy the parachute, which in this case had an especially large wingspan—and a generally heavy-duty quality—because it was designed to handle two bodies. With feet dangling and bodies floating, I turned the parachute in the direction of the tract of land Gabby represented, so that our windward movement was toward her constituency, and said, "It's pretty, isn't it?" She agreed that yes, her home state was beautiful. Under canopy, two attached humans can hear each other. It's not so windy that voices are drowned out.

We landed uneventfully, right where we were supposed to.

After I'd privately said *Thank God* for our good landing, Gabby then publicly thanked everybody else, changed back into her civilian clothes, and took her leave, saying she had to go meet with students applying to military academies. Most people go drink a beer and kick back after a Saturday jump, but Gabby was just starting her day.

That woman worked hard. She changed my whole view of politics.

Later that summer, after hosting various town hall meetings that featured screaming matches and arguments over health-care reform, she and I spoke, and she mentioned that people were really acting wildly. "I'm afraid," she said, "that some crazy person is going to shoot me in the face."

I remember her saying those words.

Intelligence and Terps

When my crew went out, there were no Democrats or Republicans. We were not sponsored by, or party to, any ideology, other than our loyalty to the U.S. The earning of promotions and the amassing of clout were not on our minds.

Why? Because we were lucky. Lucky to be focused on mission and each other. Lucky to participate in something bigger than self-interest, which is when you get gifted with love. And love is what I clearly felt for my colleagues, and the dogs.

There were others in our immediate orbit for whom I also felt it . . . just as there were some, in that same orbit, for whom I did not.

In general, during my time in the service, my unit's dedicated intelligence guys fell into the Loved category. Which is not something I can say about the larger intel community. I was skeptical of them, because I felt that some of their members had their priorities mixed up. It often seemed to me that their top priority was to demonstrate that they were smarter than I was. I also felt they had an overdeveloped fondness for the Excuse Matrix.

In my middle-manager position, I felt my job was to make sure I created the best situation possible for my crew. I wanted to ensure that they had everything I could give them. Every advantage. That was my priority. And I had one particular trait that allowed me to execute against that objective fairly well: I asked questions that others wouldn't. You might think that this ability to ask tough questions was a by-product of some brash courage. Not really. It was a result of the fact that I was unfazed by awkward moments (and maybe even enjoyed them). And I was also a firm believer in the maxim Do Not Waste My Crew's Precious Time.

Sometimes, outside leadership would look at me and say, "Why would you ask that?" just as someone on my crew was saying, "I'm glad you did." And usually the immediate leadership within my unit was happy I'd asked, too. They also wanted there to be no stone left unturned when we went to fight.

Admitting that intel can and must sometimes be an imprecise science, I believe there are nonetheless some hard and fast principles that apply. And they have less to do with the actual intelligence—whether it's good or bad—and more to do with the attitude of the people managing or dispensing it, because that is something they can control. So perhaps some helpful parables—and cautionary tales—are in order.

CLOSE-HOLD

Monday was the day we typically had our mandatory pre-deployment intelligence briefings at our compound here in the U.S. Prior to one of our trips to Afghanistan, the briefing was conducted by a junior officer who was being supervised by a senior intelligence officer attached to my unit. Going into this particular briefing, something was weighing on me.

The day before, on Sunday, I'd caught a few minutes of *Meet the Press*. On the show, a very senior member of the intelligence community made reference to the fact that a group of enemies was being trained and hosted by what appeared to be certain factions within the government of a country that neighbored the one into which we were about to go. This neighboring country's government was supposed to be an American ally. And yet here was this senior member of the intelligence community, on TV, saying that elements within its government were allegedly sponsoring and training people to fight Americans—people that my unit, in particular, might very likely end up fighting.

That seemed like bad news. But there was a silver lining, because I was pretty sure I'd find an occasion to unburden myself in this briefing, due to my willingness to weigh in and ask questions where appropriate.

I waited for a break in the junior officer's presentation, and I raised the issue. I explained that government official So-and-So had been on a major network saying there might be people getting recruited and trained by elements within the neighboring local government, our ally. "Is that true?" I asked.

The younger officer, who was serving as lead briefer, didn't know how to answer. So he looked at the senior officer, who would be going on the deployment with us.

The senior intel specialist took a moment to survey the array of people in attendance. Everyone there had a high-level security clearance. We all had that in common. But there were also some differences. Of the forty or fifty people present in the room, thirty-five were of the meat-eater, knuckle-dragger variety, and I was pretty clearly one of those.

So the senior officer turned to me and said, "Actually, that information is kind of close-hold . . . above your level."

And I replied, politely, "What the fuck do you mean it's 'close-hold'? It was on *Meet the Press* yesterday."

Everyone laughed. Well, thirty-five of the people did, anyway.

I went further, soldering some deft logic to the steel line of my inquiry: "Come on, man. . . . If anyone will be fighting these guys, it'll be us."

No dice. The senior guy moved on. There would be no more discussion.

It's amusing to see the titles of experts on TV who inform the country about the goings-on in the world, especially when their title has the word "counterterrorism" in it. Sometimes I feel they're part of a large, unofficial fraternity, whose ranks also consist of certain civil servants and think-tankers and even sometimes military personnel. I often feel that what they do is actually not about informing—the public, or us— but, rather, it's designed to keep people out of a bubble that makes the people inside it feel important.

They are the Bubbletastics.

When I raised my objection about supposedly secret things being discussed on the very nonsecret *Meet the Press*, what I was really asking, in an oblique way, was: *We are betting our lives. . . . What are the Bubbletastics betting?*

The purpose of intel is to facilitate our work inside foreign cultures and allow us to better understand the people we will meet there—both the good ones and the bad ones. But this does not always happen. When we went out and dealt with populations of people whose culture was thousands of years old, I noticed that our side would sometimes make presumptions about behavior that were based on shaky premises.

Let's say we had intel that some dudes blew up something at a checkpoint, or set IEDs in a road. We'd then go to their house and visit them. And, given the circumstances, it was not unreasonable to assume that the other people living in that particular house knew those bad guys and knew what they were doing. Right? So in the early days, we'd show up at the house and say, "You're obviously all in on it," and we'd take all the men to get questioned in a detention area.

But the truth of the matter is different. In many variants of Iraqi culture, for example, if someone comes to your home (even a man who may be, unbeknownst to you, an IED maker), your obligation is to treat him as a guest, to treat him in some cases better than family. So when a combatant flees to a home, and we assume that the folks who receive him are co-conspirators, in fact, they may just be good hosts. They may or may not know anything about the IEDs. But our initial MO was to go ahead and just treat them all like criminals, essentially. And what happens when you do that? You create hostility, which makes fertile ground for recruitment.

I am not holier than anyone, especially thou. Maybe I had some responsibility to discover those kinds of societal subtleties myself, beforehand. Maybe. But our job was not, first and foremost, to be culturally astute. The Green Berets specialized in that. And they were very good at it. We were assaulters. We punished people who'd been identified beforehand as bad. I was busy training to shoot and communicate and deal with combat, not arrive steeped in a vast array of cultural nuances. That doesn't mean we passionately pursued ignorance. We were particularly keen to know those key nuances that would allow us to operate more effectively and efficiently in a foreign land. And that kind of thing is what the Bubbletastics are paid a lot of money to tell us.

But we rarely got that kind of information from them. Maybe it was close-hold.

At any rate, we were never told about the likelihood that what might look like terrorist-harboring was actually hospitality.

Now, it has to be said that even if someone had indicated that this is how their culture works, we were, at the end of the day, dealing with an armed conflict, and there were people blowing themselves up. If we had known this fact about local hospitality—that not everyone in a home was complicit—it wouldn't have meant that all of a sudden we'd be going into a situation thinking that the only thing the locals want to do is offer us tea. We'd still operate under discipline. But having that information—having a little knowledge off the top—would have helped make things more fluid, both for us and for the folks whose homes we visited.

Do you know who helped us discover these cultural patterns about hospitality? The terps. And you should see their salaries—infinitesimal, compared to the Bubbletastics. But the money isn't even the issue. I'm pretty sure money could never fully compensate our terps for what they did. They were something.

TERPS—THE OPPOSITE OF CLOSE-HOLD

The night Spike turned me around on the guys running out of the building was a bloody fucking night.

After Spike's save, and the work inside that initial house, it wasn't over. We had to clear several more houses in the area. At one point, I was called over to a specific house (let's call it the *What If* Casa) because the scenario looked like it would require a skill set that Spike and I possessed.

In the days and weeks and months prior, the other side had been using a new tactic. They'd baited us into houses and then blown up the house, and themselves, killing a number of us in the process. My unit had lost several men, and other similar units had lost men, too.

Already that night, we'd been shot at, and we'd shot some people. There had been deaths. It was clear that a lot of folks in this neighborhood wanted to kill us. So everyone was amped up, moving to this next house. I was completely immersed in the here and now, and as I walked through the neighborhood, I tried to note where all of the friendlies were, and where the best place for cover was, in case the shooting ramped up again. It was, for the moment, eerily quiet. Even the birds were scared.

Spike and I met up with the team already set up on this next location, the *What If* Casa. The first thing I noticed was our interpreter yelling at the house. He was screaming. It wasn't aloof screaming, like a bored tilt-a-whirl operator shouting rules to kids at an amusement park. It was invested screaming. He cared about his words having an effect. He was obviously trying to make something happen. But the more he hurled words at the dark, inanimate house, the louder he became, seemingly out of frustration.

Slight of build and very intense, this terp was typically a pretty calm fellow. Cool-headed. I pictured him as a watchmaker or engineer before the war started.

Before we assaulted targets, there were always a few precious moments in which we could try to sort things out and get our bearings—try to understand the lay of the land as best we could, before we ran into a house with armed men behind the doors.

Here's what I knew about this deal: Our crew had already cleared some people out of the house, just by yelling at them to get out. Now they were directing a lot of their inquiry at the oldest woman who'd emerged from the house. They were telling her, "Hey, make sure *everyone* is out. . . . If they aren't, people are going to get hurt," because we were getting ready to assault the structure in a way that was safest for us, not the occupants.

As the terp alternated between shouting at the house and discussing details with the woman, I looked Spike over and made sure he had his kit square. I also checked my own gear and made sure I was getting clear comms from the head-shed.

With time running out, the lady was getting really upset. She was talking to the terp incessantly, pleadingly. Finally, the terp relayed what she was saying to us. "She's saying that her father is elderly, and he cannot get out of bed, and he is in there." The terp was upset, too. I don't think he liked the prospect of what was getting ready to happen in this scenario.

That's why the terp had been screaming at the house. To get the father out.

I saw two options. Option 1: If this woman (who was herself quite old) did indeed have a father in there, then he was even older, and his mobility was likely impaired, as she claimed.

Option 2: She's baiting us, hoping we'll go inside to get her alleged and aged father, only to find there is no father, just a bomb.

I was leaning toward option 2, as were most of my crew. It had already been a bloody night, in a place that was bloody on the regular, a place where we had lost other Americans. Our inclinations toward gentility were mostly gone.

The situation was a powder keg. People often use that expression figuratively, but I'm not. I was pretty sure something was actually going to blow up. Maybe us.

The woman screamed some more. Her fear looked real. But then again, maybe she was just a good actor. It's risky, letting things like this tug at your heartstrings. Our primary objective is the mission. Our secondary objective is to protect each other, and make sure we're keeping each other safe. Our tertiary objective is to protect the innocent locals. In truth, they all blend into one. But that's the official order.

Protocol said be wary of a trap. And that meant we'd be going into the house hard. Sorry, lady. I wanted to indulge in the luxury of believing her, but I couldn't. It was time to act.

Just before we did, the terp changed everything. He stopped yelling at the house and then did a very surprising thing. He turned to us and said, "I will go get him. I will get the father out."

Now, it's worth pointing out that the easy thing for the terp to have done, at this stage, would have been to say, "Hey, I gave a warning. I did my part. My hands are clean." He could have stepped back and let us go to work.

But that's not what he did. He went into the house and started searching. I don't know what happened inside, because I was on standby for my entry, outside, somewhat incredulous that the terp, armed only with a helmet and some body armor, had just gone in.

A moment later, the terp emerged, walking an old man out. It was the woman's father. He was real.

There is no doubt in my mind that the terp saved that old man some serious shock and trauma, at the very least, and spared him some inadvertent bodily harm, at the worst. For my part, I was amazed at the terp's courage. It was no joke. He read the woman's emotions. Correctly. He chose to believe her, and he was right. He had put an unknown and hypothetical old man before all other considerations, even before his own safety.

I'm glad men like that terp sometimes scrambled the order of what was primary, secondary, and tertiary.

THREE SWEET WORDS

It was 2006. I was on my second deployment to Iraq. And we were in a dusty part of the country.

Notwithstanding the guy that I now refer to as either Close-Hold or Fuckface, when we were overseas, my unit's access to existing intel was pretty fluid. I'm grateful for that. We lived in separate compounds cordoned off in a different area within American bases. We had our own basic security perimeter isolating our area, with Hesco walls and access control points. There was always an intel hut in our compound, and it was staffed 24/7. Any one of us shooters could walk into that intel structure any time of day and ask whatever questions we wanted.

This made for some funny after-hours visits. When most folks can't sleep, they go to the kitchen, get a glass of milk, and either read a book or channel-surf the breaking waves of infomercials on TV. When we couldn't sleep, we walked across a small stretch of dirt to the intelligence hovel, awash in maps, and got data on AQ guys killing civilians, which helped us go back to sleep, dreaming happily of the upcoming opportunities to punish said thugs.

At one point, one of our targets was an IED specialist whose forte was large-vehicle-borne IEDs. When I say "large vehicle," I mean dump trucks, buses, and moving trucks. In Iraq, the garden-variety truck you saw most frequently on the road was a Toyota, complemented by a smattering of larger Russian vehicles, sourced God knows how. I don't know where this particular guy got his vehicles, but what he did with them was pretty impressive, and sinister. He built the type of IED that would level whole buildings, like the Oklahoma City event.

On more than one occasion, the vehicles he built had been driven into checkpoints, where they killed scores of both Iraqi troops and Americans. Typically, the driver was a young martyr who had been convinced by a senior cleric that the best thing he could do was kill himself on behalf of the cause. The young man would drive the vehicle into the checkpoint, at which point the bomb would be remotely detonated, usually by cell phone. The driver was really just another cog in the mechanism.

The bombs were big. They would level buildings within fifty meters, killing anyone in that circle, for certain, and injuring people out to two hundred meters. This is, by the way, a technique that ISIS has adopted. It's how they often start their assaults. They drive vehicles close, blow them up, and then flood the aftermath with fighters.

The intelligence we had on this IED builder's location was not extremely specific. It was a series of homes in a small dusty suburb of a city west of Baghdad. But there was one big, glaring question that we couldn't definitively answer. As we looked at the target buildings on digitized maps in the intel hut, we were trying to determine if the place where he laid his head at night was also the place where he was storing the explosives and constructing the vehicle-borne IEDs.

This was important because if that caliber of explosive was present in and around the target area, we would have to assault the target in a very specific way in order to try and protect ourselves. Conversely, if this home was not the location of the heavy explosives and bomb-building materials, we had more liberty with the types of tactics and procedures we could use. So the question was, *Is this where he makes his bombs, or not?*

On the day when we were scheduled to hit this fellow, I woke up in the afternoon (we slept during the day) and dealt with the first order of business, which, for me, was a trip to the intel building. I wanted to get information that I could use to frontload the actual mission brief for my crew later, before we went out that night.

Emerging from my hutch and walking across our small compound, I had the feeling I always had. Happiness. I felt fortunate. I belonged to a crew that got to go out every night on direct action missions, where there was risk but also the very real opportunity to punish the enemies of decency, and I loved it. Every afternoon, I looked forward to the possibility of gunfights and violence with the same early-morning enthusiasm that I imagine a nurse or carpenter or executive feels when they love their job.

Feeling chipper, I walked into the intel center, which was a shack, not unlike all the others in our compound. It did, however, have unique features. For starters, there were two separate access doors that you had to negotiate, using coded push-button pads and other things, even though the whole place was within our already secure area inside a larger base.

Once inside the first door, I walked by the coffee mess, which featured two large percolator pots of coffee surrounded by the classic military coffee menagerie. In most of military food service, there is this notion that even the slightest hint of brand elegance or slick consumer packaging would somehow detract from effectiveness. In keeping with this philosophy, there was also always the appropriately bland sugar container and monochrome, cardboard cylinder adorned with the sexy marketing jargon "Non-Dairy Creamer" in an anemic Helvetica font. There were standard military cans of ground coffee beans emblazoned with the terse but effective identifier "COFFEE." There was also, generally, a plastic spoon or fork inside a small Styrofoam cup, for stirring purposes. This spoon or fork almost always had dried traces of faint brown drips covering its white plastic expanse, the remnant of previous stirrings. It was never virgin cutlery. Someone had always been there before you.

I took this as a metaphor: Someone was always ahead of you in the intel game, too. Someone had already been there. You are not the first to get the lowdown. The question is, will you be the first to act on it? I tried to be, as often as possible.

It was my habit to secure myself a nice Styrofoam cup of black coffee on my way into the intel shed. I could tell, the moment the coffee hit my palate, which military service had been responsible for the coffee-making that morning. There were Army, Air Force, Marine, and Navy personnel in this intel center. And their gift for deciphering enemy activity was only slightly more valued than their ability to brew joe. The coffee ranged in strength from dishwater, made by the Air Force, to light brown unflavored hot water, made by the Army, to standard diner-type coffee provided by the intrepid U.S. Marine Corps, to the mud-black tar made by the Navy personnel.

On this day, the Marines had made the coffee. After I secured a cup, and took a sip that lacked naval strength, I walked through the second access point and into the main room of the intel center, where there were several people working at plywood desks bristling with computer screens, wires, papers, and maps. There were so many maps. They seemed to cover the local area, while also reaching all the way out to Antarctica. I looked around to see who was in there. I saw my boss, the officer who was my unit commander, poring over some maps. He was basically always in there. I don't think he ever slept. I tried not to bother him, because he always had way too much to do.

I noted the rest of the intel team. There was the intelligence officer in charge. He was also extremely busy, as usual. And then I saw the Gunny. He and I had already done a deployment together, and we would end up doing a few more after this one. I trusted and respected him.

I walked over to the Gunny's slice of the table, where he was scouring maps of the intended assault area for that evening—the IED maker's home. I grabbed a chair and sat down. He looked at me, and I said to him, "So, tell me, Gunny, based on what you've read and seen, do you think this guy is making the IEDs at this location?" He smiled, looked me square in the eye, and calmly said, "I have no idea. I don't know."

I laughed. I was happy with his reply. Ironically, I found it comforting. He could have made something up and tried to sound important, theorizing for twenty minutes on all of the places that might have explosives, which anyone could do simply by looking at the array of maps and spitballing. But instead, he gave me the truth: he didn't have any idea.

It might sound strange that I was glad to hear him say that he didn't know whether or not the place I'd be visiting later was teeming with explosives. But his admission meant he was honest, and trustworthy. And that's a valuable asset, especially in a conflict. After you've spent some time in war, you're always guarded around new people, until you've had enough exposure to them to determine whether they're going to BS you or be honest. Being lied to can put you in a situation where you get killed.

The Gunny wasn't going to BS me. And that's why I laughed. After I was done laughing, we toasted "the great unknown" with our brownish coffee, which had very likely been brewed by the Gunny himself. Then I left, letting him get on with his business.

The formal pre-mission briefing for this specific target happened a few hours later, in a briefing room next to the intel center. There was a slide in the presentation that detailed the man's past accomplishments, itemizing the large trucks he used, the amount of destruction and the number of IEDs he'd been responsible for creating, and the types of explosives that had been used.

The final slide indicated that they could not correlate those explosives to a specific location, including the one we were about to assault. But one could surmise that a guy who was good at making vehicleborne IEDs was also good at booby-trapping things and making havoc for any assault force coming to try to put him out of business.

Upshot: We didn't know where the bomb maker made his IEDs, or where the explosives were being stored, but we had a general idea of where the man himself would be, and that's where we were going.

The truth is that most of the time, we didn't have all the intel we wanted. It was almost comical. We wanted to know everything. The more details we could plan for, the safer we felt. But certainty was an illusion. Things change rapidly. The map is not the terrain, to paraphrase De Niro's character in *Ronin*.

Or, to cite another fictional strategist, Hemingway's Robert Jordan, who was evaluating a plan that looked simple on paper: "Paper bleeds little."

The wars that used to be on paper are now on digital screens. And those screens went dark. We were done with the briefing.

Afterward, we ran the standard atmospherics and de-confliction procedures, which involve checking in with the element responsible for the battle space we'd be visiting later—giving the heads-up to the conventional forces who owned the real estate. They needed to know that the folks running around in their area of responsibility (AOR) that night would be us.

A couple of hours later, we put on our gear, loaded onto the helicopters, and took off in the dark. In any season other than winter, the helicopters were generally without their doors. So the air beating in from outside was usually warm when we departed, and it would seem a lot cooler on the way back, especially when you were soaked with sweat, and tired. At times, it could get pretty cold in Iraq, and that's when I was glad I had a dog.

Suzanne Somers's wearable full-body blankets have nothing on a canine. Eventually, the other guys caught on, and they'd also snuggle

Western Iraq, 2006   This is a shot of Spike and me and a couple of other shooters. It was taken on our way back to the base after a long night's work, as the sun was rising.

up with my dog in the helicopters, for warmth. The dog didn't mind it, either.

I was always amazed at how calm the helicopter crews were, even when things seemed dire. They were always so mellow. I'd even say "stoical" and a bit mysterious, because we didn't talk to them as they flew. Typically, only one of the senior shooters on the helo would be wearing a headset, listening to comms and getting last-minute updates. I was not on a headset that night, so I relied on the door gunners holding up fingers to indicate time to target. Three minutes out. One minute out. At thirty seconds out, I performed my standard pre-game ritual: donning my goggles and then checking the body language of the rear door gunner on the right-hand side, closest to me. Looking for indicators, I scanned his face in the green glowing reflection created by his night vision goggles, and I got the sense from his relaxed features that we would not be landing under fire.

I was right. The helo touched down, deposited us, and took off.

Sometimes we ran toward the objective, depending on the scenario, but this time we walked. When we arrived at the neighborhood, there were several brown, single-story structures and a handful of two-story structures. We walked toward the target house indicated by the intel. It was one of the two-story jobs.

We got set up on the target. When we were ready, we made entry—something we could do in several different ways. If need be, we could blast the front door, or we could go in quietly. This night we were quiet.

We secured the rooms, moved upstairs, and found a man, fast asleep. We snatched him out of his bed, let him rub his eyes a bit, then quietly handcuffed him. Next, we searched the home. To me, it seemed like the man was basically living like a student. There were books and pictures on the wall. The place was clean and comfortable. We found some food, his computer, and a cell phone, but no trace of any explosives or IED-making equipment.

We led the man downstairs. We'd brought along photos of our target, which we held up next to this fellow's head. It was a match. He was Mr. IED Maker, all right. When we confronted him with the positive ID we'd just made, he calmly confirmed it, even confirming his name.

He did not try to hide his identity. In fact, he actually seemed rather proud of his accomplishments.

One would never imagine that a human being who could create that kind of mayhem would live in a place so tidy and cozy. This rather extreme fellow seemed to be leading a normal home life. Just like the terror-funder in his mansion on the Euphrates.

Those of us inside the house walked back outside for a bit. Our commander got on comms and relayed the status of the capture we'd just executed. We were done.

On the helicopters, flying back, the target had an interesting expression on his face. The look wasn't a look of defeat or anger, just peaceful resignation. It was as if he knew that at some point this was going to happen. Like this was just part of the deal.

When we got back to our little base, we turned the target over to the interrogators and gave the computers and notebooks from the house to the intel-receiving team. We then went into the debrief, where I saw the Gunny. I smiled and said, "Gunny, that place was basically the jihadi version of the Jones's house. Just like your highly detailed intel report predicted it would be." We both laughed.

It was good to be home in our little shacks, and I reflected on the curious virtues of an uneventful mission. We'd successfully accomplished our task by taking this IED maker out of play with no shots fired, no injuries, no explosions.

The best missions are the ones you never hear about, because they were so smooth that nothing bad happened. The guys I worked with who were the best and most professional were the ones who could make that happen—who could make nothing happen—on a consistent basis.

The Gunny's "I don't know" helped make nothing happen that night. With respect to target location and attributes, he'd placed heavy bets on just the info he did have, not on the info he didn't. And that's valuable, when lives are in the balance.

A SLIGHT HITCH IN HIS GAIT

Another intel specialist blessed with the capacity to say "I don't know" was a fellow named Dom. When someone is capable of saying "I don't

I took this photo at about ten thousand feet in the sky over the western U.S. It's a military jumper doing some training. It was a seriously lucky shot.

know," it means that, conversely, when he says he does know, you listen. This was true of Dom. Especially on one of my earliest deployments in Afghanistan.

We were going after someone. In a remote location. And two of us—my buddy Yankee and I—wanted to go after this target in a slightly different way. We wanted to jump in.

Yankee is dead now. But back then, he and I were good at parachutes, and we felt that jumping into combat was a good option to always have on the table. A main reason we lobbied the command for the jumping option was that we felt it was safer than some of the other methods of deployment we used. I won't say exactly why, so as not to reveal tactics. In a nutshell, high-altitude jumps, opening either high or low, were two good free-fall methods for quietly commuting to the job site.

At the time of this particular mission, I was not yet even close to being a team leader. I was #6 in my crew. But Yankee and I nonetheless managed to convince our bosses that this mission we were facing was better suited to a jump insertion.

I was now slated to be the one who would lead our group out of an airplane in a HAHO (high-altitude, high-opening) jump, so that we could fly ourselves onto a drop zone (DZ) in the mountains.

Luckily, Dom was our intel contact for the planning of this mission. He worked long hours, trimming down the available information into a manageable capsule of images and intel. I could see, based on the maps and digital imagery assets he provided, that he'd plotted a path that would get us where we needed to be.

Going one or two steps further, he actually struck up a relationship with the local helo crews, who had brought along a new range-finding technology that allowed me to virtually fly from our calculated release point into the DZ and then walk into the target area. It reminded me of the old Atari, with its optical sighting and joysticks. But of course it was much more sophisticated than any Atari, in that it gave me angles—the views of the terrain from different altitudes—so I could see what I was going to be looking at ahead of time.

On the night of the mission, just before boarding the plane, I slapped Dom on the shoulder. Thanks to him and the instruments that I knew were waiting for us on the aircraft, I was feeling good about our odds of finding needle X in haystack Y.

A short while later, we were at altitude, the doors were open, and the green light to jump was fast approaching. In situations like this, you're never 100 percent comfortable stepping into the unknown, but when people like Dom have worked tirelessly to provide you with the maximum amount of meaty information that directly affects the probability of success and the probability of surviving, you feel as good as you can. Had he not worked so hard, there would have been slivers of ambiguity about the geography that would have made the odds of failure higher.

When we jumped out the back of the airplane around midnight that night, the priorities were the same as they always were when you left a plane. Get your parachute open, make sure it works, and get headed in the proper direction. Steps 1, 2, and 3.

I fell for a bit, directing my fall by flaring my arms and steering with my legs. Then I deployed my chute. It snapped harder than normal when it opened. At such a high altitude, because of the thinness of the air, the aircraft needs to go faster in order to generate the same lift it gets when going more slowly at lower altitude. As a result, our bodies were also traveling faster when we left the plane, and there was more of a jolt as our parachutes went taut. But they held up just fine. We were all under canopy.

Gliding along, wearing oxygen, with my hands on the risers, I took just a moment to do a quick inventory of the situation. We were at 22,000 feet. It was cold. And I was elated. Elation is not really part of our normal checklist. But I indulged in the emotion, just for a second. I felt like I'd won the lottery. It was so beautiful up there. And I was on my way to do what I believed was the most honorable thing I could possibly do. Many times I'd jumped at night, in the dark, to help train others and to train myself. But I'd never had the candy at the end—the reward of getting to actually engage the enemy.

There was a shard of moon, and it gave off a small amount of light, enough for me to make out some of the fellas suspended up there with me, above the mountains. We were now a part of the night sky. Undetectable from below. The slight moonglow also allowed me to make out how incredibly rugged the terrain was, beneath us. But the ruggedness wasn't its most surprising attribute. The darkness was. I realized that I'd never experienced a place as dark as this. There were no lights. Anywhere.

This made step 3—going in the right direction—more difficult. There was no room for fudge factor. One of our first in-flight priorities was to make it over three mountain peaks, which crested at about 11,000, 10,000, and 8,600 feet, respectively. As we descended, we were looking for those peaks.

And it was all just like we'd talked about twenty times. Because of Dom's work, the sights we were confronted with were already familiar. We had enough of a grasp of the terrain and topography to steer our canopies where we needed to go.

Once we'd sighted our three peaks, the race was on. If we didn't clear them, we'd be hung up on the wrong side of some pretty inhospitable summits. I did my right turn just as we'd rehearsed, flew toward the first 11,000-foot upwelling of jagged terrain, ensured that it stayed beneath my hanging legs as I traversed it, repeated the feat for the next two peaks, and then homed in on the DZ, which was lying in a 7,000-

foot valley on the other side of the craggy hurdles. We had picked a flat chunk of remote terrain, along with a few offsets, in case we couldn't make it. As we bore down on the pocket we'd chosen—about the size of a city block—we were guessing there'd be some heavy winds. The instrumentation on the plane had been pretty beefy, in terms of anticipating the atmospherics we'd encounter as we landed, but even with that tech on our side, we were still rolling the dice when it came to how Mother Nature chose to greet us.

She was blustery. As we came in, getting buffeted a bit, I scanned the terrain surrounding the DZ and noticed a flickering in the distance. Bedouins. Well, we called them Bedouins. Technically, Afghan nomads are Kochis. My first thought was *What the hell are they doing up here?* Leaked diplomatic comms would later suggest that a chunk of the Taliban's ranks might have consisted of disaffected Kochi. But in my estimation, at that moment, this particular group seemed to be doing what most Afghans spent their time doing: trying to live their lives. I didn't see any reason to think they posed a danger.

Closer in, I didn't see any additional movement near our actual pocket, so we hit it.

Although it's hard to hit a high-altitude mountain DZ in the dark, we were basically on target when we landed. And everyone was in good shape. Or so it seemed. You're supposed to report if you've been injured. The guy who was, didn't, and he somehow managed to keep his secret for the next few hours.

This was one of my first really serious missions, in 2005, and of the many things Dom did on our behalf, one of them is something I didn't quite understand at the time. He'd set the standard. For good information, and how important it was.

As a shooter who actually got to encounter the enemy up close, I would quickly come to understand that we couldn't have been successful had it not been for all the behind-the-scenes people who will not be (and never have been) recognized as vigorously as they should. There are no books for sale on Amazon about the naval intel specialist who worked for three days to compile the maps and imagery that allowed us to successfully conduct an aerial insertion into the high mountains of a rough country a long way from where you are currently reading this.

Once I hit the ground, I was back in the real world—less calm, more on edge, but in a healthy way. We were facing a new array of unknowns and challenges, starting with a significant walk in the mountains. What came next was up to us; there were no Doms to help us anymore.

Wordlessly, we set off on our hike. What struck me about the hike then, and still does, today, is what one of the terps did on our little jaunt. Or more accurately, what he didn't do. He didn't gripe.

This terp's job was not some consultancy conducted via sat phone. Nor was he doing a ride-along, or an embed, which often involve added degrees of protection, such as habitually remaining in the rear, where it's safer. He was in it, all the way. He'd jumped with us. And now he was hiking with us.

That night, we did about five kilometers, in mountainous terrain. As we walked, some of us noticed a slight hitch in the terp's gait. But he said nothing, and neither did we. He gave every indication that he was good to go. So we didn't pry.

We eventually came down a last stretch of road leading to the remote village that was our target. As we approached, we could see that the buildings were of a clean white, with a consistency like plastered adobe. There were no doors that opened or closed, just rectangular passageways framed with jambs. This mattered, because once in the village, our plan was to go into people's houses, unannounced, with force.

The way we went door-to-door was not haphazard. From the moment we actually crossed the threshold of the village perimeter, we were immediately on a schedule. We had to hit targets at specific times. Missions like this one involved hundreds of moving parts, and they were all coordinated.

A small group of us splintered off and moved toward a particular house in the target set. Three, two, one . . . We went in through a little door, which ended up being a tiny cavity that we had to crawl through. Crawling is not ideal when it comes to tactical entry. You have to be quick on these entries, because you have to cover each other as you move. Having shimmied through, we encountered an internal terrace system—with levels layered on top of each other like squat Anasazi cliff dwellings. Climbing these on hands and knees, we reached another doorway. Passing through it, we found a couple asleep on a foam mattress. They had not heard us. Two children were nearby. In keeping with our training, we cleared the area, intuitively dividing the space into zones that we scanned and searched. After determining that the cramped room was threat-free, I focused on the bodies and experienced a momentary, unexpected shift in perspective. Instead of seeing four prone humans in an upper chamber of a target building, I saw a sleeping family.

And I was in their bedroom.

A few hours prior—while I was up in the night sky, looking down at the beauty and darkness of Afghanistan—was the first time that I'd had a split-second break in the action on this mission, into which had slipped a rumination. This was the second time. With this sleeping family at my feet, I reflected that what I was doing was completely opposite from everything I'd been taught by American culture, and by my own upbringing, where the protocols associated with visiting someone's house were so different.

Back at it, we woke up the family by tapping them, and then pulled the blankets off to make sure there were no weapons. I can only imagine what I'd do if I were tapped in my bedroom by four guys with machine guns who weren't wearing what looked like clothes, but rather resembled goggle-eyed visitors from another solar system. Fear was in the woman's eyes, and something diabolical was in the man's.

We separated the men from the women and searched the rest of the house for weapons and anything valuable in terms of information. One of the primary objectives at this stage was to determine who, if anyone, was going to come back with us.

When the questioning began, it was clear the man was lying. He kept changing the basic details of his own story. The high-value target (HVT) we were after was known to have a group of henchmen, and most of us believed this fellow was one of them. He'd be joining us on the helicopter later.

The schedule beckoned. We had more houses to visit.

The homes had no running water and no power, and yet they seemed habitable, although there were some strange accouterments in a few of the residences. Some of them had cows and chickens and goats. And not always outside. Once or twice, we entered a door and found a cow standing in the front room. As strange as that was, we'd seen stranger. On another occasion, elsewhere, my buddies went into a home and were greeted by a camel. A camel is a big animal.

We continued, home to home, separating the inhabitants in the area where we were searching for this HVT. And in spite of the cultural differences, such as lack of running water and screen doors, I saw something that I clearly understood—fear and hate and resentment on a level that I did not have the ability to be prepared for. There was a profound look of horror on their faces, especially the women.

With practice, over the years, I would become a better surprise house guest, eventually achieving levels of congeniality that included sometimes putting my helmet on the children and letting them try out the night vision. But not yet.

These observations about the Horrified Ones, each time, lasted just for an instant. It was important to stay professional, because you can die from hesitation. Our medic kits have tools for most wounds, but not a bleeding heart.

We conducted our terror census house-to-house. With us, each step of the way, was the terp. His steps were more painful than ours. After we'd cleared the village, without a shot being fired, having found the HVT's associates but not the HVT himself, we turned to the terp and basically said, "Enough already." We insisted on checking out the cause of that hitch in his gait. A quick analysis revealed that he had broken his foot while landing back at the DZ.

I wish the Horrified Ones could have known about the terp. He was a Muslim who cared about America, and its mission. So much so that he fell out of the heavens and trekked through the mountains on a cracked metatarsal.

THE ART OF KNOWING WHEN TO TAKE R&R, AND WHEN NOT TO

Summer 2009. Afghanistan.

I shuffled through the sandy dirt, in the treacherous summer afternoon heat, shielding my eyes from the dust and the searing brightness of the sun. The heat in this part of the world was truly no joke. There was a real risk that you'd only realize how hot it was just as you discovered that you were also out of water, and then you'd die.

But I had to brave the heat—no matter the cost—because I knew that this particular day would likely be the day we got final position on an extraordinarily high-value target, enabling us to take him out. However, before that happened, before I could get that final batch of intel confirming this depraved maniac's whereabouts, there was something I had to do.

I had to brush my teeth.

It was late in the afternoon on Saturday. And I'd only gotten up a few minutes before. As usual, my team was on vampire shift. I'd kicked my legs off the cot that I slept in, thrown on a T-shirt and a pair of flip-flops, grabbed my toothbrush and some toothpaste, and opened and gently closed the most annoying tent door in the world, which had the tendency to slam like a mortar going off next to your bed.

I call my living quarters a tent, but it was actually a combination of plywood and fabric. The guys in my crew were still asleep inside. This was nothing new, as I was often the first one up. I'm a morning guy. Even when the morning is the afternoon. And on this one, I was particularly excited, because of the prospect of going after the big hitter.

For weeks, we'd been getting a steady flow of intel on this senior member of AQ, who was being continuously tracked. Ranked #6 on the playing card hierarchy of bad folks, he was the key individual for transferring funds and creating alliances between AQ and the Taliban in Afghanistan. At this point in the war, most of the HVTs were hiding in places that were unattainable to us. For unknown reasons, our government had decided there was a free zone for the worst of the worst, a country into which we couldn't go to get them, and where they knew they'd be safe. It was the same place Close-Hold wouldn't discuss.

However, with this particular HVT, it had become clear that, sometime soon, he was going to visit an area that we *did* have access to. It would be a rare opportunity—a window for us to get a big player on the terrorism world stage. We were all quite enthused about punishing him.

So we were trying to set up an operation where we could capture him. Every day we would get up and check the latest information on where this person was, where he was going, and where we might be able to hit him. The data flow came primarily from the many heavy-duty national assets involved in tracking him—vehicles in the sky being flown by people inside those vehicles, vehicles in the sky being flown by people back in the U.S., plus resources on the ground. All from multiple agencies.

A great deal of money was being spent on tracking this one man's whereabouts. What it all came down to was waiting for the right moment, and then being able to seize it. I had a feeling this day might be that moment.

I survived the scorching desert march and made it to the bathroom. It was a shallow tent featuring sinks with running water and real toilets, which made us some of the luckiest people in the country. After I tended to my dental hygiene, I shuffled back to my tent, threw on socks and shoes, and wandered over to the intel center with an expectation of good news.

The intel center on this deployment was a large corrugated plastic dome. It looked like a half sphere lying on its flat side. Like our intel centers on other deployments, this one was located in our compound within a compound, and it required a passcode and other access security measures to get through the outer and inner doors. As I approached the outer door, I reflected on how odd it was that in a country where running water was scarce, we had so much technology dedicated just to the opening of doors.

When you walked in past the first door, there were two small plywood cubicles with unclassified computers that we could use to contact our families. And there was also the ever-present coffee pot, surrounded by some canisters emblazoned with that helpful noun COFFEE, in case drinkers grew confused about their contents.

A short walk through that area put me into some small rooms used by the IT people and the Seabees, who built and maintained every damn thing in our world. Then, at the second secured door, I gained access to the inner sanctum of the intel center. The door swung open, I walked through, and I was quickly hit with a blast from the powerful air-conditioning. The next things I sensed were the buzz from the many computers, the glow of the large-screen TVs, the maps on the wall, the crappy fluorescent lighting, the hum of generators, and the smell of coffee, a lot of it. The intel guys didn't get much sleep, so they basically mainlined Arabica.

It all seemed just right. All this information was percolating away, along with the coffee. The best intel guys—the ones we trusted—wouldn't leave the center, because there was always information coming in. In order to keep their vigil inviolate, they'd even go so far as to send junior guys to get food.

I was the first shooter there that day, which meant I'd get the privilege of breaking any good news to my crew later. It also meant I'd be getting the intel first, which increased the chances that my little operational subset of the crew would be selected for the choice work.

I was enthusiastic about what the day would hold. Then I saw the Gunny's eyes.

He was sitting behind his computer, at a plywood desk. I could tell he was not exactly looking forward to giving me the latest developments. When I asked him, "Hey, what's up with our man?" he knew exactly who I was talking about. The high-value target. #6. The AQ money man.

Some of the intel guys turned away from me. I saw the Gunny take a deep breath.

Before he spoke, for some reason, my mind did a curious thing. It boggled, just for a millisecond. I thought about all of the money involved in this intel center alone, all of the taxpayer funds that had gone into my training and the Gunny's training, the computers, the lighting, the A/C generators, the thousands of maps, the large-screen TVs. And the many multimillion-dollar assets and staffs being used to track this one fellow.

The money. That's what my mind was dwelling on, just before he spoke.

And then he spoke. He said, "You're not going to believe this."

I felt my jaw tighten. And I looked at the others in the room, who were also now paying attention. I asked, "I'm not going to believe what?"

"Some of the assets that we rely on to track our boy are unavailable," he said.

And I said, "Why?"

"Well," he responded, "it's a holiday weekend back in the States, and the assets are not being manned because people are barbecuing."

I let that sink in.

"Are you fist-fucking me?" I inquired.

"No," he replied. "I wish that I was."

I was overwhelmed and extremely angry. *What the hell was going on?*

"I don't know what to say," I said.

"Neither do we," said the Gunny.

I went and shared the info with my crew. My boss, our CO, who always talked about "echelons above reason" and the decisions that got made there, just shook his head.

That night, and Sunday night, while certain people back home were preoccupied with their barbecues, we busied ourselves by going out and executing other missions.

On Monday, we learned that during the weekend, the big AQ money man we'd been targeting had indeed come into our AOR, performed his job of helping finance the local insurgency, and then left. Untouched and unmolested.

How did we find this out on Monday? The holidays were over, and the assets were back up.

The Why of War

Folks sometimes ask for my thoughts on the validity of recent wars. It's worth sharing some of those thoughts here, because fully understanding the extent to which I believed in my work helps to explain the crushing darkness that came later, when I was no longer able to do it.

So, were the wars worth it? In answering, it helps to distinguish between two different kinds of war: (1) the specialized, small-unit variety that I experienced in Afghanistan and Iraq, and (2) the larger-footprint variety that also went on in those places.

Let's start with my kind of war. I believe it was worthwhile, despite the negatives. And there were serious negatives. I've killed people where their brains and chunks of skull have spit onto my face and clothes. It was a horror. And so was the way many remarkable guys in our crew died. I think of friends killed because their helicopter was shot down or because someone clacked off a charge and brought down a building on top of them. Remembering their deaths, I smell the filthy rising tide of the seeming futility of it all. And that makes it easy to say, "The costs are too high. . . . It's not worth them dying." But then you realize everyone does, in their own way. And this might be the way for us. The ones who have died . . . I don't think they would have opted out, had they known it was going to end the way it did. So the question is *why?* Why did we go out and do this crazy thing—run into buildings full of likely combatants? Why, with the arrival of each new day, after nearly getting killed the night before, did we enthusiastically repeat the exercise?

Because we believed in it, in our hearts.

The Fly Fisherman has a good take on the subject. He was pre-med, and could have stuck with that safer route, but instead, he gave up going to med school in order to get into our line of work. He volunteered for it. He has seen enough—the grim realities, and what we were doing about it—that he can make up his own mind about its value. There is evil, and we need the best people to fight it. It goes way beyond mealy-mouthed talk in the halls of Congress. (In fact, he feels policy on war should start as much as possible with guys who do the real fighting, not theoreticians.) Explaining his choice, he once said, "I could have opted out. But I volunteered to re-enlist. Numerous times. In fact, I volunteered to re-enlist just as many times as other people volunteered not to enlist."

For me, this much is clear: There are people who want to do 9/11 version 2.0, and they have to be stopped on the other side of the world, before they get to this one. They want to get their jihad on and kill Americans? Fine. My former unit shows up in their neighborhood, and shortens their commute. We let them shoot at us over there, so they don't shoot at kids on tricycles over here. And do we eliminate them? No. They're a hydra. We just keep cutting off heads. But that maintains a balance, by keeping a lot of bad folks busy thousands of miles away from U.S. soil. And that's something.

People say you can't kill an idea. True. But you can punish ideologues enough that they can't fully carry out what their ideology demands.

Now, the truth of who those people are, and exactly how many of them there are, and why they became that way—all of that is up for discussion. But as far as I'm concerned, I felt we were keeping American people safe. It was the bedrock of everything we did. And there was honor in our intent.

Sure, there were times when we'd be overseas, and I'd get glum thinking that the folks back home seemed more worried about the heat in their latte than the fact that there were people dying where I was. I'd reflect, sadly, *When someone brings down another building stateside, then we will pay attention.* But the fact that no more have been blown up, so far, means we're getting lucky, due in large part to the work of a small group of Americans. They are out there right now. Not safe inside a forward operating base. But outside of it, way outside of it. In the dark. Capturing and killing the enemies of decency. I envy them.

And the rah-rah, amateur hour, body-count, tough-guy narratives don't help people understand the more important truths about this breed: that there are specific groups of talented Americans who have signed up to conduct violence on everyone else's behalf, and shoulder the darkness that accompanies such work. They've worked their asses off to earn the right to be in that position. And it's OK that there are people who are this kind of violent. They are not bad citizens. They're some of the best. They just love getting on helicopters and going to away games. They love it more than just about everything. I sure did.

We had to adjudicate bullets and shadows. In a matter of milliseconds. And you bring things into those milliseconds—remembrance of your last mission where you lost your dog, and another mission where you left a target alone who didn't seem to be a threat but who later hurt someone. All of the work you've done as a group over the years. All of the training. All of the innocents who've been terrorized. You carry all of that with you, and then—suddenly, and wonderfully—you get into a gunfight, and there is a narrow pipe through which to send all of that energy.

When you get to work in that arena, it changes you. The conversations you have there are real, and the actions you do with each other have significant consequences. There is less fluff. As members of that crew, we got to exist in a clean place and experience a frequency of life beyond the dull pulse of comfort. In a gunfight, there is no pollution, no agenda, no personality conflict. You kill the killers and make sure your buddies are OK. That is beautiful.

It's also sad—that violent circumstances were required for me to feel fully alive. And that it sometimes takes being knee-deep in savagery before we can be our best, or embody the nobler virtues.

So, yes, it's worth it. But it comes at a price, which you can't escape paying. Hemingway's Anselmo said it well, thinking of the upcoming raid on the fascists. "The killing is necessary . . . but I think the one doing it will be brutalized in time and I think that even though necessary, it is a great sin and that afterwards we must do something very strong to atone for it." I was glad Anselmo said that. I was less glad that he said this: "All that I am sorry for is the killing . . . In those who like it there is always a rottenness."

1,400-YEAR-OLD GRUDGES

One of the blessings of the specialized kind of work we did was its clarity of purpose. We were lucky in that we knew what we were up to, and why. This was no small thing, given that we operated within larger political and tactical ecosystems that were often messy.

In Iraq, coalition forces trying to secure the country found themselves having to negotiate a brutal and chronic factionalism. At first glance, the obvious source of the friction was the Shia-Sunni fault line. Shia are only about 15 percent of global Muslims, but they constitute a majority of Muslims in Iraq, site of some of their greatest shrines. The first imam of Shiism, Ali, son-in-law to Muhammad, was killed while praying and then probably buried in what is now Najaf, Iraq. The tomb of his son, the third Shia imam, Hussein, is just seventy-six kilometers away in Karbala. Despite the importance of Iraq to Shias, they have long been marginalized in that country, where they've remained mostly poor, recently because Saddam (who was nominally Sunni by birth) probably feared their numbers and kept them down.

Then, after Saddam was deposed, with the U.S. government mismanaging the country based on a misguided approach to nation-building, and with our man Maliki installed at the head of a new Shia coalition government that showed real enthusiasm for vendetta governance and bald-faced exclusion of Sunnis, one of the region's latent cancers—sectarianism—metastasized.

The general consensus is that more than 150,000 civilians have died violently in Iraq since 2003. And a lot of that death is the result of Iraqi-on-Iraqi violence. While I was in Iraq, in March 2007, a truck bomb targeting a Shia market in Tal Afar killed 152 people. This led to reprisal attacks in the Sunni part of Tal Afar a few hours later—attacks carried out by gunmen and police who were mostly Shia. In that one week, roughly 500 people died in sectarian violence across Iraq.

At a certain basic level, Shia and Sunni consider each other to be followers of fraudulent leaders, and thus apostate pollutants to Islam. Hence the tension. But here's the rub: While Shia and Sunni may sound binary, none of the battle lines were ever crystal clear, once you were on the ground. In my experience, we dealt primarily with Sunnis in western Iraq, often encountered Shia in Baghdad, and met with both, north of that city. And from what I could see, the violence didn't necessarily stem from folks fighting primarily over ideology or other supposedly heartfelt truths. In many cases, it more closely resembled opportunistic gangs jockeying for turf and power.

It was messy. There were armed Sunni factions that broke with fellow Sunni AQ on principle during awakenings, only to later renew their subfranchise with AQ, because AQ paid well and because they gave them less grief than the Shia-dominated government. There were Sunni and Shia who didn't stop at just wanting to kill each other, but also wanted to kill their own if they didn't subscribe to certain hardline ideals. Take Muqtada al-Sadr, the aspiring ayatollah and champion of the heretofore marginalized Iraqi Shias who nonetheless liked fighting the Shia-centric regime of Maliki. And when Sunnis started exploring partnerships with us in areas around Ramadi, they were targeted by other Sunnis who were aligning with AQ in Iraq or the germinal jihadist groups that would eventually sprout into IS.

People talk about "civil war" in Iraq and other places, like Syria, which has its own cloudy Shia-Sunni battle lines, with the Assads, who are Alawite (an offshoot of Shiism), sticking it to their country's majority Sunnis just as vigorously as Saddam stuck it to his country's majority Shias. But "civil war" applied to these places is a tricky term, because it's small "c," small "w."

In our Civil War, the daily holocausts of men we inflicted on each other dwarf American casualties in Iraq: 17,500 killed or wounded in a single morning at Chancellorsville; 21,000 killed and wounded in a day at Antietam. Over 620,000 dead total. But our Civil War is capital "C" and capital "W" because it ended. With eventual reconciliation.

Was the reconciliation strained? Sure. But it was real. Iraq doesn't have that. Yes, in America, you'll encounter the occasional Son of the Confederacy who still yells "The South will rise again." But, if you look closely, you'll notice that this same fellow has an American flag decal in the back window of his F-150. There's a greater allegiance. Our Yanks and Rebels mellowed.

In the Middle East, the debate over the rightful successor to Muhammad commenced in the seventh century. Since then, it's been Yanks and Rebs circa 1863, perpetually. It never mellows. Iraqi Shias and Sunnis don't have Iraqi flag stickers in the back windshields of their trucks.

Healing is hard. But in America, we grope along and find ways. In Richmond, you can visit the site of the R. E. Lee Camp Confederate Soldiers' Home for poor and sick veterans, which was established in 1885. Privately funded, with money that included donations from both Confederate and Union veterans, it came to be a hub for "Blue & Gray" reunions, where former enemies mingled, swapped stories, and took group photos, in which, if you look closely, you can see some of them clasping hands. And on our country's first Memorial Day, in 1868, thousands of people put flowers on the graves of the twenty thousand Union and Confederate soldiers buried in Arlington National Cemetery. Something bigger than "being the winner" was at work. Charity. And forgiveness.

Something I doubt I'll see, but would like to, is an Iraqi Memorial Day, or a Syrian one—where folks decorate Shia and Sunni headstones side by side. The hajj in Mecca is promising, where Shia and Sunni do something sacred together. But in places like Iraq and Syria, most of what we see is the increasing and ongoing strain.

Despite the internecine mess, I was never confused about what I was doing. We were equal-opportunity raiders. Whether you were Shia, Sunni, Tribe A, Tribe B, this gang, or that gang, if you were killing Americans or innocents, or plotting something grim, then we came to your house.

In Iraq and Afghanistan, I felt I needed to protect people who were being victimized by the enemies of decency. If people are spraying acid in the eyes of little girls because they're going to school, I want to be the guy to punish them. If men are raping women or boys or creating sex slaves, I want to be involved in their punishment. The same goes for IED makers. And for the financiers and orchestrators, the people who bring in money and weapons. And for the men who cut off the noses of young girls to punish them. And for the people who give a child a backpack and instruct him to go across the street to Canadian soldiers and ask for candy, while a guy with a cell phone remotely clacks it off, killing all of them.

This is why it's not hard to kill those kinds of people. They are fundamentally incapable of understanding decency. An apologist would say, *Well, it's their culture.* And I say, well, if raping little boys or spraying acid in the faces of young schoolgirls or putting a backpack bomb on a nine-year-old and sending him to talk to NATO soldiers is part of your culture, then that part of your culture needs to die. There is no negotiating or reasoning with someone who would put a bomb backpack on a nine-year-old child. It sounds fatalistic, but it's the truth. Most Westerners, and Middle Easterners, in my experience, do understand that.

Now, how you capture or kill those kinds of people matters. *Carefully* is best.

Civilians did die in missions I was involved in, twice, and it will eat at me forever. That pain is important. It made us ferocious about avoiding future civilian casualties. Ferocious. And while the subject of drones is another topic for another time, I will say this: In dark rooms, crews like mine are a more humane and more precise instrument than a remotely launched missile, because we can distinguish between an armed man and a child. Which we did. A lot. If you are the son, wife, or daughter of one of America's high-value targets, you would much rather have my friend with the protective right arm visit your house than a Hellfire.

THE PROBLEM WITH BIG BASES

In my own simple way, I tend to measure people's level of investment in war by the likelihood that the blood spilled is theirs. Personally, I'm leery of some of the cowardly architects of regime change and war, who push us into it knowing they won't bleed and neither will their children.

Everyone agrees on the value of preventing another 9/11. But then people split over just how we should do that. Some argue that America's campaigns after 2001 were an overreaction. I can say this: The work of my former unit was not an overreaction. But the oversized American military footprints may have been.

Sometimes, when looking at war and its corporate support mechanisms, you have to ask, with Cicero: *Cui bono?* Who benefits? The following is from an actual, honest-to-God press release put out by the DoD in 2004:

> AAFES has opened new name-brand fast-food restaurants in Iraq, Afghanistan and Kyrgyzstan, with more to come in those and other Operation Enduring Freedom and Iraqi Freedom locations. AAFES opened a Burger King and Subway in Kandahar, Afghanistan; Subway restaurants at Ganci, Kyrgyzstan, and Camp Danger, Iraq; and Burger King and Pizza Hut restaurants at Balad Air Base, Iraq . . . Army Brig. Gen. ██████████, commanding general of the 13th Corps Support Command, and Air Force Col. ████ ██████, commander of the 332nd Air Expeditionary Wing, were present for the grand opening ceremony at Balad, where the two restaurants together pulled in $22,000 in sales the very first day . . . The opening of these Burger King and Pizza Hut restaurants brings the total number of AAFES name-brand fast-food operations in Iraq to eleven with five Burger Kings, four Pizza Huts and two Subways . . . In Afghanistan, another Subway is also planned for Bagram, along with a combination Dairy Queen/Orange Julius and Popeye's Chicken. Additionally, a combination Dairy Queen/Orange Julius is projected for Kandahar and a Dairy Queen for Camp Phoenix. "A Pizza Hut in Kandahar will open in the next couple of weeks," said ████████, contracting officer for OEF/

OIF with AAFES European Region. "We also have Subways planned for Balad, Taji, Sather, Bucca and Victory South, Iraq."

So, during what was supposed to be a war, we had an American general and an American colonel staging Burger King and Pizza Hut grand openings on a base in Balad, Iraq.

That is not what I did when I went to Balad.

I question the value of staging massive bases featuring Whoppers in parts of the world where small-unit work is more effective. In Afghanistan, a land full of rugged terrain shot through with a mountain range that reaches 24,000 feet, we went to deal with people who had not long ago stood up to one of the world's largest ground armies, the Soviets. What that tells you is (A) they have every right to be confident, and (B) maybe using a ground army isn't so smart. But we did anyway.

For the kinds of wars we're now fighting, massive "boots on the ground" footprints are largely misguided. Launching big wars overseas, on what are sometimes shaky premises, so that defense contractors can build bloated military installations where nineteen-year-olds can stand sentinel at the gate and get blown up by suicide bombers is no good. I felt terrible for the brave young American troops tasked with conducting Presence Patrols in Iraq, which often amounted to wandering around cities in clunky, unmissable Humvees, or on foot, waiting for someone to take a potshot at them.

Presence Patrol for us = Target Practice for them.

And yet those Presence Patrol guys would go out when they were sent, knowing they would get shot at and blown up. I love them for that. They have principle, integrity, and balls. But because they have all of those things in such abundance, it just makes it even more pressing that we send them on the right missions.

THE PROBLEM WITH NATION-BUILDING

Nation-building is the wrong mission.

It makes me angry that in this day and age, the military is responsible for so much that it should not be responsible for. The military should be killing and destroying the enemies of the U.S., not attempting to build a new civilization for countries that have stayed largely the same for a thousand years, successfully avoiding any attempt to change their inherent structure. Look at Afghanistan. Dominated by mountains, much of that country is also dominated by a deep desire to resist central government and stay tribal and clan-managed. The country has maybe a hundred kilometers of railroad, in total, which I think is a pretty good symbolic representation of just how interested they are in our notions of unified, centralized governance.

I believe that the policies that were devised and the bases that were built to support nation-building in Iraq and Afghanistan were a product of arrogance. I know some of the nation-builders responsible, and I respect them, as people. But I believe we wasted a lot of lives and treasure in trying to implement systems in countries where in many cases the people themselves are bristling over borders artificially created by the British and French after World War I, and where too many influential groups ensure that the focus is always on new opportunities for power grabs, or old grudges (including the one that's almost 1,400 years old). Carved out of Ottoman lands in Mesopotamia, modern Iraq was, from the get-go, a volatile, clashing mix of Shia, Sunni, and Kurd—an inherent instability that was basically a birth defect, as I see it.

It's one of the reasons I believe the idea of nation-building in those parts of the world is a farce, and we will see, in the long run, that we have been duped. The evidence mounts daily. In Afghanistan, we used to help the mujahideen (we gave them Stingers). And then we fought many of them as the Taliban. Only to eventually see many locals choose a resurgent Taliban (emboldened by coalition troop drawdowns and bumper crops of poppies) over the "nation" we tried to create for them. And so on, and so on.

We mean well, but good intentions are a bad strategy.

Like Ramadi, Mosul, and Fallujah in Iraq, Helmand in Afghanistan has a lot of American blood in its soil. And after spilling all that blood, these flashpoint locales have moved through various stages of recapture by new franchisees of basically the same old gangs we fought before. No matter how many Americans we throw into these conflicts, we cannot force a people to break the habit of being subject to tyranny. We can't make people want to fight for themselves, or for new political systems that we tell them they should want.

Yes, I understand that some Iraqis and Afghans are fighting hard for their countries. But, for the most part, they're fighting with our help. Lots of it. The impetus needs to be home-grown, and I don't see that it is. Why? Because the majority of the decent people in those parts of the world are beleaguered. They aren't the squeaky wheels, and they aren't shaping the policy, and they aren't calling the shots. This is because warlords and tribal bosses rule, and a driving force for the general populations in those places is fear. I pray (and I don't actually pray very often) that we will never become afraid like those people in Iraq and Afghanistan.

I also pray our children don't make the same mistakes we did.

I do believe we should have gone overseas to punish certain people, but I don't believe building huge military bases where Westerners can get Orange Juliuses is a way to create a country that won't allow Islamic fundamentalists to run the show. In fact, I think the Orange Juliuses and Burger Kings only add to their narrative.

I hope we have learned our lesson with this type of idiocy.

MY MODEST PROPOSAL

I suggest a different approach.

In the future, when someone does us harm, we should find the people responsible and kill them. Then we should leave. Period.

And then, if we really want there to be a world where fanaticism is discouraged—if we really want to change the way certain cultures operate—the solution is simple. I clearly don't believe in forcing our way of life on them. Instead, in parts of the world like the Middle East and South Central Asia, where we see conflict and bloodshed on a massive scale, here is the formula:

First, get big deployments of Westerners out of those countries.

Then, find high-ranking government officials or tribal leaders whose daughters are attending school, and give them the weapons and hardware to eradicate the thugs that disagree with them. No Americans need to deploy and stand up Presence Patrols and die in those places. Let the locals take care of it with our financial and material support. If a man in that part of the world is keen on getting his daughter educated, he passes the test. Those people will be quick to do away with groups like the Taliban and AQ. And they know who's who in the zoo. Why have talented Special Forces folks learn the ways of their world? The tribal elders who are invested in their daughters already know those ways. Let them do the work. Those cultures will largely self-correct.

Arm the fathers of girls in school.

Death Star

On my various deployments, I knew what my unit's objectives were. And we executed them well. But, as I've hinted, I couldn't always figure out what the objectives and priorities were for some of our country's larger military components. For example, there was a lot about America's presence in Afghanistan that was just simply a bit odd. Some of the major bases were basically little cities. When you were in one, it was hard to feel like you were really at war.

One morning, about a dozen of us found ourselves in trucks, driving through one of these bases, on our way out to execute a mission. My unit had been leaving the wire pretty frequently, doing capture/kills. As we passed the Orange Julius and traveled farther down the base road that led to the gate, we encountered people jogging as part of their mandatory morning physical training. A major, wearing a shiny reflective safety belt, jumped in front of our lead vehicle, threw his hand out, and screamed, "There are no vehicles allowed on this road during PT hours!"

Rolling down our windows so that we could have a civil exchange, we reminded the major that there was a war going on, and that although his PT was important, that was not why he was in Afghanistan.

So, on this base, the Orange Juliuses flowed, and PT runs got executed safely without threat of traffic infractions. But if we needed to test-fire our weapons before a mission, which we liked to do, we had to leave the base, because there was another somewhat curious war-time rule: No test-firing of weapons on that particular base. For safety reasons. Instead, we had to leave the wire and drive several miles down the only paved road in the area—a road that we considered to be an IED magnet—to a stark hillside, in unsecured terrain, that was designated a test-fire range.

Think about it. If you were an IED maker, where would you plant your work? On the dirt roads, or on the paved one leading to and from the American base?

Suffice it to say, we pretty much avoided these bases as much as we could. But avoiding them completely was impossible. And I eventually found myself revisiting the installation in Afghanistan that had the outstanding traffic safety protocols.

It was the summer of 2009. We were back there because my crew needed to get briefed by leadership on a potential target, and I was one of the messengers who was going to relay the briefing. So, along with some other guys from my crew, I walked the well-lit avenues, and we made our way to the command-and-control nerve center, bunkered inside a sequestered part of the base.

It was a surreal room. A colonel was flanked by folks who were seated in a tiered amphitheater built out of plywood, with handsome, high-backed chairs, probably bulk-ordered from Staples.

And the people. Wow. Those people. What a strange sight. I had a gut feeling that 80 percent of the people in that room had had a carefully crafted latte in the last hour. They had perfect hair, not a strand out of place. Bright, spotless uniforms, with color-coded plastic ID cards.

We did not look like them.

I'm also pretty sure we didn't experience war quite like they did. They were all staring at four huge plasma screens of Kill TV, which were streaming live operations and drone strikes. It was inane, and comical. These folks were watching guys out there fighting, like it was a video game. They had cold drinks, clean clothes, air-conditioning. And I kept thinking, *All they're missing is the popcorn.*

We called that place the Death Star.

The Death Star's denizens were, to put it bluntly, eye-fucking us. They were checking our badges to see where we fit into the caste system. As everyone knows, when you greet someone in the military, you have to be cognizant of their rank, and badges denote rank. They also indicate which schools you've gone to. They're one of humanity's greatest visual aids for quickly decoding status. But they don't mean much when you're working beyond the walls of the forward operating base (FOB). Walking on our way to gunfights, I knew who my team leader and boss were by the way they walked in the dark. Badges didn't matter.

But here at the Death Star, they did, and we basically had some that identified us as visitors.

While we took it all in and watched the Death Star folks glance away uninterested due to the unimpressive nature of our badges, a particularly nasty piece of violence suddenly played out on the TV screens. We saw a gunship strike some people in a ditch. The folks in the Death Star had the same keen gaze I've seen in football fans at sports bars—and on the faces of customers watching *American Idol* in electronics stores. When the shell from the cannon detonated and blew up the guys in the ditch on the TV screens, some of the folks in the Death Star crew high-fived each other and let out some whoops.

There I was, with the guys from my unit, in distinctly non-shiny and dusty clothes, watching this showmanship and game-ification of death. I looked at the Death Star crew and thought, *Wow, except for the ideology, I have more in common with the guys who just got killed in the ditch.*

It was just proof that there was, and always is, a huge separation between those who actually fight and the people who facilitate it. General McChrystal is a good man, and he says, essentially, *Do not let your proximity to the gunfight determine your value.* I agree with that. The Westerners who populated the Death Star did things that made me more effective on the ground. There is, of course, value in good organization. And command decisions, which need to get made, get made in places like the Death Star. But I was closer to the business end of an AK-47 on a regular basis, so I felt like I had more skin in the game. People who don't go to the gunfight don't have to address, or live with, the consequences in the same way. When I get off the Speeding Train, the luggage I'm carrying is a little different from that of the Death Star folks.

But I recognize that we are on the same team. And I get why the Death Star folks cheer. They want to connect to what's happening, and emotions are involved. I think many of them would have preferred to be out doing business with us, if they could. Their heart is in the right place. Very much so. But war is not a video game. Killing is not clean and shiny and christened with high-fives.

Within minutes of those high-fives, the tone in the Death Star changed, as a piece of paper got circulated around. I was taken aside by the leadership and informed of a development: there had been a deserter.

PART 2

The Second War

The Chain

Kelley was out walking one of our beloved dogs, Bodie, near our home. The walk was special, because Bodie wasn't slated to have many more of them. He was going to be put down the next day.

We lived close to the Catholic parish. In fact, the priest had explained that back in the day, the area was called the Catholic Ghetto. One of our neighbors was a prolific mass attendee at this parish, and after she talked to the priest on Kelley's behalf, the priest agreed to give the dog a blessing before he was put down.

This is where Kelley had just been, at that blessing. During it, Bodie had fought furiously and strained against his leash. Now, she was walking the agitated Bodie back home. As she returned to our backyard, the other dogs, who'd been waiting, suddenly went nuts, sensing someone at the front door. My wife wondered who'd be at her door at 8 p.m. Not shy or withdrawn by nature, she made her way through the house to the front, opened the door, and saw three guys from my crew standing there—guys we'll call Avenue, the Pastor, and Suspect. This was unusual. She tended to be in her own world while I was deployed, achieving a rhythm that allowed her to move forward with the business of living, day-to-day, while I was gone playing Action Man. This rhythm did involve managing our unruly pack of multiple hounds.

This rhythm did not involve keeping in touch with the guys in my unit or seeing them when I was gone. She might run into their wives once in a while, but that was it.

So something was definitely up. She just didn't know what. She welcomed them in, and asked what the occasion was. "Well," one of them said, "we wanted to come over and let you know that Jimmy got hurt." They said it in a very untheatrical manner. After this straightforward thesis statement, the guys followed up with a few more low-key remarks on the topic, which seemed to fill in the blanks, sort of. "Yeah, Jimmy had a little something go down," they said, clarifying things, but not really.

The tough part, from Kelley's point of view, was decoding the trio of poker faces that had presented themselves on her front stoop. She scanned their eyes, in an attempt to determine if these guys were (A) generously trying to downplay the severity of a real event, or (B) joking. She was not in the mood for jokes, given that the following day, she was scheduled to put Bodie down. The loss of any dog is tough, but Bodie's would be especially tough, because he was a rescue that we'd brought back from the brink of death, and adopted.

We'd been volunteering at the SPCA. Because of my experience, I often helped the staff manage dogs that were particularly aggressive. Kelley cleaned kennels and took dogs for walks. We became friends with the volunteer coordinator, and one day, when a hurricane was bearing down on Hampton Roads, the volunteer coordinator asked if we could take Bodie home, because he was a tiny, very sick newborn and would likely die. This volunteer coordinator did not want him to expire alone in a crate in the shelter during a tropical storm. So Kelley said yes.

Truth is, the coordinator feared that Bodie wasn't going to make it regardless, even without the hurricane.

Kelley nursed that dog. No, it was more than that. She made it her mission to save that dog. Making his bed. Feeding him every few hours. Comforting him and checking on him always.

But the business of salvation is a tricky one. Despite our best efforts, the dog, in a way, progressively lost his mind. Things worsened, until finally he attacked our other dog, Pepe, who is basically the Switzerland of dogs, as nice a dog as you're going to find. After a couple of similar episodes, an animal behaviorist warned Kelley that she needed to put Bodie down, otherwise she'd be opening herself up to a lawsuit, because she (and I) didn't know what his triggers were, or when he'd go off.

Further shortening Kelley's temper that night was the fact that I hadn't called in a few days, even though she was certain that I knew she was upset and going through this rough patch with Bodie. So when these three guys showed up at her door, she was fairly pissed off at the man they were saying was wounded.

For my part, I was, in fact, heartbroken over Bodie. I felt terrible that Kelley had to deal with it alone. As cold as it sounds, even though I knew quite well that it was going to be very hard for her, I just didn't want to climb into that capsule of pain, because I was so busy. Despite the half-assed attempt to insulate myself using the highly ineffective and immature technique of spousal radio silence, the Bodie situation weighed on me, heavily. It impacted my work, and I had to fight to clear it out of my head. I knew how much Kelley loved that dog, and how she'd tried to get the dog to a point where it could coexist and live in our family.

But I hadn't told her any of that. I just avoided the sat phone.

Standing on our front lawn, she mulled the situation over, guided by her mood as much as her intellect, and chose option B: they were jokers.

"Just leave me alone, guys," she said.

"No, this really isn't a joke," one of them replied.

It still wasn't clicking for Kelley. But their faces no longer looked like they might be involved in a bluff. And she remembers thinking that these men were evidently not trained in how to relay this kind of message. On the other hand, now that she could tell it was not a joke, the delivery was not what mattered. What mattered was that they were friends of ours, and they were there with her.

"OK, then. Tell me what happened."

Avenue, the Pastor, and Suspect explained that I'd been shot in the leg and that I was going to be fine. Someone had been tasked to travel along with me as I ran the gauntlet of treatments that damaged people run—a journey that, as I look back on it, was kind of like moving through a new length of digestive tract, in the stomach of war. That stomach keeps right on digesting, long after the bullets stop flying.

The plan was that once they got updates from this chaperone on my status, they'd relay the information to Kelley. "And once they get Jimmy to Germany, we'll let you know that, too," they explained. At that precise moment, their best guess was that I was still in the initial FOB field medical facility. In fact, they told Kelley, "He's probably in surgery overseas right now."

After they'd cut my clothes away and gotten me on the table, in that initial field hospital in Afghanistan, their first priority was stopping the bleeding, and then medicating me in a manner that left me unconscious for the duration of my five- or six-hour visit.

It was the first time any bright light had been shone on my wound, the first time anyone could get a really good look. I didn't see it, because I was out cold. But here's what the doctors learned: On its path through my leg, the bullet had entered above the knee and punched out the back, carrying gore and fragments of femur, which it had shattered. Along the way, it did some selective vascular damage (ripping through the popliteal vein, but not the femoral one), while also shredding my quadriceps and severing my hamstring, like scissors at a ribbon-cutting.

The medical team did a little bit of cleaning and some stabilization on me—skillfully shunting the important popliteal vein (providing the blood flow a temporary detour around the ruined part), and then putting my leg in a high-speed splint. Loose bone shards were suspended in the pulp of my thigh, and for now, the key was just to immobilize that zone. The project of re-forming the shards into a femur would happen later. The doctors also replenished my fluids, and noted the fact that I took fourteen units of blood. They didn't need to put in an airway for me because I was breathing, and I'd hopped my way through the front door, a sign of adequate respiratory function.

Their real priority was to prep me for the bigger hospital in Bagram, where I was flown after five or six hours, on another aircraft, accompanied by the chaperone from my unit, Chris. In Bagram, I got very lucky. There was an Army surgeon named Miller who happened to be on duty when I arrived. He was a gifted vascular surgeon, and he did a vein graft on my popliteal vein, in an effort to augment the bulk of it that had been shot away. This would prove to be a key plot twist in the surgical leg-saving saga to follow.

In addition to the razzle-dazzle of the popliteal repair, my ground-up hamburger of a leg seems to have given the Bagram crew ample additional opportunity to demonstrate their medical skill. From what I can tell, fascia are the remarkable compartmentalizing swatches of fibrous tissue that keep our gooey innards where they need to be, binding the muscles and packed circulatory plumbing into the forms we recognize as legs and arms. Because fluid and white blood cells rush to the site of a trauma, swelling occurs, causing pressure to build up in those packed pockets of gooey innards, which can in turn cut off circulation. I had a lot of that pressure (ironically, it ended up being generated as much from the traumas of the surgical process as from the initial AK-47 round). When that pressure builds, you have to relieve it. And what's the best way to do that? Slashing the fascia, and then securing the opened, gaping wound as the new normal. It's called a fasciotomy.

My medical records from Bagram abound in lively accounts of fasciotomies—from analysis of the big one down the side of my leg that was already in place from the FOB field medical station, to repairs of secondary ones that were at risk of giving out under the strain, to discoveries of wound sites needing new ones. And once you start opening up the body like that, you have to irrigate it. The process of opening, flushing, cleaning, and re-closing the fasciotomies after packing them with wound-vacuuming sponges seems to have become nearly a full-time job for the team, to the extent that the write-ups indulge in a rhetorical flourish, referring to the amount of irrigation occurring as "copious." That's dramatic language in the military medical community.

Also on the schedule was an upgrade of the initial external fixator apparatus, which had been rigged in the field hospital. This involved replacing the femoral and tibial (thigh and shin) stabilizing pins inside my leg, and overhauling the architectural superstructure outside of it,

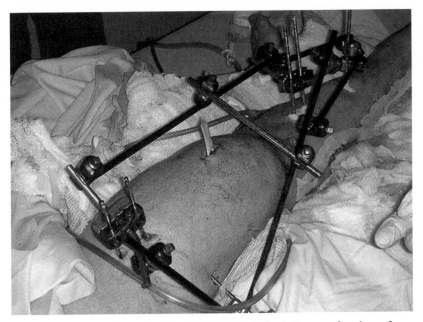

This was taken in 2009 at the Bethesda Naval Medical Center a few days after I'd been flown back to the U.S. You can see the external fixator holding my right leg together, as well as the drain inserted where the bullet entered my leg.

in this case by upgrading to a snazzier configuration of scaffolding that employed triangulation for stability.

Wrapping up their work on the "ex fix," the Bagram crew plugged the holes in my leg—at the front of the thigh wound and the pin sites—with Kerlix, and then wrapped the whole thing with an Ace bandage. Thinking about it now, I experience a bit of medical déjà vu. The Kerlix and Ace combo was precisely what the Fly Fisherman and the Mechanic had done. It's impressive: they'd been able to provide some of the same premium care, with bullets whizzing over their heads, that doctors in operating rooms provided.

Miller, the vascular surgeon, tagged out and was replaced by an orthopedic surgeon named Brad Goeke, who engaged in a bit of hamstring repair, strengthening it and encouraging it to rebuild by employing something called a fiberwire Krackow stitch. When a tendon or muscle is torn, or shredded by a bullet, surgeons use different kinds of specialty sutures to repair the damage. A pressing issue is the need to minimize gap formation in the junction between the reattached ends of the tendon or muscle, so as to facilitate healing. The Krackow stitch, a suture technique that anchors a series of threaded loops in the tissue, is known for its good pullout resistance, which in turn seems to minimize gaps.

Finished with my hammie, the medical team in Bagram gave their recommendations. From their point of view, I was in stable condition and ready to be medevacked to Germany the next day. "Stable condition" is, of course, a relative term. Biomechanically? Perhaps. Mentally? No. While in Bagram, I was in a dream state most of the time, with the dream a pretty barren and vacant one.

I do remember the bad reverie being broken once or twice. The first time, I de-fogged just enough to register a doctor's face as what it was, a doctor's face. That was an accomplishment. The second time, when I emerged from my dream state, I was alone in my room in Bagram. Drugged out and therefore prone to drama, I had an overarching fear that people were going to walk up to me and shoot me. It was bizarre. I really thought I was going to die. After that fear subsided a bit and I got my bearings, the pendulum swung to feeling lucky. Lucky to be alive. I quickly developed a strong desire to see as many people I knew as I could. Remembering that a Ranger friend, Jason, was working out of Bagram, I called for Chris and asked him if he could find Jason. He did. Jason came. I was exceedingly happy to see him. It felt like a little family reunion. Albeit a short one.

Sensing a window of opportunity during which I might be mildly coherent, and knowing that my mind would soon slip back toward the blank muddle, Chris kicked into gear on another project: trying to arrange a phone call with Kelley.

The day before, one of the three fellows visiting Kelley had asked, "Do you want one of us to stay here with you tonight?"

"No, I don't want any of you fuckers to stay here," she'd replied, employing a touch of profanity to show her love. "Why wouldn't I be OK?"

Another one of the guys asked if he should call his wife, so she could come over and comfort Kelley. "No, thanks, just go away," Kelley said. "I'm fine. What good is any of that going to do?"

Reflecting on it, Kelley has said, "I know they were trying to be nice. But there were a lot of emotions running through me. It was like it wasn't even real."

Part of what is unreal about receiving such news is that you have to keep the rhythm of life going, while handling a new disruption that's huge but also vague. It's like someone telling you "You have a new job next week!" but not saying in what field or where. You have no idea how to prepare, or what to prepare for. Kelley knew a surprisingly small amount about her damaged husband. She felt like the thing she wanted most was more information. Something. Anything.

In the absence of it, Kelley decided that the best thing to do, as much as possible, was not disrupt the rhythm. But, of course, there was a problem with this plan, because at this unlucky moment in time, not disrupting her rhythm meant going through with something that was not only not a solace, but actually a small tragedy: putting Bodie down the next day.

She went through with the euthanasia, and she was crushed. She'd loved that dog, and had nursed him back from a death sentence.

Afterward, still sticking to the strategy of maintaining rhythms, she kept her slightly less painful plans to attend a wine tasting that evening. It was being held at the home of my squadron commander and his wife, who is a big Francophile. In between sips of a merlot that was probably French and probably exquisite—but which just resembled other reds to Kelley that night, because she was numb—she got a phone call. She was surprised to learn that the call was from Afghanistan, and the person on the other end was me.

During my first deployment to Afghanistan in 2005, Kelley and I had the ability to communicate fairly regularly. But I'd never wanted those comms to get into a pattern, because I didn't want her to worry. If there were a pattern, and it were to get broken, she might assume the worst. One night, she came home from work and saw on the news that a number of Naval Special Warfare guys were dead and a helicopter had been shot down. It was the Red Wings disaster. She did the natural thing: she freaked out, because she hadn't heard from me. Little did she know I was trying to rescue the downed men. Thankfully, a thoughtful friend of mine called her and said, "Hey, Jimmy is not one of the guys who got killed."

After that, she made it a policy to never watch the news when I was deployed. Which was easy. And to not expect calls. Which was hard.

Hence the surprise when, drugged and dopey, I dropped her a line from the other side of the world. Actually, it was Chris who initiated the call. He had tracked down my home number and then brought a landline phone, on a long cord, from another room into mine. When he passed the phone to me, Kelley asked how I was doing, and was reassured to hear me mumble something about being OK. She thought I did indeed sound OK, but also heavily medicated. She was right.

I don't remember the call.

QUILTS

In the days and weeks after getting shot, during moments when I wasn't groggy from sedatives and painkillers, fear was quickly setting in.

I didn't really fear the loss of my leg, which was a possibility. I feared that I was now sentenced to a life back home, among a civilian population I didn't really understand, and that didn't really understand me.

I knew that the clarity of purpose I'd felt in the harsh moments on deployment were now pretty much gone. And so were the powerful relationships I'd had—primarily with my immediate crew, but also with the terps and the Gunnys. I hated the fact that my fighting career was over, that I was done with war.

But it turns out I wasn't done with war.

I was entering a second one. A war after the war. From the beginning, I was pretty sure I would lose this one, because I realized it was going to take place in battle spaces where I wasn't good at operating—dark hospital rooms, amid sad circumstances, where my brothers couldn't help me. I was morose and miserable.

On my journey from Afghanistan back home, I stopped at multiple hospitals before finally ending up at Bethesda Naval Hospital. The various medical staffs tried to lift my spirits, but I'm sure most of them quickly concluded that such efforts were in vain.

There were, however, two glimmers of hope on that journey, both occurring at a stopover hospital in Germany. The first, I sort of expected. The second, I did not.

Up to this point, my perspective on hospital visits, and the context I had on them, was in large part shaped by my friend the Admiral. During one outing, he'd gotten fragged in a badly aimed airstrike, which struck the vehicle in front of him, killing four Americans. It left some metal chunks in his face. Having been medevacked out of Afghanistan into Uzbekistan, he, too, had been slated to go to the hospital in Germany where I was now headed. Unlike me, when they started to stage him for this next hop, he just said, "Nope," walked out, found a flight back into theater, and returned to Afghanistan. He still has some of those frag chunks in his face. There's a bar in Arizona that he owns. You can visit him there and ask him about it.

Knowing this about the Admiral did not make me feel like much of a tough guy as I was being wheeled into the hospital in Germany, and it only added to my pathetic woe.

So the first glimmer couldn't have come at a better time.

Ace, a senior squadron corpsman who'd been on deployments with me, appeared in that hospital, sent by my unit from the U.S., with the express objective of ensuring that I wouldn't be surrounded by complete strangers. The day before, the command had told Ace I'd been shot. They wanted someone around me who knew me well (to replace Chris, who needed to get back to the crew and finish the deployment), and they'd asked Ace if he would be interested in the gig. Ace had replied, "Absolutely, tell me when we're leaving." He was on a plane to Germany four hours later.

Sitting next to Ace on that plane was an intel colleague I'll call Anonymous who was also traveling to Germany to see me, for other reasons. He asked Ace if he thought I'd recognize him when I saw him, given the heavy anesthesia I was under. Ace wasn't sure.

As Ace and Anonymous got off the elevator on my floor of the German hospital, they ran right into me; I was being brought to my room at just that moment. I made eye contact with Ace and yelled—loudly enough so that everyone around could hear—"Hey, who let this asshole in here!?" Anonymous turned to Ace and said, "I guess he does recognize you."

Watching Ace walk up to me made me quite happy, just as seeing Jason had, back in Bagram. Reflecting on it, it's surprising how desperately an allegedly tough guy like me needed those dosages of Familiar Face. Conventional medical wisdom says it's good if the first thing a patient sees, as he emerges from an anesthetized stupor, is someone he knows. Well, I can tell you that seeing a friendly face is valuable at any time, not just when first regaining consciousness. I know the surgeries to rebuild veins and bone were the priority, but if forced to choose just one remedy, I'd have chosen seeing Ace, Chris, or Jason appear. It's the better medicine, for the mind.

Ace could see that I was awash in morphine, had a pretty heavy fever from an infection I'd developed, and wanted very much to get home and see Kelley. Of those pressing concerns, he identified the one he could help with the most—finding the next medevac flight out of Germany—and set to work getting me on it. There was no guarantee that I could get a slot, given the standard red tape, but Ace's paramedical expertise helped him make the case for our prompt departure, and he got us booked on an upcoming flight to America.

With Ace there in Germany, cracking jokes and teasing me (which was merciful, by the way, because it meant normalcy), the other glimmer happened. And it was a different kind of comfort. One of the nurses walked into my room and handed me a square of overlapping fabrics featuring patriotic colors, an embroidered eagle, and hand-sewn lettering that read:

QUILTS OF VALOR—MONTANA CHAPTER

This quilt was made for you out of appreciation, admiration, and respect for your service to our country. We salute you and hope this quilt brings you comfort and cheer when you need it.

I was confused. I didn't understand. The nurse explained. "This is a gift for you, from Americans who want you to be comfortable and happy." She then told me that "every wounded American gets one of these."

This hit me hard. Like a slap in the face.

A silent group of Americans, who don't write blogs or op-eds and don't seek attention, took some time to buy the materials needed and then sew up this quilt for a complete stranger. An American who had been wounded. These people from Sheridan, Montana, did this for me. Holding that quilt in my hospital bed gave me a powerful, spontaneous sense of connection to the people of the United States of America.

It didn't dispel my fears about my new life. But it lessened the pain of re-entry. For a moment, at least.

When you're feeling like our country has gone off the deep end, think of this quilt, and let it remind you of who we are. I do.

GAUZE AND HOSES

As military transport planes leapfrogged me across South Central Asia and Europe, en route back to North America, I was receiving some good things, like medical attention and that quilt, and also a lot of drugs.

Kelley, meanwhile, was receiving a lot of phone calls. Updates on logistics and medical status poured in, but the news didn't really change. Kelley felt that everybody was doing a good job giving reports and keeping her posted, but it was overkill. Finally, Kelley told one of the status updaters, "Look, I don't need all these people calling me. I just need one source. I can't filter all this." So it was agreed that Avenue would become the main point of contact. "The plan was that he'd keep me abreast," says Kelley. And he did. He called a lot.

After about three days of zealous play-by-play, the upshot, as far as Kelley could tell, was that I'd gotten shot in the leg, I was alive, and they'd figured out my medevac flight from Germany back home. "How bad can that be?" Kelley remembers thinking. "It sounded like all was well. And nobody was telling me otherwise. So I had no idea how wrong I might be."

Ace was thrown a curveball just prior to boarding the plane that was slated to take us home from Germany. This evacuation was being handled by a branch of the military that has a tendency to stick to the letter of the law in their SOPs. Accordingly, when Ace wheeled me on a litter to where they were staging the plane on a tarmac, the personnel in charge of the flight stated that they couldn't put me on the plane, because of a mathematical discrepancy. Their protocols allowed for six walkers and six litters on the medevac, and they had me slated to be a walker. But here I was, on a litter, making for a total of seven litters and five walkers, an imbalance that blew various procedural fuses. Recognizing that these guys were just doing their job, but being also short on patience, Ace said, "Who gives a shit?" which didn't get the result he was hoping for. So he had to do some battling with the young man who held the clipboard. Reflecting on that episode, Ace has observed, "If you're a patient and you don't have someone who can speak medicine, you're screwed." He's right. The clipboard-toting gatekeeper, being human, came around, and I got to fly home that day, but only because Ace was a convincing advocate.

I was not conscious when they loaded me on the plane that would take me from Germany to Andrews Air Force Base, so I'd missed the drama of the excess litter count. When I woke up, I realized I was in a C-17. I'd flown in them many times, and jumped from them, so I was familiar with the plane. I was also familiar with Ace's face; he was on board, too. Everything else was alien.

It was a sobering cargo. I was in a bed, and there were beds over the top of me, arrayed like bunks against the fuselage. I started to look around at my fellow passengers, in their beds, and some of them didn't look like humans—just oblong mounds of gauze with hoses running into them. Up to this point in my post-gunshot life, I was so self-absorbed that I hadn't considered what it meant to be wounded in ways other than my own. Taking in what I was now seeing, I realized, *I'm not that badly hurt. These guys are.*

One of the "walkers" on the plane was a Green Beret. Having come over to speak with me, he admitted that he felt horrible, like he was cheating, because he'd been fragged, but could still walk. He didn't want to go home, but leadership was making him. He then broached the subject he really wanted to raise, asking me if I was the guy he'd heard about, the one who was shot trying to rescue that kid. I was still drugged, and not supercoherent, so I mumbled some variant of yes.

My dialogue may have been hazy, but there was nothing hazy about the way I felt. I felt massively disrespectful, discussing how I'd gotten injured, given what was around me on that plane.

I was shot July 9, and I was scheduled to arrive home in the United States July 12.

Once Kelley had been given the arrival date and time, she'd made arrangements for friends to move into our house and watch the dogs and take care of everything while she was gone. Luckily, it wasn't the first time these particular friends, a lovely couple of ladies we'd known for a while, were house-sitting at Casa Hatch. What was different this time, however, was that they didn't know how long we'd be away. I've always thought it was really nice of them to sign up for a tour with no end date.

Kelley was essentially doing the same thing.

"I didn't know where we were going," says Kelley. "I just drove my car, following Avenue for about four hours." Eventually they got to the Bethesda Naval Hospital campus, an hour or two before our C-17 was to arrive at Andrews, and they checked into their rooms at the Navy Lodge on the hospital grounds. Then they just hung around, waiting, for a spell. When they got word we were about to land at the airfield and be brought over to the hospital buildings, they headed over to the buildings from the lodge.

Once inside the hospital lobby, Kelley saw the other folks who were waiting for our arrival. About thirty people, in all. "They were randoms, non-uniforms," recalls Kelley. "And one of them was this girl with her backpack full of stuff, just hanging out in the lobby. It didn't look like she'd checked into her room yet, as I had. But she was obviously also there to greet a wounded husband or boyfriend or sibling coming back from overseas."

She was there to greet one of the oblong mounds of gauze, but she didn't know it yet.

Thirty miles away, we landed at Andrews Air Force Base, where we were off-loaded from the C-17 and driven to Bethesda Naval Hospital.

As we came into sight, Kelley could see that the ambulance she was expecting was actually a bus. I remember that bus. It was a Blue Bird school bus built in the '60s, shellacked with a dull white paint job. And being that I was situated in the back, every bump we hit during that ride resulted in jarring violence, which caused me to make constructive remarks such as "What the fuck!" I'm an average, not an excessive, complainer, but this particular instance of resource management deserves an aside: We are a country that has stealth bombers, but we can't give battle-damaged carcasses a smooth ride in a nice Prevost?

The Blue Bird pulled up and they started to unload us, one gurney at a time. Kelley was there with Avenue. It was strange for Kelley, who hadn't seen such a thing before. There was no calling of names as the men were off-loaded, one at a time. The primary noise was the clacking of roller wheels and the creak of metal gurney frames. She also couldn't really see anybody on the gurneys, in the sense that she couldn't see any part of a body that would identify it as a body. There was the gauze, but now there was also a small mountain of machinery stacked on top of the rolling beds. "First of all, I was wondering, 'What's under there?' and second, I was thinking, 'How are they even alive?'" recalls Kelley. "Obviously, you could draw the conclusion that someone was on each gurney, buried under all that equipment that was being used to keep them alive. But it was genuinely eerie, upsetting, and a shock to my system, because there was no visual indication that there was a human there. You felt horrible for these guys." And as she watched all of these massive casualty cases being taken off the bus, waiting for me to be hauled out, she couldn't help but reflect, *Oh my God, I thought all they had to do was sew up Jimmy's leg.*

She now feared that I'd be gauze and hoses, too.

What she didn't know was that there was an order to things. The more severely injured people were off-loaded first.

As I was brought off the bus, I was lifted onto a rolling hospital bed, and a young Marine slotted into position to push me. Rolling along, I saw Avenue, Ace, and Kelley, and noticed that my wife had a look of shock on her face and she was crying. But it wasn't about me or her. Yes, she was surprised by the array of rigging around me, having let herself hope that a leg wound was somehow not too severe a thing. But she was also relieved when she saw me, because comparatively speaking, I wasn't as badly off as the others.

The reason she was crying was the phalanx of men she'd just seen who needed machines to live. Also, she was crying because of the girl with the backpack, who looked like she was just out of high school. During the bus disembarkation, Kelley had watched as a young Army guy—mummified with life support—was wheeled off the bus in a shambles, and the girl with the backpack rushed up to him. He was one of the first guys off.

I often think of that young Army guy and some of the other guys on that flight—and how strange it is that I never met them, or saw their faces.

One person I did meet, and whose face I did see, was the young Marine who was pushing me. After I'd been transferred from the flight litter to a hospital bed with wheels, he took up his post at the top of my bed, near my head, and I could see he was breathing heavily as he pushed me. I teased him a bit. "You're breathing kinda heavy for a young guy." He laughed, embarrassed, and said, "I'm sorry . . . I've had twenty-three surgeries, but I'm getting better."

I was floored.

That Marine kept pushing me, onto the elevator and up to the fifth floor of Bethesda—the Wounded Warrior Ward—where Kelley, Ace, and Avenue helped me settle in to my room. I was sedated, but I was able to participate in conversation and make half-hearted quips about my condition.

Slowly but surely, I became able to listen and understand what I was hearing. This hadn't been the case of late, and it was a lucky thing now because not too long after my arrival, the Marine came to see me, and he told me his story. He was a top gunner in a Humvee when an IED blew it into the air. When the vehicle came down on its side, he'd been ejected out of the top, leaving him with fractured bones and shrapnel throughout one side of his body. When he'd been pushing me, I just couldn't see those wounds. They weren't visible.

Little did I know that I'd spend the next many years of my life grappling with my own kind of invisible wounds. And I'd come to learn that invisible wounds are the toughest, because it's difficult to target them. Nothing is bleeding, and you can't put a tourniquet anywhere.

DONATING MY BODY TO SCIENCE, IN EXCHANGE FOR CHEESEBURGERS

Subject: RE: Jimmy Hatch
Date: Monday, July 13, 2009 5:06 AM
From: Kelley Hatch
To: Christian D'Andrea

Hey Christian,

We are at Bethesda now. He got in yesterday around 5 and is having surgery again right now . . . I've attached some "cool" (according to his buddy, Avenue) pics. He was getting super pissed off in the pic with the nurse, because she couldn't get a vein. He's been stuck like a pincushion over the last few days and he's dehydrated, so his veins kept collapsing when she would try—he was sooooooo irritated, but managed to hold it together. Anyway, I know he would love to see you . . . He is much more lively when the guys are around, so obviously he really likes it . . . He's at NNMC at Bethesda in Building 10, in the 5th Wing.

Kelley

Kelley was with me almost constantly in my room, keeping vigil. The room had a ten-foot-wide set of windows on my left, framed by a lovely set of teal and pink polyester curtains, adorned with a kaleidoscopic diamond-and-heart pattern that screamed "industrial hospital chic." But even an anonymous hospital room can take on some personality, if you're lucky enough to have visitors. And Ace and Kelley were there a lot. Eventually, they developed a routine, getting up in the morning,

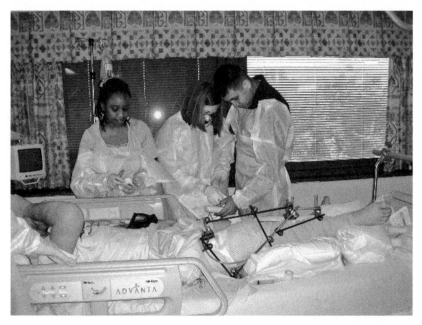

Bethesda Naval Medical Center, July 2009 These are a few of the nurses and hospital corpsmen who took care of me day in and day out for several weeks, while I underwent the surgeries to rebuild my leg.

picking up some coffee—one for Kelley, one for me—and then hanging out and keeping me company, as my leg got opened and closed and opened again, over and over.

It was a fasciotomy fiesta. It got to the point where the entire inside length of my right leg looked like the long vertical seam of a bulging woman's corset, the ends of which could no longer fit together, but instead had to be fastened with gaudy, thick, red cross-stitching.

Day in and day out, Ace was there, hypervigilant, helping decode what was happening to me medically. I was especially grateful for that early on, when they thought I might be getting a pulmonary embolism. As a surgical patient who was lying flat in bed for four to five days on end, with a lot of bleeding going on, I developed a prizewinner of a clot, and they thought it had migrated to my lungs. That kind of thing can be life threatening. I got very sick, and Ace helped me understand the treatment: administration of high-level blood thinners to break the clot.

After that bump, for the rest of the more than four weeks that I was there, much of the work on my leg involved ongoing wound cleaning, structural maintenance on my fixator hardware, and some vascular maintenance on my popliteal. But three or four of the surgeries were dedicated to something new: the rebuilding of my leg, mostly the thigh bones, which were largely shrapnel. This required painstaking assembly of scattered skeletal puzzle pieces, and exquisite new configurations of my external fixators. These therapeutic exoskeletons now became elaborate frames from which bolts radiated internally into my leg, through the flesh and into the bone, securing the pieces of femur—which consisted of two major fragments plus lots of smaller chunks—and keeping them under a kind of tension that would help the leg heal properly. The idea was to basically work a miracle and encourage splinters to recommit to the idea of being solid bone.

All this time, Ace was away from his family, and he refused to be spelled. It was clear that he didn't really trust anyone else to come in and start at the beginning, in terms of being my chaperone and advocate.

On days I had surgery, I encouraged Kelley and Ace to take advantage of my absence and grab some air. They went for walks on the peaceful grounds and observed the unstressed lifestyle of squirrels lucky enough to live on this fenced-in military reservation that had a great deal of untouched nature and was really quite beautiful, as far as Navy bases go. One morning, Kelley spotted a doe and two fawns, and then that night saw the family again drinking at a stream. These bucolic jaunts were refreshing for Kelley, but they would only happen after she and Ace made sure they'd seen to my every need, before I went into surgery, each and every time.

And how else did my devoted wife and this dear friend evidence their love and concern? By screwing with me. They loved to egg me on while I was heavily drugged. They'd make me say crazy things to strangers, because apparently I'd say anything if instructed to do so. "You were so morphined up, it was easy," recalls Ace. Kelley indulged in the teasing with the same vigor and aplomb as any one of my buddies would have. She was cut from the same cloth.

One of their favorite gags? They'd tell me that people had specifically requested to see my junk. As a result, a lot of folks who came into the room were treated to a private viewing of my manhood.

Kelley and Ace were such regulars that they scheduled and bought supplies for a routine happy hour, which typically took place in my room, without me, even though I was right there. They'd have margaritas while I had my cocktail of debilitating drugs. Apparently they were quite good at making margaritas, because it could get kind of lively in my room, and it's possible that once or twice we were reprimanded for loudness. Happily, there was a terrific male nurse that Kelley grew rather fond of, for many reasons, a key one being his ability to figure out diplomatic ways to mitigate the fallout from our illegal happy hours.

For thirty-two days, Kelley kept this vigil. And while I know that I tried her patience, I suspect that some of the monotony did, too. Every other day, I was moved out of the room so my wounds could be cleaned with a debriding, which involves cutting away dead tissue and sucking it out with vacuum tubes. My medically astute friends, like the Fly Fisherman, have subsequently informed me that gunshot wounds are some of the dirtiest wounds you can get. And when you get them on a battlefield, it's even worse, especially from a close-proximity shot. The tissue that was burnt or destroyed right away is removed, but with a big wound, some of the tissue continues to die due to circulatory complications and other issues. And that's why the Bethesda staff was always clearing away the newly necrotic stuff, because they wanted to promote circulation in new tissue, and also because each time they sewed me up, they wanted to stitch into fresh tissue, which provided clean margins and better bite for the thread.

Kelley recognized the necessity of this routine, but she started to wonder why we had to be in Bethesda for this endless battery of cleanings and surgeries. Why couldn't we just go home, maybe get transferred to Portsmouth Naval Hospital?

I also think there were some facets of Patient Life in Bethesda that may have begun to strike her as flat-out odd. For example, who knew waste could have value? Or result in a gourmet meal? At Bethesda, we learned that it did. One day, a medical researcher poked his head in, said hello, and then promptly dove into the real reason for his visit: horse-trading. He made me an offer. He said that if I agreed to give him priority dibs on sucking the festering fluids from my wounds on a regular basis, for his research, he would get me a cheeseburger. While at first blush this might seem like an unappetizing proposition, it was actually just about as appetizing as a proposition could be, because they didn't serve cheeseburgers at the hospital cafeteria. And it was a doubly big deal because he promised to pay me in Five Guys, which I had yet to try. So, with the prospect of pus-harvesting actually making my mouth water, I cheerfully donated my fluids to science. He gathered that vile infected serum for two weeks, and then brought me a double cheeseburger. It was the best burger I ever had.

HELD CAPTIVE IN KOREA

In the year after I was shot, there would be two projects: saving my leg, and saving my mind. These two projects involved me undergoing eighteen surgeries and being admitted to six different hospitals in twelve months.

I think it's fair to say I was a handful at every one of them. But, starting with Bethesda, I became something more than just a handful. At Bethesda, the hours may have been happy. But I wasn't.

The problem with modern medicine is that there is no debriding tool for the mind. You can't surgically remove the very bad stuff. You can't cut away the morbidity that sets into the psyche, where it festers and swells. All you can do is learn to live with it, and mitigate its power over you, by looking at it honestly and clearly.

I wasn't yet aware of that option.

Despite the remarkable commitment of my wife, the guys in my unit, and the hospital staff, I started to do things that would probably qualify as ominous foreshadowing, if this were a Greek drama. Hinting at what would eventually become a crushing defeatism, I looked at my leg, which in its salvaged state was a monument to the love and good luck I'd experienced, and instead just saw a monument to my failure. As such, I started informing all the people working to save my leg that I wanted it cut off.

This was pretty much my battle cry for a while. I even buttressed my negativism with some half-assed rationale: I'd seen a lot of veterans living with prosthetics—and some Olympians running with them—and it looked as though they were able to function just fine, without pain. Then one day my overall commanding officer (CO) came to the hospital and said, "Listen, I hear you're talking about getting your leg amputated. You need to keep your leg. I know it looks cool to watch those guys run on TV with the springy prosthetic, and living what looks to be a normal life. But it's really not that way. Just think about when you have to go take a leak at night. You're faced with a decision: either go through the five-minute process of putting your leg on, or pogo-stick it to the bathroom. It's less cool then."

My CO knew whereof he spoke. He was an above-the-knee amputee.

Let me pause for a second, and correct something. I just described my CO as an above-the-knee amputee. And he is. But that's me committing the minor sin of identification-by-malady. It's like introducing someone as a cancer survivor, or a paraplegic, or a "homeless vet," before giving any of his other attributes. Isn't he a hundred other things besides his affliction? My CO was.

He was a terrific leader who was decidedly uninterested in career progression, or "boot-licking," as we called it. Instead, he focused on doing his job well, and on caring deeply for the members of my community under his command, and their families. With that leg, he did PT with us, just like everyone else. And he was one of the most humble men I know.

I loved that guy, so I took his advice, relented, and let the doctors go ahead and try to win the battle to save my leg.

This meant we'd gotten past the amputation drama, which was itself just a small psychological glitch, a forgivable little error, all things considered, right? The ship was righted. All was well. It was very important to me that this was how it was perceived. You see, in those first days and weeks and months, what I wanted to be was the living, breathing incarnation of the wounded veteran success story. I thought that's what I needed to be, and I didn't understand that to be the wounded veteran success story, like my CO, you have to go through, and work through, some things. There is a circle of hell, or two, en route. And I didn't understand that. I just thought, *I'm already there, the successful vet. This is my new status.* If you wanted to introduce me that way—*successfully recovering wounded vet*—that was just fine, because I was a shiny exemplar of exactly that. Hurray for me.

However, it started to become clear that my donning of the Super Vet mantle was premature.

For example, early on during my thirty-two-day stay at the Bethesda Naval Hospital, I found myself in bed 24/7, but unable to sleep. You might laugh, but these little difficulties—like not being able to sleep—rankled. They didn't feel like inconveniences, or side effects; they felt like failures. Which fed a growing vortex of self-condemnation.

During the day, I played hero pretty well. People would visit and be enthusiastic about my recovery and me. But at night, when I couldn't sleep, I began to suspect they were lying. In the darkness was where I reckoned with myself. And now it wasn't just the separation from my former crew that plagued me. It was also the weight of my failures. I'd killed Spike. And in the end, I was too slow, and won a limp for it, while also getting Remco killed. I thought about these things constantly.

Previously, I'd been pretty capable in the darkness. It was my preferred environment. Not anymore.

Making matters worse, lack of rest plus heavy meds had me in a state where I was groggy and hallucinating. Sometimes these hallucinations were harmless. For example, on one occasion, while in bed with my laptop, I made an executive decision that a certain supply order needed to be placed for a critically important item. Stat! So I jumped on eBay, did some swift cost and quality analysis, and ordered three Dick Butkus jerseys. I mean, I like Dick Butkus and all, but upon mature reflection, that was probably an impulse buy that would have benefitted from a lower dosage of drugs in the purchaser's cranium.

Sometimes the hallucinations were more serious. At one point, I emerged from the haze a bit and returned to an imperfect kind of consciousness in my hospital room. I say "imperfect" because on this occasion, although I was alert, I was also certain I was being held captive. In Korea. How the hell I got to Korea, I'll never know. I looked up at the medical staff in my room, and I informed them that I was going to kill them. From the looks on their faces, I think they believed me.

In order to execute my plan, I grabbed my external fixators and tried to heave them and my leg over the edge of the bed. If I'd succeeded in that effort, it would have been a very bad thing.

It was a dicey situation for the staff, and it was complicated by the fact that nobody felt safe getting close to me. Before I could get my leg out of bed, the youngest medic in the room, nineteen years old at the time, put his hands up and said, "Hey, if I could get your wife here, would you believe you were not being held captive?" Mind games, eh? I could play those. So I blurted out some clever rejoinder like "Yeah, whatever."

The phone in Kelley's room at the Navy Lodge started ringing, and it woke her up. This was jarring, because she hadn't slept in days, and she'd finally, mercifully, been given a window to grab maybe five (but nowhere near forty) winks, in her own bed. The person on the phone told her that "we're having some problems with your husband. Can you come and help us calm him down?" She was pissed. "I was finally getting some sleep!" she recalls, with a smile and also some lingering and appropriate bitterness.

In that moment, she did not consider me a successful wounded vet.

She got dressed and ran up the road to my hospital room.

When she came marching into the room, some of the staff were still in the throes of trying to negotiate with me. I think it's safe to say those negotiations were breaking down. Quickly taking it all in, my wife was feeling a bit frenzied, and she said, loudly enough to silence the room, "Hey, it's 3:30 in the morning, what the hell is going on here, Jimmy?" She was not happy. And I was ashamed. After her entrance, the hospital room and its inhabitants did start to strike me as being distinctly American. Because of that, and because a deep-down, unforgetting part of me knew that my wife's wrath was not something I wanted to face in its full effect, I was able to shake some of the cobwebs loose. I suddenly became acutely aware that I was not in Korea, but that maybe it would be better if I were. It might be safer there. In the spirit of maintaining détente, I told my wife that I believed her assertion that I wasn't imprisoned on the East Asian peninsula.

The reason I wanted to be the successful wounded vet is the same reason we often desperately want to be something new or different—because we don't know what we are. I didn't have a clue. I used to. But what was I now? In the absence of evidence or a clear path, I told myself that I'm a guy who is positive and who can stand on his own and doesn't need help.

This idea of the successful wounded vet was something I genuinely admired. But now it was also something that tormented me. I desperately wanted to be one, while steadily growing in the conviction that I'd fail in my attempt.

I was starting to sense the first early whiff . . . the stink . . . of liability. And that I probably was one.

On the other end of the spectrum were the assets to humanity, like my wife. I refer to her as "Her Highness," because I feel it's a title she's earned after all I've put her through.

WHAT PURPLE HEARTS AREN'T

A few days after I had to look Her Highness in the eye at 0330 and acknowledge that I'd caused a bit of an unnecessary ruckus due to unfounded fears about being abducted in Korea, the secretary of the navy and the secretary of defense visited me at Bethesda.

Secretary of Defense Robert Gates came to my large and comfortable hospital room while I was in between surgeries. Most of the rooms in Bethesda were designed to have two beds in them, but in the Wounded Warrior Ward, each room had only one bed, and that made them unusually spacious, which worked well for me and the others because of the heavy visitor traffic. I had an electrical tilt bed that allowed the top section to move, while keeping the lower section rigid and flat, so that it could support the two external fixators, which now resembled Erector Sets around my leg.

I hadn't even gotten around to extending Secretary Gates the courtesy of tilting my bed all the way up when he visited, because he was very quiet when he appeared at my door, and I was a bit surprised. He asked if he could come in, and I responded, "You're the secretary of defense . . . Am I allowed to say no?" He smiled at that. My wife and I were deeply impressed by his humility and matter-of-fact questioning. A gentleman, he began not by focusing on me, but by focusing on Kelley. He asked how she was doing, and how she felt my treatment was going. When he was satisfied that she was OK, he turned his attention to me. He asked, "How long did it take, from the time you were wounded to the time you were in a field hospital, getting treatment?" And I told him. It was twenty-eight minutes. And he said, "That's good." It was a concern of his. In fact, it was a bit of a mission—to ensure that no matter where someone was wounded in Afghanistan, they could be in a field hospital within the Golden Hour.

The Golden Hour is the window of time in which saving the life of the wounded is most possible.

I was impressed with his priorities. Later, when I read Secretary Gates's book, in which he discussed the fights he had with people inside the DoD who were protectors and promoters of projects that did not directly benefit the wars we were fighting, or the warriors who were fighting them, I'd realize that my suspicions about how things worked were indeed true. Curiously, although I was an enlisted fellow, I felt a fair amount of kinship with Secretary Gates. And the same goes for the other secretary who visited me.

When the secretary of the navy, Ray Mabus, visited, he mentioned that he'd heard I'd been making noise about cutting my leg off, and that he was glad I'd decided, in the end, not to. I asked if I could give a little impromptu speech, and he replied, "I wish you would." It was pretty moving. For me, at least.

Secretary Mabus was there to give me a Purple Heart, and I was conflicted about receiving it. In my speech, I mentioned that I had heard that the Purple Heart was sometimes called "a shooting medal for the enemy." That didn't sit right with me. But another thing that didn't feel right was the fact that I was receiving a Purple Heart at all. For getting shot. I was embarrassed. So I tried to shift the focus. Away from the enemy. Away from me. I tried to make it clear that the Purple Heart wasn't for me, and it certainly wasn't a shooting medal for the enemy.

The Purple Heart actually stands for something else; it stands for the long line of people who dragged me out of that battle space and back to life. The guys in my crew. The helicopter pilots. The medical staffs in the overseas military hospitals and the medical facilities state-side. The surgeons and vascular experts who were putting in long hours to save my leg, against the odds. All of these people didn't just extend their time and energy. They extended their love to me.

They were the layers. Of dedicated, professional people. "Those layers run deep," I told Secretary Mabus and the others. "And they are why we will not lose this war."

I cried. I think Secretary Mabus was moved, too. Maybe not to tears. But moved.

I now realize that I was describing to the secretary how I was a spectator. I'd become incapacitated and had no choice. I had to watch. I couldn't change the channels. Even though there was a morose self-loathing inside of me that was growing, dangerously, there were none-theless moments like this, rare moments of clarity, where I couldn't ignore the incredible show that was playing out right in front of me. What I now see, and understand, is that I had a front-row seat to the human spirit. I believe I still have that front-row seat. Many of us do. If we care to recognize it.

UNTOUCHED BY ANGELS

I believed in my good luck and the layers, and I tried to force myself to derive some comfort from those things. But I was losing my ability to feel them. The salutary things in my life just weren't registering. My soul scale only felt the heft of the negatives. They had weight. The good stuff did not.

One day, a couple of men in their sixties showed up and offered to help. "With what?" I asked. "Anything," they replied. "We're Vietnam vets, and we're just here to make sure you don't get treated the way we did." I loved them for that. And I promptly repaid their gesture by lying and saying I was good to go.

When Cale, a friend and dog handler, came and brought Duco and Hags, I perked up, at least for a moment. Hags was a former LAPD

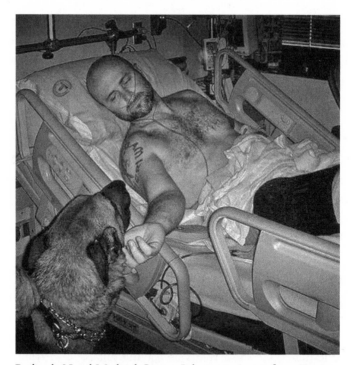

Bethesda Naval Medical Center, July 2009 A visit from Duco,
a K9 I'd deployed with previously. Duco was an amazing K9,
and seeing him made my week.

cop, and a real friend. Duco was a dog, and it was a miracle the hospital
let him in. Actually, the same goes for Hags. I remember them entering
my room. I was genuinely shocked that they'd let the dog in, but also
really pleased and emotional. The last dog I'd seen was Remco, when
he was killed. So now, I was glad for the opportunity to touch another
one. Duco had the decency to be very friendly and civil, given that he
was, in fact, a badass. I had done deployments with him, and he was a
hero, a fierce one. Hags was also heroic in his own way, but less civil.
He made fun of me. Lying in my bed, I showed him my junk. He
called me an idiot. It was great.

Like all of my visitors, Cale and Hags asked how they could help.
I thought about it for a second. I was feeling that constant sorrow at
being bereft of what I thought was my core family (even though this
visit from Cale and Hags was momentarily lessening it). And I was also

feeling the agony tied to the loss of my dogs. But, as usual, I was unable to speak my fears. Or my heart. Or the truth. So I told them I was fine and sent them on their way.

Something was deeply wrong with me. I was alive, surrounded by amazing people, receiving amazing care, and yet I was secretly despairing. Crumbling inside. Masking it the whole while. And when you know, logically, that you are enjoying every advantage and should be nothing but grateful, yet still feel rotten, that only adds to the misery. Because on top of everything else, you feel guilty about feeling rotten.

It's difficult to describe the mechanics of a deepening depression. But I'll try.

I think of it this way: The structure that I considered to be me was being dismantled and taken apart, piece by piece. "Elite." "Special Warfare." "Asset." All those critical facets of Jimmy were gone. And without them, I wasn't much. How did I see things playing out? Not well. I knew intuitively that at the end of this process, I would be either a shattered hulk or rubble.

My leg had swollen to the point that I could no longer pull on a pair of regular pants. So Bethesda Naval Hospital outfitted me with the latest in post-operative couture: absurdly huge baggy pants that closed with Velcro on the sides. They fit over my swollen leg, with its elaborate fixators.

These pants played a small but memorable role in maintaining Kelley's sanity, and momentarily distracting me from the loss of mine.

Kelley's life was hijacked by me the minute those guys came to the house. For the next several years, her life was dominated by "Jimmy has a problem." No matter what she did, she was constantly forced to ask the question "What about Jimmy?" And not only did Kelley have to be concerned about what I was going through, she had to actually bear the brunt of it. She had to see, smell, and taste it. When I broke down, she couldn't afford to. She had to be responsible, while I focused on things like defying my Korean captors.

Sometimes, guys who got hurt were left by their wives. If Kelley had left me, I wouldn't have blamed her. I was a pain in the ass.

One of the challenges is that there is no manual for what to do. But I see now that total vigilance is not the answer for people like us. What's important is a break, and I'm amazed Kelley survived our ordeal, because she rarely got one. Kelley was at Bethesda the entire time, and with me everywhere else afterwards. Maybe too much, for her sake. But I guess one thing I can say is that she was very smart about seizing even small opportunities for respite, if and when they materialized. It was never one long break, which would have been best, but at least she engineered some small moments of relief.

I'd been hurt early in the deployment, about three weeks in, so my squadron commander (a different person from my leg-salvaging overall commander) was still over there. But his wife—the one whose in-depth knowledge of wine was lost on Kelley that night I'd called—drove a considerable distance to visit us in Bethesda, say hello, and take Kelley out. I think they had a great time. I wasn't with them. But I was there when they came back.

They were in a rascally mood. The ladies spotted my super-sized Velcro shorts sitting in a drawer, took them out, and eyed them mischievously. The twinkling in their eyes suggested something was about to go down. Would it be a joke? A quip? Come on, let's have it.

They proceeded to squeeze themselves—both of their selves—into my pants. My wife and my squadron commander's wife are not big women, so they could each fit into one of the pant legs. One stood in the left pant leg. The other stood in the right pant leg. And they were dancing, with the clock behind them reading 2:30 in the morning. I was laughing . . . laughing . . . laughing.

You know that expression "drink to your health"? They had. To mine. And it had worked, granting me the reprieve of a moment's mirth.

Even though I knew that they'd ultimately be ineffectual, the ambassadors of love and goodwill kept trying.

Like Gabby. She spent time with me and my wife at Bethesda. I don't recall how she knew I was there. I probably sent her a message in my drugged-out state. Congress being right down the road, she didn't hesitate to visit, coming in very quietly and being very kind, as she always is. She and Kelley spoke at great length, and I remember telling her how lucky I was, because of the support I was receiving from my unit and community. Here at the hospital, I was being treated like a king. I knew that not everyone was so lucky.

She was glad to hear of my positive care experience, but I think it was bittersweet for her, too, due to the fact that she's unable to turn off her concern for the less lucky. She confided that she was worried about the veterans in her district, because many of them were reservists who didn't have the support, safety net, or tight military unit that I had. Kelley shared Gabby's concerns, and mentioned the girl with the backpack. Kelley had discovered that the girl was living out of it, essentially camping in her man's hospital room and sleeping in chairs. Gabby indicated that she was working on the issue, and then focused on comforting me.

Among other things, she told us that she was going overseas soon and would probably see my guys. I wasn't in great form—groggy, partially coherent, and fading a bit. But I did say I wanted her to give the Fly Fisherman, the Mechanic, Mr. Clean, and the Texan a hug for me, and thank them for saving my life. She accepted the charge.

Even though after Gabby left I quickly forgot about those things I'd told her I was grateful for, and sank further into my self-absorbed depression, this visit she paid me, post-shooting, meant a lot. I would never have guessed that two years later, I'd be returning the favor.

In those early days of my damage, I did some solid groundwork laying the foundation for what would become a bad pattern of not being able to ask for help. But with respect to one nagging problem—my sleeplessness—there was a certain visitor who insisted on helping me, even though I was too confused to ask for it. Most nights, I'd be grateful if I was able to achieve even a partial doze. But even if I did achieve that half measure, I'd usually wake from it with a start, not knowing where I was, but fully expecting someone to sneak into my room and try to kill me. Destabilized by pain meds and feelings of helplessness—which was something I'd never felt before—I was revisited by the fears and emotions I'd had the night when I really was helpless, shot, and just a short distance from the folks I fully expected to kill me while I screamed. It became a serious problem, this habitual inability to sleep. It was causing things like the Korea episode.

Taking the initiative, one of the young corpsmen volunteered to visit me every night and stay with me. He spent the nights in my room, awake, reading books, cramming for a promotion exam. Making the rank of petty officer second class was something he wanted quite badly. I admired that, but I'm not sure I was a great study partner. When I'd snap out of my semi-sleep and cause a ruckus, he'd say, in his calm Oklahoma drawl, "I'm here, Senior Chief, everything's cool." For some reason, hearing him say that was the one thing that allowed me to actually fall—and stay—asleep. At least for a little while.

I've noticed that a distinguishing characteristic of the good people of the world is their intolerable stubbornness. They just simply do not relent.

It had been a week or so since Gabby's visit when I got the phone call from one of my superiors saying, "You're not going to believe this." And he told me the story.

A plane bearing a congressional delegation had landed in Afghanistan. In a room waiting to greet them were all the senior officers. It was wall-to-wall brass. Plus guys from my crew. Gabby deplaned, and when she came in, the first thing she did was walk up and ask, "Who is the Fly Fisherman?" which is not what anyone was expecting to hear. After he identified himself, probably sheepishly, she went over and hugged him.

She then named everyone else on the Love Roster I'd given her, not forgetting a single name, and doled out hugs to each of them.

I sure was grateful for those hugs Gabby gave. Hearing about it deeply touched my heart . . . until I hung up the phone and let the narcotics reassert themselves.

WHAT I SAW IN THE WARD

Sometimes, the fog of drugs would lift just enough to allow for a semi-coherent thought. On one such occasion, I realized I was tired of being the Visited. Bedridden. Pathetic. Passive. Deep in my tanks somewhere there were some last drops of gumption, so I tapped them and decided I wanted to be the Visitor. I wanted to get the hell out of bed. I wanted to take my mind off myself—the fake heroic wounded vet—and meet some of the real ones around me.

First, I had to learn how to walk again.

During my Korean captivity, I'd decided I was ready to go for strolls, but I wasn't. So I consulted the nurses, and they told me what success in the area of mobility would look like. Success would be me leaving the hospital on crutches and not on a bed. So that became my target.

After the doctors decided I was up for it, the specialists came to teach me how to properly use crutches. Their tutelage began with demonstrations, simple ones. How to position the body. How to shift weight while protecting the leg. It felt a little strange to be getting a lesson about crutches. What could be more straightforward? Well, my initial movement on those crutches turned out to be neither straight nor forward.

I was outside the door to my room, perched on those metal girders designed for hurt humans and staring down the gullet of a long, carpeted hallway. I set forth, and began to wobble. Anticipating that wobble, the therapists had put a belt around me, with one end in their control, so that they could hold me up if I fell. I didn't, but I was quite dizzy. The first objective was just to walk to the end of the hallway and back. It was hard. I became nauseous. My leg was still scaffolded in fixators, and in order to avoid hitting them, I had to swing the right crutch in a wide arc.

The therapists were good teachers. If asked, I suspect they'd say I stuck to the rehab schedule, and that I was mostly compliant. Apparently I was still able to commit my mind and body to something. And eventually, I was doing laps around the ward, tallying progressively more every day. When they graduated me to the next level and taught me to do stairs, I was scared, massively dizzy, and almost fell.

So, as much as I could, I preferred to limit my perambulating to the floor I was on—the fifth-floor Wounded Warrior Ward.

On my laps, one of the first mileposts was the nurses' station, which was always buzzing. I said very witty things to them, which generally made their day—or that's how I choose to remember it, anyway.

Past the nurses' station, there were eight to ten rooms that made up the rest of the length of the hall. Walking down it, I could often glimpse behind open doors, and see the folks in their beds. There was a lot of damage.

It was a very serious place to be. But it was also a place of defiant vitality. Some of the doors stayed closed, and you could hear machines pumping away inside. Those closed doors, which shrouded some of the most damaged vets, were not featureless. They were message boards for the people laid up behind them. On one of those doors hung a small whiteboard, featuring the ghosted lines of erased writings, and then one day this text, which didn't get erased . . .

> *Quite strange*
> *to see the grit*
> *and splintered mess*
> *and still seek shelter and comfort*
> *from the same that you know*
> *will hurt you the most.*

Amen. I missed the Speeding Train, too.

Nearby, another door featured a framed note on a brown piece of paper, this one penned by a recent graduate of the fifth floor, Jason Redman. Even though his face had been shredded by bullet entry wounds, I think his note made it pretty clear whether or not he shared my sentiments about being dismantled:

Attention to all who enter here: If you are coming into this room with sorrow or to feel sorry for my wounds, go elsewhere. The wounds I received, I got in a job I love, doing it for people I love, supporting the freedom of a country I deeply love. I am incredibly tough and will make a full recovery. What is full? That is the absolute utmost physically my body has the ability to recover. Then I will push that about 20% further through sheer mental tenacity. This room you are about to enter is a room of fun, optimism, and intense rapid regrowth. If you are not prepared for that, go elsewhere. From: The Management. God bless!

Not only was his structure not crumbling, that bastard was adding floors. I loved him for it. And hated myself. As foretold in his posted proclamation, Jason would indeed recover. And he'd go on to help a lot of people, eventually even attempting to become part of my recovery, too.

Although I was awash in self-loathing, that didn't mean I'd lost the capacity to admire others. It was an honor to be in the same place as these other wounded. These were guys whose crises far exceeded my own. Guys whose character far exceeded my own.

And also a gal whose crisis and character exceeded mine. The girl with the backpack. While her young man from the medevac was there in the hospital, she was there all the time. She was truly committed. Having grown accustomed to seeing her in the hallways, Kelley realized one day that the girl had stopped coming around. I didn't see her on my walks, either. Curious, Kelley asked a nurse about her and the man she'd been visiting, and who he was to her.

He'd been her husband, and he had died.

What visitors saw was a person keen on learning to walk. Because that's all I showed them.

And I've already made the point that while my body publicly showed some signs of recovery, my soul privately did the opposite. I was deteriorating in the ways I've described, while sharing it with no one.

But there was another peculiar aspect of my woe. The problem wasn't just a matter of me being the passive victim of malign outside forces—a bullet, bad fortune, and sadness. My malady wasn't just occurring to me. I was making it occur. I was actively causing it. My suffering? I chose it.

I was enfolded by Duco, Hags, Vietnam vets, cabinet secretaries, corpsmen, Gabby, and quilts. And although I did acknowledge these people and things in the moment, I did not let the good that was around me sink in, or touch me. Was this because I was a hapless puppet of fate and despair? Nope. It was a choice. I rejected their gifts the moment the givers were gone. And I preferred, instead, to continue crumbling.

Why? Why would someone make that kind of choice? Why would someone give the negatives in their life more weight than the positives? Attrition of the spirit. Aided and abetted by opiates. Pain meds and shame conspired against me. In spite of all the good things that people were doing, I felt the much more salient fact was that the whole reason I was in this position (where people had to visit me and do kind things for me) was because I had fucked up. I was ashamed that I'd screamed, gotten hurt, forced guys to risk their lives to save mine, and gotten another dog killed. I was more than a liability. I was a hazard. And a sham. These disgraceful failings were the true portrait of what I now was. I did not deserve saving.

These were the thoughts I woke up with, and fell asleep with.

TUMBLING BULLETS

Late in my stay at Bethesda Naval Hospital, while I was recovering from the umpteenth surgery to fix my shredded nerves and shattered femur, the doctor in charge of rebuilding my leg asked, "You must have been close to the guy who shot you, weren't you?"

"And how the hell would you know that, Doc?" I asked.

Once a bullet leaves the barrel of a gun, after a certain distance it starts to tumble, and when it's tumbling, it causes more damage. I was actually familiar with this phenomenon; I was just surprised that the doctor knew it, too. It turns out that he was with Marines in Fallujah, where he'd worked on guys who had close wounds, and he'd noticed that their bones were largely salvageable, unlike other guys who were hit farther from the barrel. So he started puzzling things out. It was impressive that he'd taken the time to figure out the ballistics on his own, and make the distinction.

"So basically, I can tell from the wound that you were close," he said. "If you hadn't been, you wouldn't have a leg."

Yes, being shot from close-up was one reason I still had a leg. But doctors like him were the other. My surgeons were amazing. They reconstructed my femur, and fought 24/7 to cultivate clean new tissue in my torn-up leg, thereby saving it.

That was a good thing. In fact, to anyone looking at me and my situation from the outside, a lot of things seemed good. I'd hit the PT so hard, with Kelley's help, and listened to my walking coaches so intently, that it was now a sure thing that I'd be leaving Bethesda on crutches, under my own power.

Yes sir, a lot of things were looking good. Even I was, once in a while. When the secretary of defense visited, I'd made a point of cleaning up, to such an extent that Kelley had remarked about how "super fresh" I looked, and what a marvel it was that I'd taken the time to get dressed for the occasion.

But these good things were small physical things. Surface things. Things that could mostly be cleaned with detergent or a suction hose. It was, after all, part of a guise. The guise of the happy, successful, recovering wounded vet. My door did not have writings on it. And why should it? It was fairly obvious that I was a shining, sterling silver war hero.

The extent to which I'd put on that guise, and just how convincingly I was doing it, can be seen in a note my wife sent to friends in late July.

Hey people,

Quite a day today for Los Hatch's. Got good news that we will be blowing this popsicle stand quite soon—maybe by Monday . . . and maybe straight home instead of a layover at Portsmouth—wooooo hoooooo!!!! Still have to do PT every day somewhere though, but just the thought of being in our own home with our family is so awesome. I was informed today that Phat J would like a jeweled cane if he ends up having to use one, so I am going to go online and look for one of the most pimped-out pieces of equipment I can find! SECDEF Gates swung by our room for a chat/photo op. What a humble, genuine man . . . I hadn't even showered after my morning workout! Nice way to welcome a guest! . . . Jim is in good spirits, so feel free to call him if you want to chat. Every day gets better and better. He had surgery this morning and they closed up the entire fasciotomy, and switched him from the heparin drip to lovimax shots and then he will be on an oral anti-coag before he leaves. He doesn't need oxygen anymore, and . . . he looks really good now—his color is back and he's there mentally . . . he's just tired from PT.

One of the upsides of all this, is that we have met some great people here, reconnected with people we just lost touch with, and developed closer relationships with people that are already a part of our lives. We are lucky.

xo

Kelley

Either I'd managed to trick her, too, or she was actively wanting to believe my ruse, for my sake. Maybe it was a bit of both.

GEL BALL MINES

Once the doctors had won the battle to save my leg, I left Bethesda Naval Hospital—on crutches—and went home, where I lost the final skirmishes in the battle to save my mind.

People talk about the sympathetic response between body and mind. If your mind is down, your body is prone to run that way, too. This applied to me.

Basically confined to bed, I was forced to use crutches when I walked, due to the fresh surgeries. The external fixators were gone, but that's not because I was no longer in need of scaffolding. It was just that the external hardware had been moved inside. I now had thirteen bolts in my leg. And shortly after those pieces of metal took up residence in my limb, I got the sense that something wasn't right. Recalling how the Fly Fisherman had palpated my thigh in order to judge the severity of broken bones, I occasionally prodded the pulped flesh of my leg, in an attempt to judge the severity of possible infection.

I wouldn't say I was great at it. One morning in mid-August, about a week after leaving Bethesda, and while high as hell on drugs, I noticed that my leg looked a bit red and felt a bit hot. I didn't have a sound baseline against which to judge such things, so, medically, my assessment was of course piss-poor. My assigned civilian home-care physical therapist also took a gander at the throbbing limb and said immediately, "Dude, you need to go to the hospital. This is no small thing." I thanked him for his read on things and wondered if there was a way I could ignore it.

There wasn't. The swelling was indeed no small thing.

I was still technically based at my unit, so I had the good fortune to be able to call the medical guys at work. They jumped in a truck and came to get me pretty quickly. Once inside my unit compound, I met with Jay, one of our doctors, who later became our head surgeon. He sat me on a table, took a look, and echoed what I'd heard earlier: "We have to send you to the hospital, right now."

I was seriously demoralized by the news. A hospital was the last place I wanted to be. It seemed like my new status as a Liability was something I was destined to never shake. Jay decoded my emotions somewhat and said, "Look, man, this is a long journey, not a one-stop deal. And throughout all of it, remember that you have lots of good things going for you. The best is your wife."

I knew he was right. But in my disordered mind, the dejectedness quickly crowded out any gratitude.

I was undergoing surgery at Portsmouth Naval Hospital within four or five hours of talking with Jay. One of the things they did was insert anti-bacterial gel balls into my leg—basically planting little land mines for the rampaging bacteria swarms. I was out cold for most of the surgery, but before I conked out, I could see that the doctors were going back inside the scar tissue around my knee. It was a heavily trafficked tract of skin. Those layers of epidermis had been opened and shut like tent flaps for the last five weeks. And this time, when they were pulled back, they found an infection-palooza.

The body does not like invaders. It fights them. And that's good news, when the invader is a bacterium. But it's bad news when the invader is the hardware holding your bones together. The thirteen bolts were invaders. Even though the implanted metal was helpful, my body's systems attacked it, causing a general commotion that compromised surrounding tissue and allowed for a bacterial bloom.

That is an important concept: our bodies reacting wrongly to the things that are there to help us. It's precisely what I was doing to the people who were pouring their love out on me.

And, as history suggests, there's a price to be paid for rejecting angels.

THREE BULLETS

After three days laid up at Portsmouth, at the end of which the reduced redness in my leg suggested the mines were finding their targets, I swapped the hospital bed for my couch at home. And after about a week of lying on that couch with my leg elevated, Kelley mentioned that there was a gentleman coming over with his wife to talk with us. I was still pretty drugged up, and all Kelley would say was that this man was another wounded fellow.

The doorbell rang, and Kelley let the couple in. The first thing I noticed was that his face was all torn up. Because my manners were as hobbled as my leg, I asked him, "What happened to your face?"

"I got shot in it," he replied.

Then, without missing a beat, he moved on. "But here's why I'm here. When I got hurt, I didn't have a clue, and neither did my unit, about all of the things that would help me. All of the resources. And when you don't know the resources that you have at your disposal, that tends to make the challenges you face seem insurmountable." He reached out and handed me something. "So here is a notebook I made. It's full of things you should do. Organizations to be in touch with. They will help you and your family. Because your life has changed."

And while he was talking to me, his wife was talking to Kelley. Not once did they mention anything that would have hinted at the fact that he was somewhat famous. They were from a different Naval Special Warfare unit, not mine. Regardless, here they were, extending themselves to help others, without any regard for notoriety, and under their own steam. All they knew was that I'd been wounded, and they knew that I was not in a position to manage the fallout intelligently, because of the absence of a usable resource hub.

There had been no Wounded Guy Handbook, so this guy had literally written one. Just because he gave a damn.

I started to understand why so many people admired Jason Redman.

Legend has it that he started his nonprofit, Wounded Wear, because other vets sparked to a T-shirt he often wore, which said, "Stop staring. I got shot by a machine gun. It would have killed you." That shirt is accurate. During an HVT snatch and grab in Fallujah, he'd been shot in the side of the face, and the arm, with an AK-47. Per the algebra of violence, those three bullets triggered a bunch of follow-on statistics: 37 surgeries, 1,500 stitches, 15 screws, 200 staples, and 20 skin grafts.

And it did make him look quite different. The structure of his face, the way he breathes, the way his eyes work—they all changed. My femur only punched out the back of my leg, courtesy of a bullet that wasn't even tumbling. He got shot in the face. I think of that a lot.

As he took his leave, he gave me his number and said, "Hey, listen, there will be dark times. When they come, call me."

"No, I'm good, man," I lied. And then, laughing feebly, I assured him, "I'll heal."

"Well," he said, "maybe in the future you'll need it."

Boy, was he right.

Even though I continued to defiantly stand by my lie, he came to see me a couple times afterward, just to check in. One time, when he stopped by, he was on his way to the airport, to fly to Chicago, to see a private doctor for more work on his face. Jason took out a picture and showed it to me. "This time, when I go in, I'm holding up this picture and telling the doctor, 'When I come out, I'd better look like this, or else.'" It was a picture of Brad Pitt.

Chock-full of relentless optimism, wit, and generosity, Jason was a one-man resurrection machine. When you were with him, it was clear that he was committed to helping lift you out of the doldrums and start you on a healing upward trajectory. I knew without a doubt that he was a sign of hope and promise. But for others. Not for me.

SETTING RECORDS AT THE MAYO

Depression allows you to cultivate some morose worldviews, which you stick to doggedly, like credos. My favorite was that, because noncombatants and other civilians couldn't understand me or my experience, they therefore couldn't do anything to help my soul. Could they help fix my body? Maybe. But not my soul.

Gunfights are good for a lot of things—like dealing with trouble-makers, and burning away the fluff. But they can also become an artificially restrictive wicket for those of us who've been in a lot of them. I had a hard time trusting anyone who hadn't. I guess I just presumed that the only people who were invested were the ones that I had been in battle with, where all of us knew what it felt like to rely on each other. Where each of us felt like we were part of the equation, believing oddly in the safety net that existed when you were overseas and fighting, so that we were more comfortable there than here. Being back home, I just simply didn't think that any civilian safety nets or recovery methods could ever be sufficient or up to snuff. I know: it's a strange kind of snobbery. But I'm confessing it. I was arrogant.

It took a visit to the Mayo Clinic to smash some of that arrogance.

The Mayo Clinic in Arizona looks like a high-end office park on a Mars colony.

As you enter the campus, you see buildings that are a mix of glass, steel, and what seems like space-age adobe. There's also a prominent sign that says "The best interest of the patient is the only interest to be considered."

And that's not just some mantra. It's real.

It's also a philosophy that presents an opportunity for drama . . . when the patient in question is headstrong and delusional and thinks he understands his best interests better than the medical staff does.

I went to the Mayo in October 2009, thanks to the generosity of a benevolent organization that had decided to get involved in my rehabilitation. My leg had already received a good amount of tissue and structural reconstruction work, but one of the outstanding issues was a particular nerve in my right leg. When the bullet punched through above my knee, it chewed up a large tract of my peroneal nerve, which runs the length of the leg and is what you use when you dorsi-flex your foot. When muscles in your feet lift your toes as you walk, that's courtesy of your peroneal nerve.

With mine damaged, I had what's called "drop foot." I couldn't lift the front part of my foot, and couldn't feel any of it. I also couldn't feel about 85 percent of my leg below my newly rebuilt knee.

After some examinations, the Mayo team decided to go ahead with nerve graft surgery in an attempt to reconnect it.

My nerve graft surgeon was Anthony Smith. He was an accomplished guy. Former Army. He was also humble. After studying my leg, he tipped his hat to the guys who'd worked on me prior, remarking that nobody could have done a better job of putting my leg back together. Getting the sense that I was interested in his résumé, he told me of a marathon twelve-hour surgery he'd done where he sewed a man's arm back on after it had been cut completely off in a factory accident. I think this was his version of getting me in the mood.

He took only seven hours to complete my surgery. A lot of that time was spent just trying to find my nerve endings. Luckily, he had help, from an anonymous prior surgeon who'd left a good deed buried in my body.

Somewhere along the way in the earlier surgeries, a doctor had realized that eventually someone would try to repair the nerve, so he flagged the bottom of the upper part of it, for later. This was thoughtful, and gracious, and Dr. Smith found it, but it still left him with the challenge of having to find the distal end of the lower part of the nerve. This took quite a while, because it had retreated into the mess of damaged tissue, like a very small, but very important, moray eel.

After a couple hours spent digging around delicately, Smith found the nerve.

Because a chunk of the nerve was now just no longer there, they performed what's called a cable graft, where the gap is spanned by bundled ropes of less important nerves from elsewhere. The nerve they decided to insult with the label of "less important" was the sural, from my left calf, which they removed and then sewed to the previously flagged top part and recently discovered bottom part of my peroneal.

I wonder if it was a Krackow stitch.

The upshot is that we basically robbed from Peter to pay Paul, neurally speaking. Once they closed me up, the incision stitches on my left leg ached a tad, but the pain wasn't bad. And the good news was that I was told I'd be capable of some cool parlor tricks, such as showing folks that when I flexed my left calf muscle, parts of my right leg would now twitch. Things seemed to have gone well.

The thing is, with surgeries like this, it's a long time before they declare you out of the woods. And I wasn't. A few days later, a problem cropped up. They'd had to restitch the backside of my right leg, reinforcing the skin over the exit wound that had been traumatized so badly by the bullet and surgeries. Now, that skin was beginning to fail. It became necrotic, and began dying. It was clear that this skin would not be able to protect the nerve graft. So three days after the first surgery, they opened up the leg again, this time taking a chunk of muscle called the gastroc—which is often used as a remedial flap in microsurgery—and flipping it up to protect the nerve graft. Next, they took a sizable patch of skin off my right thigh and covered the dying skin on the back of the knee.

Talk about recycling. It was pretty sweet. And these guys are so good that you don't really end up looking like a Frankenstein, even when you are one.

It turns out that what Dr. Smith did was actually something that most folks didn't think could be done. But his primary impact on me wasn't medical. It was human. I was most impressed with his interactions, and not just the charming campfire stories about arms severed by industrial machinery. What I remember of him now is that he was a caring human, who was always asking me if I was OK, in a way that I knew to be genuine. I still wasn't accustomed to that, especially from strangers.

It was truly amazing, the mysteries these doctors could solve. My lead doctor at Bethesda could intuit whether a bullet had started to tumble on its millisecond-long journey into my leg. My unit doc could divine the hidden cellular warfare being waged inside my swollen thigh. Dr. Smith could detect and find small, missing nerve endings.

And yet none could tell that the man right in front of them was dying from a wholly different wound.

My thumb was tired.

During my three-week in-patient stay at the Mayo, they rigged me to this great apparatus that allowed for a patient-controlled analgesic (PCA). In my case, this meant that the inmate was essentially running the asylum, as far as administration of pain meds went.

Dilaudid is a brand name of hydromorphone, a powerful pain-killing narcotic with a high risk of addiction. Accordingly, when you're on a PCA, you need to be on pulse ox, an automated guarantor of sufficient oxygen that kicks in if you overdo it with the drugs and knock yourself out. I was attached to a Dilaudid drip feed, on an eight-minute cycle. If I was really hurting, I could press a button with my thumb and get an additional hit during the eight-minute interval.

The skin grafts were OK, but the insides of my legs hurt all the time. I had a lot of nerve pain, which I felt mostly around my knee. The femur hurt a bit, too. So I pressed the Dilaudid drip over and over and over.

Every four hours, the system locked out, because I was hitting it so much. The staff could see how many times I pressed the button, and they were taking notice of my Thumb Olympiad. Once I pressed it over a thousand times. A psychiatrist was promptly notified.

I was supposed to be a tough guy, and yet there I was, with my thumb worn out. I actually switched hands, and put my other thumb into the rotation. A nurse came in and said they were submitting the system for review, because it clearly wasn't working. She then informed me that I'd set a record on the button.

See? I told you I'd share a Most and Only.

THE MACHINE

At Bethesda, there were times when I'd wake up from surgery and not know anyone around me. The night of the Korea incident, the hallucinations were so bad that I told the unfamiliar staff I'd kill them.

At the Mayo, I didn't want a repeat performance. In order to ensure that I wouldn't be violent or hostile, a handful of guys from my unit traveled to Arizona and did shifts. It was gracious. These were men getting ready to go on deployment. They had families of their own they needed to be with. And yet they spent a week at a time babysitting me. I remember the Admiral appearing, wearing denim overalls and bearing a platter of sushi. Not to be outdone, Jason, my Ranger buddy from Bagram, also showed up and presented me with a cheesecake he'd made from a secret family recipe.

But I also had help and camaraderie from someone—a civilian—who did not initially seem to fit the bill for such duties. She started as basically a scary commandant, but ended up becoming someone I relied on. Her name was Shirin. She was the nurse who'd informed me that I'd set a record with my thumb.

And she's also the one I now refer to as the Machine.

When she was first assigned to me, she was a cyclone of healing. She'd fling the door open and immediately start scanning digital readouts and checking everything, all while talking animatedly to me. I once asked her to please come in the room less violently, because it was all a bit much.

And here's the catch: even while she was doing all those things, you knew she gave a damn, like Dr. Smith. Not that I admitted that in the beginning. I was just trying to avoid getting knocked over, or pushed around, by the cyclone.

One of her strengths was that she was not impressed with me, or scared, whereas I think a few of the others were.

In my part of the hospital, it seemed like all I heard was alarms. Most were monitoring vitals, and they'd sound when someone's oxygen or heart rate dipped below a certain level. It was eerie, and horrible—the shrill symphony of human system failure. At night, mercifully, the alarms didn't sound as often. That was my time to sleep. But uninterrupted sleep was difficult, for a few reasons. They had to check on me every four hours, there was nobody on staff with an Oklahoma drawl, and there were significant challenges involved in going to the bathroom.

They'd given me a bedpan, because I was not supposed to walk. Walking was inadvisable, due to the large number of stitches crisscrossing both my legs. But, because I hated the bedpan, and because I knew better than they did what was in this patient's best interest, my mentality was "Fuck it, I'm going to use the bathroom whenever I want." The moment they put an emergency walker in the room with me, I started hatching big plans for the illicit nocturnal adventures I was going to have with that walker.

One morning around 1 a.m., a night nurse, who was about my age, came into my room, paused, and did a sensory scan of the place for about thirty seconds. She must have had some kind of crazy Spidey Sense, specially attuned to the small signs of patient rebellion, because she noticed that my walker had been moved, ever so slightly. She said, "Have you been up?"

"No," I replied, evidencing my facility with Jedi mind tricks.

"Well, that walker has been moved," she said.

"You know what?" I barked. "I did get up, because I'm a commando, and I'm not using that bedpan." It was delivered in a macho tone designed to communicate the general idea that "I'll do whatever the hell I want." (I blame the Dilaudid.) She stopped cold, looked at me with lasers, and said, "I don't care who you are. I'm the nurse, and you're going to do what I tell you."

She was not one of the nurses that was scared of me.

Hearing about these goings-on with her patient, Shirin swept in and added some nice, draconian touches to my little domicile. She put a different kind of alarm on my bed. Not a medical alarm. A noncompliance alarm, designed to keep the patient (me) from unauthorized exits. I was frustrated. It messed with my head. I felt like a three-year-old being chastised. After taking a moment to remind myself that I was a commando, I screamed something about wanting to leave my bed without a goddamned alarm going off.

As is the case with the rest of the women in my life when I try to persuade them of something, Shirin was not having it.

In my corner room at the Mayo, I was fastidious about cleanliness. I've always been that way. When I was overseas, the windows on trucks in which I was riding had to be spotless. Although dust was everywhere,

I made sure the glass was clean. The guys gave me grief. But the way I figured it, we spent so much time looking through toilet paper tubes, we didn't need secondary things further cluttering up our vision.

This penchant for cleanliness led to some trauma for me at the Mayo, because I couldn't maintain that standard. For starters, because I had too many antibiotics sloshing around in my system, I had C. diff, which produces toxins that lead to diarrhea on steroids.

In describing how yellow fever ravaged Spanish troops during the late-nineteenth-century hostilities in Cuba, an author named Evan Thomas wrote the following: "The mosquito-borne infection essentially melted soft tissues so that sufferers bled from the nose and gums, rectums and genitals, and vomited up something that looked roughly like coffee grounds, but was actually stomach lining and intestine. Howling and ranting as they bled from every orifice, patients had to be tied down in bed so they would not splatter the infection around the wards."

You might think that in our modern age, such horrors are just oddities of medical history, endemic only to the tropics and previous centuries. But they're not.

My C. diff symptoms were toxic, and explosive, so the nurses and staff had to wear gowns in my room. Well, gowns is a nice way of saying it. They were actually fully enrobing yellow hazmat suits. Like the field medics who took precautions in Cuba over a century ago, my team also had to guard against the splatter.

Each visit, they had to shed the suits before they left, which involved depositing them in a dedicated trash bin. More than once, I called out to departing staff members, "Hey, can you stuff those suits farther down into the bin? I can still see them, and I don't like a disorderly trash can."

It's a funny story, but of course it masks a lot of embarrassment. In one instance, I had a blowout of explosive diarrhea, where I'd tried and failed to use the bedpan, and those hazmat gowns were actually put into service. Imagine how I felt. Here's a hint: not like a war hero.

And that's where the Machine came in. She understood things on a different level. Realizing that C. diff was no fun, one day she did something very simple, but very meaningful. She yanked my big bed from its resting position, pushed it out into the hallway, and wheeled me toward a doorway. When the bed proved too wide, she transferred me to a gurney and pushed me through the doorway, into an open space, a little mini-courtyard within the building. So that I could get some sun. I hadn't been outside, or breathed fresh air, in a long time. I remember thinking it was a waterfall of warmth. And because I suspected that the light and warmth were fleeting (they weren't the hallmarks of where I felt I was headed), it was an emotional experience.

I've always had a taste for Perrier, and it only intensified after getting shot.

In Utah, when I was in first or second grade, I went to the state fair. There was a large sampling table full of clear plastic cups, about the size of shot glasses, and each was filled with Perrier. I tried the mysterious elixir, and I was hooked.

I think I was predisposed to like it, because another thing I loved as a boy was *Where the Red Fern Grows.* In the story, the kid, who was poor, had taken the train into town to pick up his dogs, dogs he'd eventually spend a fair amount of time training to hunt. After he got into a fight in town with some kids who teased him because he had no shoes, a kindly sheriff came to his aid and then bought him a soda pop. The way the author described the soda pop is something I've never forgotten. As I read that description, I felt like I could taste it. I thought about the times I'd tasted soda and the sweet and the bubbles. The description was powerful. The words on the page were themselves carbonated. The soda and its sensations felt clean.

There's obviously a pattern here, having to do with cleanliness. Witnesseth:

- My penchant for clean windshields.
- A fastidiousness that rebelled against bio-hazmat suits sticking out of the tops of waste bins.
- My strong reaction to the clean literary renditions of soda pop.

And Perrier was clean, too. That's why I liked it. So much so that whenever I deployed, I made sure there were a few cases of green plastic Perrier bottles stashed in the supply container that got sent over with us.

While at the Mayo, Shirin kept me stocked with bubbly water, which was good, because it turns out my military supply of Perrier had been compromised. I discovered this because the guys in my crew who were still deployed occasionally did something wonderful: they called me. One call was initiated by a friend I've nicknamed Peace Corps, because of his tendency to prefer less-violent solutions to problems. He said hi, and then passed the phone around to four or five different guys. It was a cavalcade of emotions. It was something I needed. It was like I hadn't been able to talk to my family. We'd experienced things together that were so rare, nobody else could understand. I was worried about them but couldn't help. The thing I especially admired about them was the fact that they were talking to me at all, because I was a scary reminder of exactly what they did not want to be—wounded in a hospital, far away from everyone else. I was anathema, and yet they chatted.

I know, those are a lot of jumbled emotions. But I was bundled up into a syrupy narcotic-infused emotional disco ball. The somewhat mixed metaphors are appropriate. They reflect my status.

Sensing my delicate emotional state, Peace Corps then commandeered the phone and switched to an earnest tone. He had something serious to tell me. He explained that he was genuinely sorry I was shot, but considering that I was now gone from the crew, he wanted me to know that he had requisitioned all the Perrier I'd left behind, and that he would be drinking every drop.

I was getting calls and visits from guys in my crew.

My wife was a stalwart hero.

My leg had been saved by wizards, miraculously.

The Machine really cared, and she was a civilian.

But somehow the depression was deeper and worse.

Not content with simply refusing to feel or internalize the good around me, I now went further, and started finding the negative in it.

The dark underbelly of things—that's what I was good at sensing. Dr. Smith gave me a book recommendation, *Mountains Beyond Mountains*. I took his advice, bought the book, and read it quickly. It's about Paul Farmer, who grew up poor, dedicated his life to fighting infectious disease in Haiti, Peru, and Russia, and made overcoming insurmountable odds pretty much a daily routine.

It's a powerful treatise on unrelenting hope and dedication. It made me feel like a piece of garbage.

Maybe my condition wasn't just a proclivity to *see* the dark underbelly of things. Maybe it was also a proclivity to *seek* it. And maybe it always has been. I think about my favorite books, even as a boy. They constitute a certain kind of reading list. *Call of the Wild. Old Yeller. Where the Red Fern Grows.* All about adopted dogs, who share a particular fate.

At the end of *Where the Red Fern Grows*, the brave dog—beloved by the soda-rewarded boy—dies, as a result of wounds incurred while saving the boy from a mountain lion. At the end of *Old Yeller*, the eponymous dog also dies, as a result of rabies contracted while saving his human family from a diseased wolf.

I was now certain that my ending was going to be equally bad.

COPS

I never once glanced at the notebook Jason Redman gave me.

When he'd dropped it off, I'd lied to him, saying I was good to go. And in the months afterward, I'd been vigorously sticking to my story.

After my in-patient stretch at the Mayo, I did an outpatient stint there, too, and then commenced a number of months laid up back home, where I pretended I was recovering, put on a happy face for my friends, and continued to spin the good wounded warrior yarn.

The happy vet story had long ago stopped being something I actually aspired to. Instead, it was now just a smokescreen that I occasionally conjured, in order to keep my shame a secret.

One day, while the Fly Fisherman was deployed, his fiancée was nice enough to take a break from her work and visit with me over lunch. We met at a Greek joint. I had souvlaki. She had a salad. She inquired about the status of my leg and its long-term prognosis. I sat upright and talked about my medical good fortune—how it had begun with the ministrations of her fiancé and the Mechanic that night. How they stopped the bleeding in the dark—a critical first step in saving my leg and life. How, after saving me, her fiancé stayed with me on the medevac and accompanied me to the surgical field hospital.

As she listened, I noticed that she was looking a bit shocked. I'd built up a head of steam, so I kept going. I elaborated on the story of her fiancé covering ground to get to me, although I didn't elaborate on the shooting he had to do (and the fire he had to withstand), because I didn't want to scare her unnecessarily.

Her surprise deepened. It started to dawn on me that she didn't know anything about what I was discussing.

"You didn't know he saved my life?" I asked.

"No, he never told me," she replied. She knew her fiancé was on the same deployment, and that's it.

That's so like the Fly Fisherman. He was in a gunfight, in the dark. He had to kill people to get to me, in order to save me. And he never mentioned it to his fiancée or family. Thinking about his grit and humility made me love him more, and like myself less.

During this period, a fellow named Mike Day was assigned to me as a peer counselor by the SOC Care Coalition, a model organization that I believe the entire military should emulate. Mike Day was a Naval Special Warfare guy from a different unit, and he had his own story. Overseas, he'd gone into a building, gotten knocked unconscious, and been shot twenty-seven times. When he woke up, he was lying in the middle of a room, and he noticed there were four or five guys there, so he killed them with the pistol he still had. The four or five guys had made the mistake of thinking he was dead (which, under the circumstances, was not an unreasonable assumption). Mike then got on the radio, and his team came back and got him.

Looking back, it's pretty clear to me that he was more honestly traveling the tough road required of a wounded vet. And he could probably see that I needed a lot of help in that department. So he offered it. If I needed anything, all I had to do was call. If I was having a hard time with the military or the VA, he'd get into it. At one point, he ignored my claims about not needing anything and helped secure a fancy leg brace for me. Even if there wasn't a crisis, he'd nonetheless make sure we got together every other week to have brunch, go to meetings, or just check in.

He was one of many good, concerned people who tried to help, and I'm sure there were times when I was genuinely positive, or at least seemed that way. "I'm good" was what visitors like him heard me say. "Now leave me alone" was what they didn't.

As far as I was concerned, the people trying to help me were pointlessly putting up scaffolding on a disaster site. *Abandon it already! I'll play along, but there's really no hope here.*

I remember one of my buddies visiting and telling me to get some fitness in, espousing the value of getting physical again. I was polite. I made some misleading nods of the head that seemed to suggest I thought his advice was great, while secretly I remained committed to my regimen of feeling sorry for myself. As he left, I selfishly reflected, *Yeah, you're lucky; you and the other guys are still part of the community where people like us have value, whereas I'm a worthless pile of human material.*

No man is an island? I was. I was skilled enough at bullshitting people that, despite being surrounded by them, I was able to make myself entirely alone, when that was the last thing I needed. But isolation seemed desirable because I was so ashamed and didn't want to be more of a problem. I didn't want to keep being the man who needed visits from concerned friends.

The ironic thing about depression is its associated self-absorption. I know that's not true for everyone, but it was true for me. I was obsessed with myself, not as an object of vanity, but as an object of contempt. Tweaked brain chemistry only further hijacked my mind and my faculties, to the point that the only things I could feel were the heavy sorrow of being out of my crew, and self-loathing. And the only thing I considered worthy of my attention was an unending re-evaluation of my own failings.

There was a hierarchy of misery. Yes, my job was done, and my purpose was over. And that was sad. But what was much worse was the fact that I was to blame. I was continually mourning the loss of my previous life, and damning myself for having caused it. I thought about my errors and failings continually. They terrorized me. They were monstrous. They loomed larger and larger. It was clear that they would eventually destroy me. And I started to see the value in beating them to the punch.

When you want to kill yourself, you're in a tunnel that is forever narrowing. At the end of the tunnel, you dimly perceive your own extinction, and it appears entirely appropriate.

In May of 2010, I decided I'd had enough. It was 7 p.m. I was in my home. The walls were wobbling, not still and solid like walls were supposed to be, and everything was hazy.

I didn't want to be alive any more. I was high on meds, drunk on booze, and had a loaded pistol in my mouth.

My wife was terrified, but not helpless. She called a couple of the guys in my unit and let them know what was happening, and they told her to call the police, because the police could get there faster.

Before she could call the police, I threw all the dishes off the dining room table and stormed out to the backyard, where I took up a position standing over the garbage cans, still brandishing my gun and threatening myself.

My wife came out and asked why I was standing over the garbage cans.

"Because I don't want to make a mess in the house," I said.

She got close and snatched the gun from me. I was shocked. She quickly bolted around the house and through the front yard gate, sneaking away so that she could call the cops without me knowing.

I've been asked if the gun was really loaded. And my answer is, *Of course it was loaded. . . . Why the hell would you put a gun in your mouth if it wasn't loaded?*

It was pathetic.

I know how to use a gun. If I'd wanted myself dead, I would have been dead. I was definitely suicidal, and I'd reached a point where I could no longer understand why I was alive, but something inside of me was still committed to indulging in that saddest of all clichés—making a cry for help.

Cry for help or not, my wife was a little afraid for her own life, and very afraid for mine. I don't blame her.

I quickly made up for the loss of one weapon by going into the kitchen and grabbing another. A knife. My need to brandish weapons, but not use them, sheds light on why the episode qualifies as suicidal "ideation" and not suicidal "success." I didn't want to live, but I also didn't quite want to die.

My wife was taking no chances. Having come back inside after her 911 call, she saw the knife and quickly knocked it out of my hand, capitalizing on the fact that I was a bit woozy and unsteady on my feet. (Remember how I said she was cut from the same cloth? She is. She can handle herself.)

Then the police showed up, and they were in a tough spot. My wife had explained to the 911 operator who and what I was. That I was dangerous, by trade. So they came to my door, knowing that the heavily medicated man they were confronting was a special warfare guy who was likely armed. On top of that threat factor, there had been a shooting nearby in the city that same night, so tensions were extra high.

Those cops had every right to shoot me, or at the very least taze the shit out of me.

But without hesitation, they pulled up and met my wife on the front porch, where they quickly discovered at least one little bit of good news—that my wife had disarmed me in the meantime.

Those officers were amazing, just walking up to my house like they did, knowing that I was in a state of drunken, violent confusion. They handled things professionally and treated me with respect.

My wife says the scenario was actually a bit surreal, because as soon as the cops showed up, I joined them all on the porch and "shifted from Mr. Insane to Mr. Normal in a nanosecond." I welcomed the police with a friendly "Good evening, fellas!" And then I sat and chatted with them, acting like everything was normal, as if hosting police for tea and crumpets was an everyday occurrence. At one point, I apparently even asked, "Hey, fellas, can I get you a drink, maybe a cup of coffee or a soda?"

Playing the Successful Wounded Vet was so second nature that I did it even after having just had a gun in my mouth. But now, finally, someone was going to call me on it.

My wife. She was not thrilled with my charade. She found an opportunity to take one of the cops inside and explain to him that I was putting up a false front, and that, in truth, I was very unwell. From that point forward, my wife and the cops essentially stood vigil, just talking with me, waiting until two members of my unit arrived.

They arrived in a personal car owned by one of them. This was not formal military business. One of the guys from my unit who came for me was Doc, a physician's assistant who had formerly been an operator. I'd done deployments with him. The other was a psychologist attached to Naval Special Warfare, who'd been working with me in the months prior. I'll call him the DragonTamer. When they arrived, they came in the house and sat down with me and Kelley. I reprised my charade as jovial host and offered them espresso. My wife shook her head in disbelief, amazed and disgusted at the Jekyll and Hyde transformation.

"No thanks, we're fine," said Doc. He quickly cut the crap. "Hey," he said, "I heard things are a bit out of control, and your wife is uncomfortable. You're making her scared. So we're gonna take you to a hospital, where we can get you checked out."

I grudgingly agreed. Fact is, I was glad to see them. So was my wife. Even when she understood that they might be taking me away for a few weeks. She was weary, exhausted from having to constantly worry about my instability.

Doc and DragonTamer took me to their car, and we started driving to Portsmouth Naval Hospital. Doc had called ahead, and he told me that Jay was on duty that night, which made me happy. Jay had been a hero of mine for a long time. Hailing from South America, he'd become an operational member of Naval Special Warfare, then decided he would go to medical school. He'd been on deployments with us on many occasions, supporting us as a doctor. He was also the guy who'd sent me to Portsmouth previously, for my gel ball visit.

We arrived at Portsmouth. I was not keen on being back in this hospital, but I knew I needed to be locked up somewhere. I was so confused about life that my outlook was basically "fuck it." Walking and escorting me gingerly, without touching me, Doc and DragonTamer brought me into the hospital's emergency room, which was pretty calm that night. The staff had already set aside a room for me in the back, away from all the "normal" folks. In that room, people from my military community were waiting for me. When I saw them, I was overcome with a mix of embarrassment and emotion.

There was Jay, full of care and concern. But that is not what I was thinking about. All I was thinking about was how hard it was to stand in front of someone you admire when you are covered in shame. I lowered my head, and did not meet his gaze. I was finally at the end. I had become the most pathetic version of myself I could be.

It was clear that everyone there was worried about me. I felt completely out of control, surrounded by so many good people that I knew, all of whom were now trying to figure out Dysfunctional Jimmy. My life with them, my love for them, was predicated on my being able to contribute. I was not supposed to be the problem; I was supposed to be the remedy. And here I was. The basket case. It's difficult for me to think of another scenario that could be more antithetical to what I held dear.

They were looking at me. And I felt they were looking at a ghost. The man who once was.

What they were actually thinking wasn't quite so condemnatory. It was, *What's the best way to help this guy?* They faced a dilemma. They wanted me to go to the psych ward, on the fifth floor, but they didn't want to force me, even though they would have been well within their rights to do so, given that I'd put a gun in my mouth. So they tried to talk me into being admitted. They wanted to see if they could get me to go willingly.

And that's something another one of the guys was there to help with. Mike Day. The fellow who'd been shot twenty-seven times.

Twenty-seven.

I had been shot once.

Once.

I looked at him and said, "Mike, you were shot twenty-seven times. I was shot once, and I'm still losing my mind."

"You're not losing your mind," he said. "We all have our own path through this stuff."

Truer words were never spoken. Ever.

I don't remember much else from that night. I don't even know how I got to the fifth floor (I've been told I went voluntarily). What I do remember is that Mike mentioned the word "path," and looking at him, and knowing what he'd been through, I felt a vague sense of comfort. Even though I was drugged, drunk, and deeply ashamed of being so messed up in front of him, something in Mike's words made me feel that, maybe, just maybe, with the help of all these people who still cared for me despite the fact that I'd just shown them the worst version of myself, I was going to be able to find my own path out of this mess, and travel it.

People had told me before that there was a path out of all of this. But it didn't matter to me then. So why did it matter now? Why did I feel a tinge of hope?

Because I had stopped lying.

Shame that stays a secret will kill you. But my secret was now out. I was clearly not the successful wounded vet. That gun in my mouth was me telling the truth. Yes, it was a pathetic and sad way to communicate, and it showed I had miles to go before I was even close to being in the clear, but at least it was the truth. And despite the fact that Mike knew the sad truth about me, he was nonetheless saying I might have a path.

But finding that path was not going to be easy.

It had become pretty clear to everyone around me that a huge part of my problem was that I was unwilling and unable to ask for help.

Two of the main reasons were Stigma and Pride. When it comes to mental illness, we're afraid of being embarrassed or offended, and afraid of offending. And that's why we spiral. The truth is, offending someone is way better than letting someone eat a bottle of Ambien or suck-start a shotgun. Sometimes offending is the best thing in the world.

In the ensuing months after the suicidal episode, my buddies and my wife basically said, collectively, "Hey, Fuckface, you need to do this. You need to get help. We don't care if you're offended."

And I was. It began the night of the suicidal drama, when my buddies took me from my home straight to the Portsmouth Naval Hospital psych ward. From my room, I could look out the window, and across the water. I could see the city of Norfolk, which represented what I no longer was: a citizen of something. I just felt empty. At that point, I had no clue who I was. I didn't want to be alive. I didn't know why I was alive. I was in a world I'd never been to before. I just could not see a purpose. I hated myself. I was a waste. Stealing oxygen from people who needed it. Not a contributor. I brought nothing to the table, except troubles, pain, drunkenness.

But ego is a relentless demon. So I made sure that the main thing I felt was offended. Offended that my friends had brought me here. That was the thing that was truly offensive to me. *Who are these people to tell me I need help?*

I ended up staying at that hospital for three weeks. While there, I spent a lot of time finding occasions to be offended.

I was offended by the recovery regimen. A number of the programs they had were cousins of various twelve-step recovery plans, and one of them was art therapy. There was a counselor who'd studied it. I had no faith in it, so of course when she gave me colored pencils and asked me to draw a "scene of peace," I did the adult thing: I made some scribbles, which eloquently demonstrated my protest, and then I engaged in an enthusiastic round of feeling sorry for myself, while pooh-poohing the whole damn thing. *Seriously, we're going to sit here and draw for an hour?*

I was offended by the lockdown they put me in after I checked in. Here I was, a grown man with multiple combat tours, and now I was forced to be in this place, wearing purple pajamas, while all these young Navy corpsmen—kids, basically—were milling around, keeping a close watch over me. They watched me when I went to the bathroom. They watched me when I slept. My small room with two beds had its door permanently fixed in the open position. Adding to the degradation, the furnishings in my small room consisted of a sheet, blanket, pillow for the bed, and a towel. No, "towel" is too generous a term. It was a swatch of worn cotton piling that amounted to little more than a hand rag. And it was all I got, because a bigger towel would have constituted a suicide-enabling risk.

The place was barren. The only thing there was in abundance was time. And quiet. I sat with myself, avoided other people, and thought about the decisions I'd made that had landed me there . . . or tried to, anyway. Truth is, at the beginning of my stay I was still so foggy from booze and pills that my internal monologue was fuzzy, fractured, and not very constructive. I remember saying to myself, *This is what you get for being a pussy.* I realized that I had myself to blame for the pajamas. I'd put myself in a position where my actions were so questionable that I needed folks to watch over me.

One of them was the psych from my unit, DragonTamer. He's the guy who made me touch the dragon. And this hospital is where he made me do it. Previously, he'd thought I was too fragile for the exercise, but now he knew I'd be less likely to hurt myself, because I was under constant observation in a controlled environment. He also thought I'd mellowed a tad. So he used this opportunity to help me.

I was offended. It was offensive to have to sit in a psych ward in pajamas, feeling pathetic, and have my buddy come in and make me undertake the dragon-touching. I did it because I respected him, trusted his judgment, and was secretly happy that he was there visiting me. But, at the same time, I hated and resented him for making me do such a painful thing.

"So I need you to write down all the details about the experiences that are hard for you to revisit," DragonTamer said, "especially the night you were wounded." I had told him that that was the key trauma, the source of my destructive self-loathing and shame. I felt I had made mistakes. I wasn't quick enough; I should have processed things more quickly. I had not identified the people who were there, and had failed to discern whether they were armed. That is why the dog was killed. My getting hurt altered the mission, having a negative impact on whether or not it was successful.

You have heard this already, so you are not impressed. Neither was he. He basically said, "OK, go further." He wanted all the details—sounds, smells, what I could see, what I couldn't see.

He handed me a notepad and a regular, not very impressive pen.

I was reluctant. I agonized and wrote. And when I handed him a full page of scrawl detailing what was tormenting me, he looked right at me and said, "OK, do it again." What I thought was a magnum opus was only a mediocre first draft.

I did do it again. And again. Over the course of three or four days. Until he was satisfied.

I started to wish I'd done the damn drawings with the colored pencils, instead of what I was having to do with this pen. Given the enormity of the exercise, I remember thinking that it deserved a more impressive writing implement. Not just a crappy leftover ballpoint.

I finally got to where I could do the exercise with some investment, and my later drafts ran to five or six pages. He was satisfied. I hated him.

What happened is I stripped it down and broke it down into tiny pieces, as I was writing it. And I was angry, writing it. *This motherfucker! I have to write about the weeds crackling, which I know gave us away, and the dog, and what I smelled, and how I watched his ears and tail go up, which is how I knew . . . I should have just started shooting . . . but no, you can't in a hostage rescue . . . and because of those rules, the dog took two rounds, and I saw the muzzle flash . . . and then. . . .*

And then I had to go to a place where I couldn't remember the details so well anymore, and that was infuriating. The last thing I remember clearly is putting a laser on the guy's face, pulling the trigger, seeing the bullets hit, and taking a step with my right leg, which didn't exist anymore.

He made me read it to him, and as I did, I remember him looking at me and saying, "Hey, what would you change? Did you make mistakes based on the circumstances? Was there something that you neglected? Was there something you were aware of that you foolishly chose not to take into consideration?"

And there wasn't.

Based on all the details, I had done the best thing I could have done. And the odds are, given all those circumstances again, I'd do the same thing.

"OK," he said, "are you done punishing yourself about it?" I got his point. And shortly thereafter, in a rare moment of lucidity, I hatched the nickname for this painful process: *Touching the dragon.* Touching the dragon involved touching the thing that tormented me over and over until I realized it wasn't going to burn me. It's how I saw that the facts didn't jibe with my damaging, fearful, and tormented feelings about what had happened. It's how I saw that my self-loathing was not fully justified. The best descriptors of me on my final night in Afghanistan were not "liability" and "failure." I was holding on to a bad, guilt-driven, and false version of the truth, which was poisoning, maybe even killing, me. So I had to renounce that bad and false version of the truth, because it just didn't hold up.

I'm not sure if it's in the textbooks, but, in my opinion, one of the core principles of mental healing is this: When you hate yourself, really hate yourself, no other good thing can ever take hold—not advice, not treatment, not the truth. And you hate yourself for flawed reasons. So expose them.

When you face it, the dragon that you think is going to incinerate you, doesn't.

I was a week into the Portsmouth adventure, and I actually had something to show for it. Courtesy of DragonTamer, I now had the theme—confront your sources of pain—and a workable mechanism.

But I also had more than one dragon. So DragonTamer made me poke all of them, provocatively.

In order to start analyzing why I was still tormenting myself, he made me confront the six or seven big things that were lingering and that I couldn't let go. The two really big ones at the top of the list were, number one, the Bergdahl mission where Remco died and I put the lives of friends in jeopardy, and, number two, Spike. Then came an assortment of other torments, including the memory of the handful of innocents that had gotten hurt over the years. It was difficult to write down those big, tough things. But I did.

And by forcing me to admit that, although I was fallible, I was not a total waste, the dragon-touching helped me start to address the pain rooted in my past. But it was only ever going to get me so far, because it still left me with the very real problem of the present.

In the present, all I felt was sorrow at being detached from my crew, and shock at what I'd become. I may not have been the horrible liability I'd imagined, but I sure as hell was not back to being an asset. These ongoing woes were exacerbated by the fact that I was drying out. Pain meds and booze were like the grenades on the night of the 500-pound bombs. Until I admitted they were a serious threat, too, and addressed them, I would never be able to deal constructively with the bigger problems.

Continually looking across the water from my room, I would just stare at the city I used to live in, and reflect on how I'd messed myself up so bad that I was now imprisoned in a place where I dried myself with a hand towel. I could not get past that analysis. *How the hell did I get here?*

Up until this point in my life, I'd always known exactly what the plan was for me. I knew the drill. I'd work at home and then deploy, which was reassuring and steady, although not really fair to my wife.

Now, I had no clue what the plan was.

"You wanted to go home, but other than that you had no objective," recalls the Fly Fisherman, "and that was clearly a problem." He walked through my doorway one day, wearing his khakis. The fact that he had to don his uniform in order to visit me in this mental ward just made me feel further away from what I was, or had been. He could tell that it took a while for my considerable embarrassment to subside. But after talking for a bit, he then noticed some overall changes in my demeanor. He compared my new state to the one he'd witnessed a few months prior, when he'd been driving a van on our compound and saw me sitting on a bench, staring at a particular memorial wall, smoking.

The wall was a granite slab adorned with a flagpole and engraved with the names of men we've lost. Sensing not all was well—because people don't just go to the wall to hang out and have lunch—he got out of the van, talked to me, and noticed that I was pretty empty, barely there. Now, even though I wasn't specifically verbalizing it, he could see that I was opening up to the idea of getting serious help, beyond Portsmouth. When asked for his take on things by DragonTamer, the Fly Fisherman said I was obviously hurting, but at least now he could tell I was "still Jimmy."

There were some indicators that the Fly Fisherman was correct in saying I was still me.

As I slowly sobered up, I started observing the staff and clientele around me a bit more closely. There is no doubt I still had serious mental issues. The administration of my pain meds and sleep meds continued to be strictly managed by others, not myself. But I remember seeing people who had mental problems on a different scale—people who had to be drugged so significantly that they couldn't lift their feet. They just shuffled, and they talked to themselves. When I saw this, I selfishly pitied myself and thought, *Wow, this is the crew I'm in now.*

There was a fixed, specific time in the morning when we had to be out of bed. One morning, I noticed that another patient didn't want to comply. Instead of trying to deal with him in a way that was constructive, the young staffers lined up at his door and got ready to rush the prison cell and make him comply. It didn't feel right. So just before the raid kicked off, I waded in and sat down on the bed, looked the prone protester in the eye and said, "Hey, why don't you just get up, because otherwise this is going to turn ugly." The patient agreed. We walked out together, and there was no drama.

Despite such heroics, I doubt any of the staff were writing things like "patient of the month" or "what a swell guy" on my forms.

They watched me less. The towels stayed the same.

One day, I was given some skydiving magazines by a friend to read. As they were handed to me, a hospital staffer intervened and seized them, saying, "Hey, Jimmy, listen, we have to take them away, because they have staples, and you might harm yourself." I responded poorly.

"If you think I need staples to kill everyone in this room," I said, "then you're the one who's crazy."

Here's some advice: Don't threaten the staff at a mental ward. It's not a good call. You might end up staying in that ward a little longer—say, for example, an extra week. You may even start getting a different kind of shot in your arm.

I should have done the drawings.

Having inadvertently extended my stay, I started to notice that my buddies were coming to see me quite frequently. At first, I thought nothing of it, and the visits from the guys did what they had always done: they triggered both gratitude and what was now a routine terror. *They're going to kick me out of the military. I'm pathetic. I'm unhinged. I'm embarrassed. I've gone from being a guy who was trusted with all this heavy responsibility, to being a guy not trusted with a full-size towel.*

It took me a while to learn that something else was going on.

It turns out that I wasn't the only one who didn't have a clue when it came to what the plan was for me. The hospital didn't either. None of the professionals working around me really thought that spending a few weeks in a lockdown unit in Portsmouth was going to be the solution to my problem. Endlessly touching the dragon in a psych ward was not a sufficient game plan. So they were trying to figure out what the next step would be.

They were good, committed people. But they were basically confused as to what to do. The regular military didn't really have a method that was working for guys like me. And the Navy, specifically, didn't get many people with my history showing up in a psychiatric facility. I stood out. Part war celebrity, I guess, and part science experiment. So the Portsmouth Naval Hospital folks consulted with psychiatry pros in some of the other services that had dealt with heavy post-combat issues—people that were a bit more familiar with my type of situation. They also consulted extensively with members of my unit, both medical staff and friends, especially the Fly Fisherman, who was brought in on more than one occasion.

True to form, the first thing the Fly Fisherman wanted to do was figure out how bad things were, so he could take action. He wanted to measure the bloody sand around me. But there was nothing quite that tangible this time. From his point of view, what was striking was the absence of any template when it came to solving this problem. Yeah, people were keen to open the dialogue on what to do with me, but after that, it quickly became clear that the real project was figuring out what the hell the dialogue should even be about. It was all unfamiliar territory, because nobody at our unit had ever hit my unique and precedent-setting low: injured and suicidal, with a gun in my mouth, while still technically active duty.

Hmm. Another Most and Only.

I did not know these discussions were going on around me—discussions that sometimes even included Kelley. Over the course of about two weeks, the conclave of medical professionals distilled the large array of questions down to one: *Where should we send him next?* The Fly Fisherman, DragonTamer, and two other doctors from my unit appointed themselves unofficial fact-finders, researching and exploring various places. They deputized the Fly Fisherman to start broaching the subject with me, and then afterward treated him like an oracle—asking him what he thought my response would be to this or that option. He'd give his two cents. He felt that, in my new state, I was open to getting help, but I was also going to be very particular about where I'd agree to go. He knew me well.

One of the options I would not consider was yet another military facility, for a number of reasons. First, I was fearful of the big Navy mechanism making decisions about my care. Portsmouth Naval Hospital had many good folks, but not a lot who'd seen combat on the regular, and I was worried they might continue to own me and push me through their channels, without understanding me. Even though by now I had trusted some non-gunfighting military to help fix my body, I did not fully trust them to help heal my mind. In my heart of hearts I still really believed that unless you were one of my buddies, who'd volunteered to live a certain hard way, you didn't deserve to talk to me about anything that had to do with why I was troubled. Unless I had seen your progression into our world and approved of it, you didn't have any right to try to help me or know what my feelings were. Whereas, strangely, I now thought certain civilians might, thanks in large part to my experience with the Machine.

The bigger reason I wanted to steer clear of military psychiatric facilities was the dick-measuring that occurred when I was around other military people who were also struggling. It would happen at VA hospitals, Portsmouth, Bethesda . . . anywhere there was group therapy. In those settings, we had to establish certain things about ourselves at the outset, and when people found out I was from Naval Special Warfare, it seemed to provoke some of them to tell stories, not all of which were true. If you were to have the same experience in therapy groups that I had, you would think that the military consisted entirely of humans who served in some form of special operations unit. There were no cooks, no mechanics, no computer techs. Everyone was a Recon, Special Forces, Ranger, Green Beret death-dealer. It was counterproductive, because this dick-measuring seemed to take precedence over being real. At least with men.

And it's not just the enlisted guys in the group who yielded to this temptation. I saw a therapist who was running a group do it, too.

So the two big criteria for my next facility were (1) it should be civilian, not military, yet still have folks adept at dealing with military patients, and (2) it needed to have an alcohol treatment program baked into the rest of the therapy. Another important requirement was that it had to allow for visitation from family and unit members. My command was worried that my not being able to see Kelley would damage our relationship.

Eventually, the recommendation was that I be sent to a civilian drug rehab facility in the South. I actually thought this was a great plan, and my opinion mattered, because this time, it was 100 percent voluntary. I'd ended up at Portsmouth because I'd looked people in the eye and said, *I want to hurt myself.* In the military's mind, this kind of behavior merited a psychiatric hospital visit that was not optional, and they would have forced me to go to the fifth floor if I hadn't been compliant. But it was different now, with this civilian hospital down south, because, technically, I had to self-admit.

I could also self-remove. And that was the real threat.

I chose to go. But before being sent down south, I really wanted to go home for a night. And they let me. I wish I hadn't done it.

Nobody said anything to me, but I could tell that every single person involved in my care thought going home that night was a bad idea. In fact, they said no. It turns out that my wife overruled them. She forced her way into the head doctor's office at Portsmouth and launched into a spirited conversation, the upshot of which was that she was liberating me. Apparently, Kelley employed some skillful negotiating tactics. She started high, asking for three days with me, which raised hackles, then came down to the one-day ask, and got it. In addition to this smooth compromising, there may have been some yelling.

Her tirade bought us one night together. But not before the chief doctor and other medical professionals made it very clear to her that I was basically a bomb on the verge of going off. I would eventually get better, they said. But this path I was traveling would be a long one.

Kelley is tough, but when threatened, she is also defensive. My illness was an unknown, and therefore a threat. So she acted accordingly that night. She made a nice dinner. It was awkward. I wanted everything to go back to what I used to think was normal. But instead, it was almost as though I was a stranger and she was being courteous. That was quite upsetting. Still, to my credit, I exerted some serious self-control. For example, when I looked at her mother's china in our china cabinet and wanted to throw all of it on the ground, I didn't.

Hurt that night by her words and deeds, which felt cold and antiseptic, I see now that it was only because she was scared to death, and she was trying to establish a dynamic with me that she could handle.

After that misbegotten homecoming, I climbed into my bed, which provided none of the familiar comfort I thought it would, got up early the next morning, and was picked up by the Fly Fisherman. He was *again* rushing to my aid, even though he was still training, coming down from one deployment while preparing for another, needing to spend time with his own family, and not obligated to do any of this as part of his duty. Later, I was told I had actually requested that the Fly

Fisherman escort me, which makes sense, because it was really no different from the night I'd asked him to join me on the helo.

Whatever the origin of the idea, he sure as hell committed to it. And not just fully. Disproportionately.

That's it. Disproportionate commitment. That's what he had for me. And I think that's what it takes, for all of us, if we're going to have a hope in hell.

PEANUT BUTTER PIE

The Fly Fisherman drove me to the airport, ready to join me on the plane and help me commence my "Down South" chapter. He was aware of my trepidation. As we approached the airport parking lot, I said, "I don't want to go." But he just kept the car moving. He was in the woods, to a certain extent, when it came to the exact nature of my mental state and what to do about it. But he was not at all confused about his commitment to the project of ensuring it got figured out.

He genuinely cared about me. And because he did, he wasn't there simply to be a happy chaperone, pal, or sidekick. He was there to be an enforcer. He was there to force me to get help. Not ask or recommend. Force. That is what disproportionate commitment looks like. You go beyond well-meaning bromides like *I hope that person recovers* to *I am going to play an active role ensuring that he does.* When you stop at the normal level of investment—having a heartfelt desire for that person to get better—it's easy to go on with your life. But the Fly Fisherman was interrupting his. In a big way. After dropping me off down south, he would immediately be boarding another plane to re-deploy overseas and get back in the fight.

Overseas would be more pleasant for him. He had massive amounts of training for that. It was his wheelhouse. Where he was now, with me, was a funhouse. Helping me when I'd gotten shot in Afghanistan was a breeze compared to this. As he got on the plane with me, he was again feeling very acutely that there was no specialized training for anything that had come after the wound.

Which is exactly how Ace had been feeling back in Bethesda. He felt it was great that he was there, but he wished he could have done more.

From a medical standpoint, he was as well trained as they come, but he had minimal to zero training in dealing with PTSD. And he could see it unfolding in me. I was having nightmares and sleep issues. The writing was on the wall that it was going to manifest. And yet he felt he couldn't really help. He says the feeling he had watching me was analogous to hearing that someone had died, wanting to offer condolences, but having no idea what to say to make it better. All of Ace's training had focused on what to do right now. Not what to do four weeks afterward. Millions of dollars had been invested in me, as an operator, and in him, as a medic, but not much had been invested in managing the fallout from what those millions trained me to do. And Ace had seen that fallout be brutal. "Guys get shot," he says, "and we put them on pedestals. Make them heroes. But a fair number get addicted to pain meds. And then they go from Purple Hearts and Bronze Stars to being degenerate drug addicts, in their own minds, and maybe even in the minds of others. It's not fair. Medicine bears a lot of the responsibility. Medicine prescribes those opioids."

A goodly number of those opioids were still coursing through my system as I buckled into my seat on the southbound plane.

As patchwork tracts of the South flowed by beneath us, the Fly Fisherman could sense a small piece of progress: even if I wasn't in love with the idea of the trip, I at least seemed more resigned to it once we were airborne.

The trip, though, was not what worried him.

He knew he'd get me to the hospital, but his fear was that once he dropped me off, I might not react well to, or interact well with, the other civilian folks, "the people who weren't us."

It was a legitimate fear. I harbored it, too. After the Mayo, it would be only my second experience with a civilian facility—of any kind—in nearly two decades. But as we journeyed south, something took the edge off these fears. It wasn't anything that the Fly Fisherman said. It was a place he took me. Big Daddy's place.

When we landed, deep in the heart of Dixie, we picked up a rental car, and the Fly Fisherman started driving me to the new civilian hospital. With just one stop en route. For lunch. At a legit southern barbecue joint.

Big Daddy's BBQ is a humble one-room restaurant situated on a small-town Main Street, which has maybe twenty storefront businesses of the kind that still rely on stenciled window-lettering for most of their advertising. The restaurant features ribs that don't fit in their tinfoil platter, industrial-strength plastic table coverings with a watermelon pattern that isn't really trying that hard to trick you into believing it's cloth, and meats being grilled by a man who is not much smaller than the huge smoker he's tending.

All of the standard buzzwords of good barbecue applied at Big Daddy's. *Fall off the bone tender. Sweet Jesus. Slap your mama* (which, for some reason, is what you'll want to do). But there's more going on here, too.

When we walked in, they greeted us with warmth. We were the only white dudes, and it was all they could do not to hug us, their love and good hearts were so apparent. Their greetings didn't just get uttered. They got served up, like food, because their *hellos* were sustenance, too. I remember one woman sending a "Hi, sweetie pie" my way, and it sounded as good as words had for me in a while.

After we'd eaten, we used napkins to scrape the sauce off our hands, and the Fly Fisherman turned to me and said, "Hey, man, you oughta get a piece of some of that homemade southern pie they have here . . . because you're not gonna have any of that for a while."

They had quite the array—some of the standard pie flavors, plus some exotics, like Peanut Butter, Million Dollar, and Heavenly. I opted for Peanut Butter.

That pie. Such a simple thing. And yet what an effect it had. It was show-stopping good. And my sad little drama needed some stopping.

The Fly Fisherman remembers that particular moment of shared pie consumption as the first time a genuine calm came over both of us. We joked (something I hadn't done in a while), and it occurred to me that I was still human, and that others considered me to be, too. Just like when the little girl put her hand on my neck in Afghanistan.

It's funny. That barbecue joint was a clean pocket of time. And I'd never had one of those outside of war before.

DISPROPORTIONATE COMMITMENT & MERRY CHRISTMAS

I was initially slated for an eight-week stay down south. But I would end up spending twelve weeks down there, in an intensive rehab program.

It didn't start auspiciously. As I sat in the hospital's waiting room, about to check in, watching a woman dig through my gym bag to ensure that I didn't have any weapons or drugs, I became indignant about the fact that I was clearly being treated with less respect than I deserved. I thought, *I've been through all those deployments, and now I have to go through this? I'm too good for this.* So I looked at the Fly Fisherman, shook my head, and said, "I'm outta here. I'm running." And he replied, "First of all, you can't run anymore with that leg, and secondly, you need to do this for yourself, and for your wife . . . and for the rest of us who are coming down the tracks."

He paused for a second, and then added, "You're doing the ADVON."

That was a heavy prophecy, and an accurate one. A lot more guys would be coming after me, hurting. It was inevitable. We've had thirteen to fourteen years of sustained combat—more consecutive years than ever before in American history. And there's a handful of guys who've been knee-deep in the heavy side of that combat for all of those years. I did 150 direct action missions. And I know guys who've done three times that. Not patrols. Direct action. It's a serious volume of fighting. It will be a serious volume of aftermath. Marriages falling apart. Alcoholism. Guys getting kicked out of their houses. Guys drowning in opioids.

The real recoil hasn't even hit yet.

Standing there, at the hospital check-in, I looked at the Fly Fisherman, this guy who had saved my life in combat a short while earlier, and I realized the only option I had at that point was to do what he said. Take the embarrassment. Take the shame. Let people dig through my bag, and my mind, for dangerous things. Try to understand my brokenness the best I could. And debunk the anxiety of confessing it.

I would come to understand that when people save your life, you owe them two things. In that moment, with the woman rummaging suspiciously through my bag, I was hit with the first thing: You can't disrespect them. You can't do things that would make them regret having saved you.

The second thing you owe to people when they save your life—well, that one only became clear to me later, after being at this hospital for a few weeks.

The hospital was billed as a drug and rehab facility. But I distinctly remember sitting with one of the doctors and having him explain, "This is rehab, yes, but make no mistake, this is also a psychiatric facility, and you are a sick individual." He was right. And I'm grateful for the Fly Fisherman's insistence that I stay there. In that place, for which I initially had contempt, I had my worldview radically adjusted. And it sent me on the path that I'm on right now, the path that Mike Day promised me I'd find, the one that makes me want to live and do something constructive.

I'd always liked being deployed—with intermittent breaks to be with my wife, sure—but I liked being in fights. I enjoyed the purposeful violence. And that is expensive, because when I look around a room of "regular humans" now, I think, *If they knew what I'd done, they'd fucking run.* The same thing happens when I'm waiting for a train here in the U.S., standing in a crowd at a station. I wonder, *What the hell am I doing here? I don't belong with these people. They are nice, good people, and they don't have the same desires I do.* I always felt, and still do, that if I could move and be an asset to my crew, I'd go join them right now and get in a gunfight. I love it, and I miss it.

Upshot: I did not feel I was the kind of person that rehab facilities reach.

And then I heard the woman's story.

She was also at the facility, and she shared her struggle with our group. She'd been raped.

By two of her uncles.

In front of her drunk father.

On Christmas Eve.

When she was eleven.

I'd gotten shot, but I had volunteered for it. Here was this woman who hadn't volunteered for anything, and she'd been put through a ringer that made mine look like a trip to Disneyland.

I kept wondering how she must feel when everyone says "Merry Christmas" each year.

I realized that you don't have to be a commando to suffer severe trauma. Life is combat. For most of us. We go from conflict to conflict, with most of the conflicts occurring inside of us. And as long as they remain that way—internal and unshared—you're at risk.

Life is combat. And this woman was fighting. She was trying to be strong. Since age eleven. She was hurting. But she was in the ring, swinging. Every day. I saw it.

In the Mechanic and the Fly Fisherman, I'd seen that there was a combat level of commitment, and there were very few places in society where I ever expected to see that same level. But here it was. In this woman. Her honest telling of her story was an act of courage.

You have to make a choice to want to get better. For me, this jarring experience was the thing required to get me to the point where I could. The woman's story didn't just give me perspective; it smashed me in the face with it. It knocked me out of the sad little cloud I was traveling in, by getting me to stop feeling sorry for myself—really stop, not just acknowledge that I was doing it. And it forced me to look at what had happened to me in the past year.

It was more than just layers—which was the idea I'd explored in my speech to Secretary Mabus. There was a Chain—a chain of selfless heroes who'd helped me, and who were still helping me.

Yes, it starts with those guys from my unit and the helo crews who saved me in a gunfight in Afghanistan. And it continues with the doctors all along the way.

But the Chain also includes quilt-makers in Montana. Vietnam vets. Cabinet members. Machines. Family members of the men I fought with and civilian volunteers, who kept showing up at the hospitals, offering to help in any way they could.

And of course there is my wife. She is smarter than I am. And thanks in large part to her, I now know that love isn't just forged in war. My wife loves me, and she never went to war. But she was in combat with me. I was the one with the gun.

Throughout my post-gunshot life, because of the narrow-mindedness of despair and depression, I'd only focused on my sorrow and shame.

I'd politely acknowledged and then dismissed (without ever really feeling) the good things being done by all of the people around me, even as they were very obviously multiplying. Now, it was impossible to do that. Because of the woman's story, and other ones like it, I stopped focusing on the misery of what I'd lost, and started focusing on what I was blessed with: the love I had been shown by my companions, and also by complete strangers.

Marcus Aurelius recommends, "Accept the things to which fate binds you, and love the people with whom fate brings you together, but do so with all your heart." I had always thought that fate had only bound me to my unit and other folks who had been in combat. Period. But now I was unable to ignore how many others there were to whom I was bound.

There was also the new way in which I became bound to my unit. They had always been there for me on the battlefield, but they were also there for me in this second war in ways I never could have imagined. To this day, I don't like being at a new yoga studio and having to explain, for the hundredth time, what happened to my leg and why I can't do things like other people. And it's not that the yoga teacher is prying; she just wants to know my limitations, so she can accommodate them as she instructs the class. Still, it's easier just to stay at home and avoid people and think *poor me*. In short, I suffer the humiliations and self-pity associated with being human, and I've been, at times, a real pain in the ass. But the guys in my unit have forced themselves in and snapped me out of those funks. More than once.

Their interventions were always serious, but that didn't mean they were always gloomy. Halfway through my stay down south, Doc, DragonTamer, and the Mechanic showed up. Their visit brought the expected relief and also the expected guilt (because I was again taking these guys away from their families). I had to ask permission to show them where I was staying, and once I'd been given the go-ahead, I enthusiastically toured the fellas around. I wanted to convey to them that I was being taken care of, and that they had made good choices in bringing me there. For their part, they had to ask permission, too—for the right to take me to lunch. That was a bonanza for me. When DragonTamer jumped in the driver's seat and fired up his rental car,

Doc and the Mechanic quickly jumped in back, courteously affording me shotgun privileges. Getting in the car, my excitement about going off campus dimmed slightly as I immediately noticed a protocol violation that needed to be addressed. With what I'm sure was just the right amount of repudiation and scorn evident in my face, I looked over at DragonTamer and said, "Dude, you need to clean this windshield."

I had a long-sleeved shirt on, so I grabbed the wristward hem, which turned the forearm into a makeshift rag, and started buffing the windshield from the inside. The smear marks were unacceptable. I cast a quick roundabout glance to see who was sharing in my irritation, and the Mechanic burst out laughing, shaking with real belly laughs. "See? I told you!" he said to the other occupants of the car, apparently happy that he'd won some kind of wager about how I'd behave.

His laughter meant a lot, not for the reasons one might think, but because it was happening in an unsexy car in an unsexy place with an unsexy friend who was on restricted medical leave from a psychiatric hospital. The irony was not lost on me that the two guys—the Mechanic and the Fly Fisherman—who had had hands on me the night I was bleeding to death were now also embroiled in this procedure to keep me from bleeding to death inside, with poisoned emotions and drugs and booze. They were jamming Kerlix into my soul wound. Those two men, examples of the dramatic and celebrated type of heroism, were also there when what was required was the inglorious and embarrassing type of heroism. When helping was uncomfortable and disturbing, because we were supposed to be tougher-than-nails guys, and there I was, a reminder that we could break.

The Fly Fisherman once pointed out something interesting to me. He said that a fair number of surgeons are fly fishermen. These guys who specialize in surgical Krackow stitches also tie the kinds of knots that fly fishermen tie, many of which are similar, and some of which require the same tricks and techniques. At the end of a fly line, you're using a filament leader—something less than the width of a knife—and you're nonetheless able to land a forty-pound fish. The knot you use to tie the fly to the barbed hook, and the hook to that leader, is what matters. It's similar with sutures.

There's an angling expression the Fly Fisherman shared with me: shock-loading. It's when your line goes from slack to complete tension, and the well-tied fly takes that shock, without the line breaking.

Thinking about the Fly Fisherman's role in my life, I see that the ties at the end of his fishing line weren't the only ones that were shock-loaded.

So why did the guys in my unit and the civilians who helped me in the second war do it? For a simple reason: they're just plain good people. They didn't get paid bonuses. They received no medals on their chests. They just gave. Over and over. As I left the hospital down south, I knew I needed to return the favor. I needed to give something back. And that's when it hit me. The second thing you owe to people who save your life: You've got to live your life fully. You've got to get back to being an asset.

I wasn't exactly sure how I'd do it. But taking stock of my situation, I did know this: although it was true I had lost the ability to be in the kind of combat I loved, I still had a lot of serious fighting ahead of me. I'd just be assaulting different targets now.

PART 3

The Debts I Owed

Stranger in a Normal World

WHAT THE "W" ON HER WRIST WAS FOR

J immy, we want you to know that she's dead."

It was January 8, 2011. I was sitting at home with my leg up on a couch—a favorite posture—when my phone started blowing up. A lot of the inbound calls were being lobbed by my buddies out in Arizona, and it was the Admiral who finally reached me, to tell me Gabby was dead.

Some of my friends out there had talked to the cops, with whom they were close. The initial word was that there had been a shooting at a "Congress on Your Corner" town meeting, held in the parking lot of a supermarket, and the consensus was that there was just simply no way Gabby could have lived through what had happened. She'd been shot right in the head. My buddies wanted to be the ones to tell me.

Sitting there with Kelley, I started crying. I was crushed. My buddies kept up the phone vigil, calling a lot, asking how I was doing. The ensuing minutes were somewhat merciful, because the reports changed, indicating that Gabby had lived.

Six of the eighteen others who'd been shot were not so lucky. They died.

Gabby had been shot point-blank in the front of the head. The 9mm bullet had traveled through her brain, after entering near her left eye, and now the neurosurgeons at University Medical Center in

Houston faced some heavy work. I knew the pressure was on her and her husband, Mark Kelly, so I sat back.

I had a little insight into what she was experiencing. After my parachute accident where I impacted the ground, I was paralyzed on the right side for a little while, due to the bleeds in my left frontal lobe—the same area in Gabby's head that the bullet had hit. After some rehab, the swelling in my brain had decreased, and I'd regained more use of my right arm and right leg. It was pretty obvious that Gabby's trauma was much more severe, and as a result, her right side—which was heavily paralyzed—would not bounce back nearly as quickly.

But I drew a measure of solace from the realization that Gabby would do a much better job protecting her brain, on a go-forward basis, than I had after hitting the ground in my air accident. That event was my first documented traumatic brain injury (TBI). My second official one came years later, from the grenades going off right next to me the night I was wounded. But the truth is, the intervening years were also not very kind to my mind. I think people in our line of work incur much more damage than the documentation reflects, in large part due to all the blasts, which were such a critical part of our repertoire.

I remember some of the bigger blasts probably in the same way that football players recall their big hits. One night, in a fairly urban area in Iraq, we were using a large breaching charge to blow a heavy set of doors, and the shock wave was considerable. I was standing on the edge of a low second-story balcony, the floor of which was slick marble tile. When the blast thumped me, its concussive force, coupled with the poor footing, blew me off the balcony. Happily, it was grass that I fell onto, on my side, meaning I could shake it off, scramble back up the ladder to the balcony, go back to work, and help round up some of the fellows inside. As we gathered them on the floor, I remember noticing how much debris there was from the walls. It had been a serious explosion.

Being very close to these types of blasts is a fairly common occurrence for all of the guys who do this kind of work, because explosive charges are how we go into places. All of us could operate them, but generally it was the responsibility of one operator in particular. And it had to be quick. You can't mess around at the door, because that's where the bullets are being directed. The folks who are good at it have developed hyper-efficient systems, where they can get the charge ready, set it up, and clack it off surprisingly quickly. It's a bit of an art form.

The Fly Fisherman has observed that for the shooters ready to rush in, the breaching MO was often a three-part sequence: (1) get bell rung, (2) shake it off, (3) get back in the game. Concussions were probably routine, but we never did checks for them afterwards.

This unkind treatment of our cerebella wasn't restricted to overseas work. Everything you do in war you have to train for. So, as with everything else, you have to blow doors open when you train, too, not just when you're overseas in a fight. You need to know the effect it has on people inside the structure and outside the structure. That meant being in close proximity to bell-ringing force as we blew doors daily in kill houses here in the U.S.

I wonder what the acronym will eventually be for "TBI and then some."

From my ground impact, and from years of proximate blasts, there was essentially a pipe into the central part of my brain—a tract of neuron-linking axons—that got twisted. Now, take these dramatic little accounts of my TBIs, wrap them all in a bundle, and understand that they are minuscule compared to what Gabby experienced. The metal object moving through the interior of her head at high speed didn't just twist some pipe; it carved a tunnel.

Actually, I can't believe she survived it.

Three weeks after the incident, she was transferred to Houston's TIRR Memorial Hermann hospital, and Mark asked if the Admiral and I would come out and see her. "Yup" was our reply. They gave us a schedule of feasible times, and we worked it out.

I grabbed some of the medals I'd been given—the Purple Heart and Bronze Star that the secretary of the navy had given me—and stuffed them in my backpack. I also took a moment to write a particular kind of letter, which I planned to read to her.

In Houston, I met up with the Admiral and we drove to the hospital. A member of Gabby's staff met us and explained that they were concerned we'd be shocked when we saw her, and that it would upset us. We were warned that she might not remember us. In order to relieve the swelling of her brain, part of her skull had been removed, which meant that she had to wear a helmet when she was out of bed, and she couldn't speak.

I wasn't expecting the Admiral or myself to be shocked by any of the gore. But if Gabby's spark had somehow been extinguished inside its punctured flesh suit, yes, that would be a sorrowful thing, and hard to take. We walked up the stairs and were led through three or four rooms into a sequestered area of the hospital monitored by two guards. She had security now.

Getting closer, we noted that one of the rooms was where they had put all of the well-wishes. And then we came to her actual door, on which Mark had hung a printout offering guidelines for interaction with Gabby. I remember one of the imperatives was to look her in eye. *She is still Gabby. She can't speak like before, but she completely understands what is going on around her.*

Gabby was a lot. So this statement—that she was still herself—was no small claim. I was eager to vet the assertion and also just see her, but I was scared, too—scared of what the failed assassination attempt might have nonetheless killed. I pushed the door open, walked in the room, and saw her lying on her bed. Her right arm was paralyzed. So she lifted her left arm and said, "Jimmy Hatch!" She said my name. And smiled. When she did that, it was overwhelming.

Her spirit had actually gotten bigger.

The Admiral and I sat with her. We embraced, hung out, laughed, and practiced words with her. All throughout the hospital room, she'd hung flashcards of everyday items that were easy to ascertain, like a baseball and a cat. The cards were designed to trigger her mind's ability to identify something and cultivate her ability to speak it. While we were there, she was trying to read some of the flashcards. It wasn't easy, because she had debilitative after-effects associated with her brain trauma. So although she understood what was on the flashcard in her mind, she struggled to get the word out. She didn't give up, though. Even if it was a baseball and she was fighting to say just those two syllables, she would not stop fighting. She still won't. To this day.

Amidst the sea of flashcards, I spied a picture of my buddies overseas—the guys she'd hugged. They were holding a flag that they'd folded up and then sent to her. This folded flag was nearby, on a shelf at the end of the bed, where she could see it all the time.

When it became time for her to start a part of her daily physical therapy regimen, we were told we were welcome to stay and watch. We did. She donned her bike helmet and proceeded to be amazing. There was no way she was going to let the small issue of half a skull interfere with her learning to walk again. A therapist assisted her as she perambulated, and she had to drag her right foot, something I knew a bit about. Analyzing her foot-dragging technique, I gave her high marks for frontal lift and slow-swing sashay (because style counts). There was also a music therapist present, to help Gabby coordinate her movement. And you could see it—a rhythm to her movements, created by guitar. She worked tirelessly, and smiled as she did.

When people ask me who my heroes are, I always mention Gabby Giffords. I was shot in the leg. Gabby was shot in the head. I suffered my wounds poorly and sat in a hospital feeling sorry for myself. Not Gabby. She was a machine of positivity and strength. She was the anti-me.

During the afternoon, I was able to sit with her at a table, at which point I pulled out the letter I'd written. It was an award citation letter, describing her grit, based on my own personal feelings about what she'd gone through and what she was now doing. I read it aloud, and then gave it to her, along with my medals. Another vet had already dropped off a Purple Heart, anonymously. But I wanted her to have mine, too. She smiled at me and seemed happy. Beyond that, it was hard to read her emotions, because there was so much swelling on her face. I do remember looking at her intently and thinking, *Gabby, this is good for you,* and then quickly getting the sense that she was probably thinking the same thing about me.

Because I was now quite close to her, in terms of physical space, I noticed the bracelet on her wrist. There was a "W" on it. I grabbed it, pointed to it, and asked, "What does this represent?" She looked at me like I was crazy and said, "Wonder Woman." Of course.

IN SEARCH OF

Gabby was hardwired to be an asset.

Not me. In my case, getting back to being an asset was a process, and it was complicated by the fact that one of the first items on my new agenda involved leaving the military, which had been the only place, to date, where I'd ever felt like one.

That feeling had ceased. I was an E-8, and it was clear I was not going to be an E-9. I just felt like I was done. Plus, I was simply too selfish to try to help out my unit by doing a less-than-action-man type of job.

I remember my last day in the Navy: May 1, 2011. I took all of my uniforms up to my team room, dropped them on the floor, walked out to the memorial wall, looked at the names of the dogs and humans I knew, walked to my truck, and drove home. I had my DD214 (certificate of discharge) and a folder with my service record. It was amazing to me that all of my twenty-five years and eleven months were summed up in less than two pages of paper. That is telling. It let me know how easy it was to replace me. Like taking your finger out of a glass of water. The spot it vacates fills right back up.

It wasn't that my former crew didn't still have love for me; it was just that they didn't have a role for me.

A few of my buddies had collected money to have a shadow box made for me. It included all of my medals and a flag and a few patches. I was supposed to go to a short meeting and have it presented to me, but I couldn't bear the thought of standing in front of people from my former crew. Even though I knew my last mission wasn't the fierce dragon I'd made it out to be, I still viewed it as a failure, and it was also undeniable that I'd been a disgrace for a couple of years. I told them I'd be there at the ceremony they were performing, but I lied and just went home. I stood them up.

The guys, of course, didn't bear a grudge, although I would have forgiven them if they had. A few weeks later, one of them actually met me for coffee and dropped off the shadow box. I still can't look at it. It's in a closet somewhere. I haven't chucked it, but it may go. I don't know.

Now what.

There was a day when I woke up and no one was calling me, no one needed me, and I had no place to be.

I took this as a hint that it might be time for me to employ that time-honored remedy for aimlessness: getting a job. I needed to find a new way to earn a living, anyway. So I tried my hand at working with a company that sold things to the military. Because I was still in touch with people at my former unit, and other units, and had some experience with different types of equipment, I was an attractive hire. It didn't take long for me to realize I'd made a serious mistake.

I was out of my element. When I tried to convince some manufacturers to produce something that I felt could be a help to the people in my former line of work, I was met with questions like "How many of these units do you think we can sell?" or "Is this viable for an international market?" For me, it was just confirmation that the things we use in war are almost more important for their ability to make companies money than for their effectiveness. It was seriously disheartening. One day, while wearing a suit and being introduced as an Action Man in a board meeting, I hit the limit, experienced clarity, and politely excused myself, never to return.

My heart was not in it. And I had to admit that if my heart wasn't in it, I probably had no business wasting the time of these corporate sophisticates, trying to be a part of their world.

OTHELLO

Once you are no longer what you were meant to be, it is very difficult to understand what you are, or should be. I stumbled about, searching. I still fought the *what ifs*, and I only seemed to remember the bad things I did. I felt a lot of regret. Regret that I didn't suffer more admirably. Regret that I'd spent so much time regretting.

And then, not for the first time in my life, a lifeline was thrown to me by a poet.

After I retired, one of the things I decided to do was use my GI Bill. I took a college theater class, and during that class, our instructor asked us to read *Othello*. We read a lot of the play aloud, in class. As my fellow students took turns reading the play, I tracked the storyline with interest as it reached its climax, where Othello kills his love because he's been tricked into believing that she'd betrayed him. And then it became my turn to read, and as fate would have it, I got the final lines.

Those last lines that Othello spoke hit me like a Hellfire missile.

> *Soft you; a word or two before you go.*
> *I have done the state some service, and they know't.*
> *No more of that. I pray you, in your letters,*
> *When you shall these unlucky deeds relate,*
> *Speak of me as I am; nothing extenuate,*
> *Nor set down aught in malice. Then must you speak*
> *Of one that loved not wisely but too well;*
> *Of one not easily jealous, but being wrought,*
> *Perplex'd in the extreme; of one whose hand,*
> *Like the base Indian, threw a pearl away*
> *Richer than all his tribe; of one whose subdued eyes,*
> *Albeit unused to the melting mood,*
> *Drop tears as fast as the Arabian trees*
> *Their medicinable gum. Set you down this:*
> *And say besides, that in Aleppo once,*
> *Where a malignant and a turban'd Turk*
> *Beat a Venetian and traduced the state,*
> *I took by the throat the circumcised dog,*
> *And smote him, thus.*
> *(Stabs himself)*

When I read those words aloud to my professor and a bunch of students who were all younger than I was, I stopped and the world kept going. They (the class, the university, the state, and the nation) kept moving and I stopped. All of those things stopped, because those words could have been my words. I feel foolish quite a bit in life these days. I feel like an alien. It seems like I am expected, like Othello, to get back into the typical social and cultural places and make everyone believe I am normal or acceptable. But then there are difficulties.

I'm often so uncomfortable in my new world that I feel like the only way others will have any respect for me is to talk about the old one.

And in the end, when I'm feeling like a buffoon, trying to establish the respectability of my conduct in dark otherworldly places where most of the people close to me these days would never go, I tell a story that ends in a modern version of *I took by the throat the circumcised dog, and smote him, thus.* Othello stabbed himself and died there, next to the woman he loved and killed. It's a sadness that's also my sadness. I killed something, too.

Whatever the best antonym is for the word "alienating"—that's what Othello's lines were for me. If you are going to read something that gets at the truth about the people in the Special Operations community, turn off *Call of Duty* and read Shakespeare. For my money, he wrote the truth about me, and us, in a fiction four hundred years ago.

ELEVATING THE CONVERSATION

I'd been Tier One in war. But I was clearly not Tier One in regular life. I was bailing on retirement ceremonies and sulking about feeling like an alien. My behavior was dishonoring the men who'd risked their lives to save mine. The situation had to change.

And then I caught a glimpse of how it might.

Some folks had heard about that little medal ceremony speech I gave to the secretary of the navy at the hospital, and they asked if they could get a copy of it. So I shared it. And I learned that it helped at least one other suicidal person. It's really just my story of how good people helped a stubborn man. But I realized that, in its own small way, it was elevating the conversation. It's not the rah-rah, Action Man, body-count-palooza, which is the wrong narrative. And it's not just, *Hey, the VA sucks, and I'm a victim.*

Elevating the conversation. That's what I wanted to try to do. But how? I took a cue from Othello, who was still reaching people daily with that interesting tool—the soliloquy.

I'd give talks.

One of my early ones was a speech to sailors on a Navy ship. They were good-looking, spit-polished young folks. But standing in their midst, and in front of them, I could see right through their masks. Having been in the same boat, I could sense that many of them were hurting, but also firmly committed to remaining clammed up and shiny. I wanted to break through. So I employed a sophisticated countermeasure: spilling my guts. I dumped them all over the ship's freshly swabbed deck. I told the sailors just how broken I was, and just how badly I needed help. It shocked them.

It turns out that because, in theory, I was a tough guy, and yet I was nonetheless up there in front of everyone admitting how ruined I'd been, there were sailors that felt OK approaching their leadership afterward and confessing their pain. Some said that they had turned a corner, because if an Action Man could be so broken that he needed help, well, hell, maybe it wasn't so shameful if they did, too.

That is the single best use of all this Action Man veneration that I can imagine. Seriously. It was a revelation that my sad, embarrassing story could have this effect. That by sharing it I could maybe do for others what had been done for me.

For most of my life, I had tried to find a way to fill a hole in my soul. The only thing that worked was being tight with a crew of guys who were vetted and hell-bent on punishing the enemy. After that, I doubted anything else could ever come close. But when I started telling my story to people, I was surprised to find that it, too, filled the hole in my soul. And looking back, I see why. Was it because I was getting something off my chest? No. It was because of the effect my story was having on folks in the audience. The deep-down soul medicine—the true healing—comes when you stop focusing on helping yourself and switch to helping others. Mother Teresa was right.

When it comes to understanding why my raw, imperfect speeches sometimes reach people, one of the factors I point to is a particular oratorical technique that I employ. I refer to it as "wearing my ass for a hat." I open up and admit my failings and weaknesses and patheticness. I give them what you're getting in this book. And it helps them relate, connect, and lower some of the defenses we as humans have when the topic hits close to home.

The important thing is that once people recognize that I'm not a shiny person trying to create an identity that's polished, it creates an environment where real communication can occur—and sometimes allows me to reach the people in the audience who are truly hurting.

Another good trick is telling people I got shot. That's typically when they stop checking their phones.

STIGMA

After I'd given a few talks, the ideas in my head started to get distilled, and I honed in on my core message. Here it is:

I believe some suicides happen because time runs out before people realize that they need to insert themselves into that person's life.

The person suffering doesn't say anything, and his friends hesitate to do anything. Why? Because of Stigma. Both sides of the equation fear the awkwardness of raising the issue.

I believe a step in the right direction is to make a large but simple demand of both the sufferer and those who know him. If you're hurting, say something. Ask for help. From a friend, or a hospital. There is no shame in it. I thought there was, and I was wrong.

And for the person who knows someone else that's suffering, it's important to realize that Stigma is holding you back, too, and preventing you from helping. You don't want to make a scene in a coffee shop when your friend makes a sad joke with a pained smile and says something that your instincts tell you is a sign of trouble. You don't want to say, "Hey, man, are you OK?" for fear that the folks next to you sipping cappuccinos may overhear, and that the magical but fictional fabric of Propriety, which we're always supposed to wear, might be torn.

Stigma. When you succumb to it, you've succumbed to fear. It's cowardly.

But because you can't medicate away Stigma, we need to break its hold in different ways. So I assault it. I would like to help destroy Stigma, so that for others, a suicidal moment isn't required to get help. I realize it might be grandiose of me to want to help people with this. But there are little everyday experiences that are constantly compelling me. Many of those experiences happen at the speeches I give.

Something I talk about a lot is the importance of making that big, seemingly awkward step of opening up and saying "I need help." I also share that I was unable to do it . . . and that, instead, I stuck a gun in my mouth . . . and that people in my life had to force their way in, and make me see that I needed help. When I describe these problems and fears, I'm hoping they will be familiar to some of the people in the audience. They tend to be. What is *not* familiar to those same people, however, is the way I share my failings and talk about them openly.

Everyone feels completely comfortable discussing a physical ailment. *I'm getting older. My hips ache.* But nobody applies the same tolerance to the mental or psychological issue. So when our soul is hurt, what do we do? Often, we clam up, too afraid of humiliation to admit our deeper fear—that our pain might drive us to do something dire. That silence is a mistake. How can we fix it? By finding someone we trust, and talking. Admitting. Opening up. In my speeches, I try to show people what it looks like when you do. Stigma is a killer because we don't.

If someone is lying on the side of the street, hit by a bus, you'd run over and stop the bleeding. You'd stabilize that person until you could get help from the pros. But when we see someone who might be exhibiting signs of trouble mentally, do we rush in to help them? No, out of fear of embarrassing them. Or feeling awkward ourselves. And also because, when it comes to psychological trauma, we can't immediately see a place to put the tourniquet. It seems there's no specific place to put pressure.

But there is.

If someone is drinking themselves to sleep every night and showing up late to work, we need to go to them and say, "Hey, is everything

OK?" And when they lie and say yes, we need to then reply, "OK, cool, well, just come with me, and let's go knock this out." And find professional help. When you approach someone who seems like they are hurting, you are not creating an awkward situation. You are exhibiting something that I believe is the only real hope for these kinds of problems: love.

That's it.

The reason I have a chance at recovery is because a set of links in the Chain interfered in my world and snatched me up, and those people told me they loved me and that they would help me and not let me fail. That's what gets people to the other side. It was shared with me, and I want to share it with others.

And the point I want to make is not just for war guys. You don't need to have been in a gunfight to have trauma. Everybody's got some combat in their life. I volunteered for the fights I was in. The young woman in my support group didn't. And Gabby Giffords didn't choose to get into the gunfight she was in—a gunfight that killed her friends. Both groups—those of us who did volunteer for violence and those who didn't—need you to force your way in and help us sort it out.

If you see someone hurting, intervene. And for those of us who are suffering, we have an obligation, too. We have to ask for help. Fight through fear of Stigma, and ask.

I've been surprised to discover that, sometimes, my little talks help people do exactly that.

BOSTON FIRE

The raging electrical fire didn't have a lot of respect for the fact that the place it was incinerating was a synagogue.

Congregation Tifereth Israel in Everett, Massachusetts, was aflame. Father Dan Mahoney, a Boston Fire Department chaplain, was on scene, and he was fixating on something: the Torah scrolls, which were still inside. He'd grown up with Jewish friends and neighbors, and he knew how sacred the Torah was. So he did a reasonably Bostonian thing. Along with two other Catholic fire chaplains and four firefighters, he risked it all and ran into the smoke-filled, burning temple.

Rushing in, the firefighters carried their heavy gear, while Mahoney carried the key to the ark that housed the Torah. As he turned the key in the ark and opened its doors, a backdraft hit him. He recalls the "terrible explosion" blowing him back twenty-five feet and depositing him in the synagogue's first row of pews. Undeterred, he regained his footing, got what he came for, and rushed the holy parchments out of the building, into the arms of the rabbi.

In Mahoney's opinion, it was "a miracle" that the scrolls were unharmed. A year later, in 1983, at the rededication ceremony of the newly rebuilt synagogue, the three fire chaplains returned the scrolls to their home, on the bimah.

Firefighters see beauty. And they also see horror. There are ceremonies—like carrying scrolls at a synagogue rededication—that allow their souls to assimilate the beauty. But there are fewer resources that allow their souls to assimilate the horror. It's like the rest of life that way. Yes, we mark a loss. But we don't always cope with it.

I think that's why I was asked to speak to the Boston Fire Department.

An officer who'd been a leader at my former unit had left the military and started a business in the Northeast called O2X. Part of his business was geared toward helping other groups of people improve their organizations by implementing some of the human-performance-related techniques that he felt had made us successful in the military.

One of the groups that he was invited to help was the Boston Fire Department. There had been some recent tragic deaths of firefighters, and, not unlike the military, there were issues with booze and drugs and the soul-straining exposure to the ugliness of humanity. The leadership felt that a lot of the frontline guys were suffering from traumas and stress and were poorly equipped to handle it. In most cases, they didn't even want to admit it.

That kind of brokenness was my wheelhouse. So my friend asked me to come and speak to a group of the Boston firefighters and their leadership, as part of a one-day workshop. The objective of the event was to candidly confront and discuss the signs and symptoms of PTS, suicide, and depression, and then discuss some resources for handling them. I was all for it.

On the plane up to Boston for the talk, picking through a sparse in-flight lunch of peanuts and citrus soda, I didn't feel pressure, in the sense that I needed to figure out my audience, the firefighters. I figured that the circumstances they found themselves in were somewhat similar to those I'd been in, and as a result, I felt it would be a place where my ideas might be welcomed even more readily than, say, in a corporate setting. I'd tell them something they knew: that because they work together in such a tight group, and have to be firing on all cylinders, if somebody is not able to perform at the level necessary, then it puts everybody else in danger. And then I'd tell them something they didn't know: that one of the most important ways to take care of one another is by getting over the stigma and shame of raising the issue, if they're hurting or see someone else who is.

I knew it was likely that someone in the audience would be quietly suffering. There had been the recent loss of life, and I knew there would be residual effects from it—just as there were in my world, when loss struck. And I was guessing that there would be people who were feeling those residual effects acutely, while also smothering those feelings and attempting to deal with them by going it alone—a dangerous mistake I was hoping to help correct, by spilling my guts.

There was another component to this situation. One of the psychologists who had counseled me would also be speaking at this Boston event. I remember sitting with her once, during a session, when she said, "Tell me one thing that you like about yourself." I couldn't, and her eyes welled up. She had a good heart, and she was highly intelligent. I was excited to see her, and when we met the night before the Boston event, I told her that I tended to be "wide open" about my struggles when I spoke, and that if she thought that relating any of my story would benefit the people we were speaking to, she was free to do so, at least as far as I was concerned.

If you're going to hang it out there, you might as well hang it all the way out there, right? And how much more can you hang it out there than by authorizing your psych to open the sluice gates? Obviously, my granting that authorization had less to do with information that I actually thought she'd share, and more to do with wanting to show her how much I trusted her . . . and maybe also how far I'd come.

All in all, I was ready for the talk, and pretty much prepared for all eventualities. Well, all except one.

The BFD event was being held in a good-sized meeting hall used by retired firefighters. A small stage had been erected. I was slated to be one of four speakers. A Vietnam Medal of Honor winner and I came before lunch. Two folks specializing in the psychology of trauma came after.

It was all well planned and orchestrated. There was just one small detail—a notation on the event flyer—that made me wonder a little about how the dynamics of the event would work. This notation indicated that "spouses and firefighters will be present (no separate break-out groups)." On the one hand, it was great that spouses were going to be there. Family support and involvement are key. On the other hand, sometimes the presence of family members can complicate matters by inadvertently compounding the fear of Stigma. Would the firefighters want to ask the kind of questions or make the kind of admissions that would allow them to start the process of handling traumas, given that it wasn't just their colleagues surrounding them, but their wives and husbands, too?

When I stepped up to speak, there were probably a hundred or so firefighters and family members in the room. As I started talking through my history, sharing some of the stories of trying out for the teams and doing my shipboard penalty lap, I could sense people in the audience loosening up. I moved on to the heavy stuff. How I abused substances and engaged in suicidal ideation. How, in spite of my wanting to isolate, my friends forced themselves into my life and helped get me on the road to living a life worth living. Without them, I would have been either dead or wasting away in a hospital for the rest of my life.

I told the room how I've viewed life in terms of an either/or: You are either an asset or a liability. Reductionist? Maybe. But also kind of true. And while there is no excuse for opting to be a liability, make no mistake, sometimes in life circumstances will conspire to make you one. It will not be your own doing, or your choice. And when it happens, here's the thing: You just simply cannot despair. You must seek a team to rally and help you. And when you see it happening to someone else, you need to help that person get back to being an asset.

One of the main ways you do that is by killing Stigma. How do you kill Stigma? Direct action. Ask your buddy if he needs help. Or ask for help yourself. Is it scary and embarrassing? Sometimes we tell ourselves it is. But more often, it's actually the opposite of embarrassing, because honest admissions are, in fact, hallmarks of a particular kind of bravery. When I need to remind myself of that, I think of a woman I once met down south.

I explained that I try to demonstrate the virtues and healing power of honesty by delivering a dosage of it myself, in speeches such as this. For a guy like me who has spent a lifetime trying not to suck at things, it's very hard to stand in front of a big group of hard-chargers and articulate the vastness of one's suckage. But then there's always that point in the confession where you switch over. Being as open and honest as possible sets you free.

I frequently get asked, *Was there one thing that made the difference?* Not one event, no. But one overarching phenomenon? Yes. Love. It was gifted to me. It was forced on me. When someone knows your deepest shame and still loves you, that's when you will feel the restorative power of family. Mine was bigger than I thought.

Conversely, when you remain isolated—hating yourself but masking that fact—despair gets a progressively stronger hold on you. Eventually you succumb. Unable to feel anything other than the shame of your own brokenness, failure, and apparent status as a liability, suicide seems like an option.

And that's why I make sure to talk about one of the tools that proved effective against this brokenness: Touching the dragon. It's something I initially pilloried, but later praised. It helps you understand that you think you know things, but you don't. I thought I knew things. I had the reality nicely parsed, and it was bleak. I'd failed. There was no proof that there was anything positive about the processes I'd employed on that night. Just look at the evidence: my shot leg, no Remco around anymore, the lives of my friends put at risk because of me.

The record was on repeat. All the negatives playing over and over. I've come to learn that this applies to many who are depressed or traumatized. Because of work problems. Painful experiences. Mistakes. Broken relationships or lost love. Bad outcomes of all kinds.

But then, with touching the dragon, you're forced to do something else over and over: reckon with the facts. Until you see that the packet of evidence you think you've assembled is incomplete. You touch the dragon, over and over, until you realize that the horrifying dragon, which you've been fearing, actually can't burn you. When I sat down, wrote on the notepad, and considered the circumstances—what I knew at the time, my tendency to be aggressive, that I was using the dog in the way I had used dogs in the past—I had to conclude that I wouldn't have done things differently. I had to conclude that the truth is not how you feel. The truth is the facts. No, you can't dismiss your feelings. They are important. But the facts? You have to admit that they are more true than your feelings. And even if all the results are negative, that does not mean that your method was deeply flawed. Or that you are.

It's largely an exercise in correctly modulating the hierarchy of feelings versus facts. Yes, I felt like a miserable failure who was to blame for almost all the grim outcomes. I felt this deeply. But the facts didn't support what I felt. And I needed to roll with the facts.

It's just surprising how hard it is to do that.

As I wrapped up, I was hoping that my story might be convincing these firefighters, slowly but surely, to see the value in treating each other the way I'd been treated. To see the value in being open to someone wanting to help you. Telling my story, I was emotional. I always choke up talking about the quilt and the Vietnam vets, but this time it was more potent. The more I spoke, the more I felt, in my bones, that these people in front of me were actually at risk, like my former crew.

But had I reached them?

I can almost always tell exactly how things are going by how honest the questions are after my speech. And some of the questions that were asked on this occasion were so personal that I knew I'd hit a nerve.

To my amazement, people in the audience seized the opportunity to do some Stigma smashing, right then and there. Two or three of the wives stood up and said they were struggling with certain issues—including the sleeplessness of their husbands, which was sometimes tied to booze, and sometimes tied to the firefighter's inability to remember the good, only the bad. They asked how they could help their partners—the proud fellows who were sitting next to them. I was amazed. The wives were essentially standing up and publicly revealing what these guys might have thought were dark, shameful secrets. But I noticed that the husbands didn't mind. They didn't look embarrassed. Their wives were intervening on their behalf. And something in them must have known it was time.

As these wives asked their questions, I thought of Her Highness. I thought of how she was untrained, and yet she utilized what she thought were the best tools and techniques to help me. And when she ran out of things to use, she called my crew for help. She had intervened.

One firefighter raised his hand, with his wife next to him, and said, "Most nights, I can't sleep after drinking a lot, and then I lie there looking at the ceiling, hating myself." I had certainly experienced what this gentleman was experiencing. But early in my struggles I didn't have the courage that he was now showing in his. He had just made this admission in front of a hundred colleagues and spouses. I told him that I admired his courage, and that clearly we weren't the only ones who've been in this spot.

I got the impression he wasn't so much asking what to do; it was more that he was 'fessing up. As for advice, I left it to what I had said in the speech. If you see someone falling apart, you need to step up. If you're the one who's suffering, you need to help yourself, and if you can't, you need to have people in your life that will. People like my former psychologist, who, a few moments later, joined me on the stage for her segment. She talked about PTSD and how to tell if one of your teammates might need some help. She went over signs suggestive of someone who is engaging or about to engage in self-destructive behavior, like suicide. I watched the crowd, to see who might be fidgeting.

She then regaled them with stories of me. She said people were concerned when I first learned that my leg would not be optimally functional. They were concerned because I was such an avid skydiver, and they worried that my new status would be a depression trigger for me. They were right. I knew (A) that nerve tissue is the connectivity between brain and muscle, (B) that the nerve tissue in my leg was badly damaged, and (C) that therefore control of my legs (which is critically important in skydiving) would very likely be iffy at best. This was indeed a trigger.

But she helped those close to me set up a plan of action for how to work through this problem. The plan of action was predicated on having the guts to make an admission that is probably just as hard for a medical pro to make as it is for an intel pro. The plan of action was to honestly and forthrightly say, "We don't know if this nerve graft will work" and "It will take a lot of time." To me, those phrases were curious things: they were cop-outs, but they were beautiful. I could trust the people saying those things. I'd be able to deal with the outcome, whichever way it went.

As I watched my former psychologist at the BFD event, I felt distinctly grateful for her link in the Chain. The fact that I could now see this—the fact that I could appreciate her gift—made me feel good about myself.

There you go, Doctor. There's one thing.

After the speeches were over, a lot of folks came up and shared personal things. I was surprised at the wide-open and honest feedback. I spoke with the man who'd raised his hand, and we chuckled at the crazy position we had put ourselves in. I remember his wife saying "Thank you" as they were leaving. In short order, the organizers, firefighters, and I all said our goodbyes, and I got on a plane.

Here's a rule of thumb about these speeches, based on my experience: The ones who are really hurting are not always the ones who walk up and share, during or afterward. And I wondered about those guys, because in my gut I knew there'd been a few.

When I reached La Guardia, my layover airport, I was thinking about how unique it was that I'd been on a dais with one of the psychologists who'd treated me, and that I'd given her complete permission to say whatever she wanted. I was wondering to myself how often that kind of thing occurred—a patient and therapist talking publicly on the same day about struggles and solutions.

And then, as I waited for my plane, I started getting texts from my friend, the organizer of the event. He told me that after I'd left, two firefighters, who were apparently struggling badly, had gone to their boss and asked to be checked into a facility to help them get better. I remember one of the lines from his text messages: *I never thought I'd see someone save a life with a speech.*

Neither did I. I really didn't think my words could have that kind of effect. I was genuinely moved, and grateful. I remember reflecting to myself, *Man, I'm glad those guys actually asked for help. Why, in my struggles, did I have to be such an asshat, and never ask for help?* I think one reason I hadn't asked for help was that I'd never heard from someone like me, or my psych.

I WAS RIGHT BACK THERE

There's a question that people often ask me when I give speeches: *Am I Mr. Happy Guy now?* Hell no. I'm not "good" now. I'm not fixed. The sadness is never fully gone. I just keep it at bay. With constant effort. And I realize that even with that effort, I'll never be 100 percent in the clear.

On missions, I was always charged with a feeling of hyperalertness, which was generally a good thing, almost comforting, because it kept you alive.

This time was no different. Having just entered the building where I was scheduled to do my next bit of work, I found an angle that allowed me to look back outside and monitor a man who was loitering out front, leaning against the building near the doorway. He'd just been dropped off by an accomplice in a truck, which was now parked nearby, with the driver still inside. The loiterer had a fairly large backpack, and he seemed out of place. In my experience, people who seem out of place can be dangerous.

He was looking down at what appeared to be a phone, and he was avoiding eye contact with me. Had he and his buddy been following me? People who know how to follow never let you see their eyes. I scanned his backpack, trying to discern its weight and looking for bulges, shapes, wires.

Then something unfamiliar crept into my thought process. Doubt. *Is this threat real, or am I crazy?* I was battling. I had to do something. So I steeled myself and walked out through the doors.

As soon as I broke the threshold of the doorway, I immediately tried to decode as much of the situation as I possibly could. First, I looked around to see if someone was standing across the street with a video camera. Because that's how they do it. One guy always films. When people perform terrorist acts, they need keepsakes for those hellish scrapbooks of theirs. To scare people on YouTube.

Next, I turned back to our friend at the doorway and tried to force eye contact. But the man was still averting his gaze, even when I closed the distance and walked within two feet of him. It got weirder. As I passed him, he walked into the building. *Is this the signal? Is it about to go down?*

My heart was racing, which was unusual, because normally my ticker is at peace in these situations. Despite the atypical tachycardia, my mind and instincts were taking me to that place where I'm most comfortable: evaluating everything I'm seeing to help me understand something explosive that's about to happen, and how I can manage it. Identifying who's who in the zoo. Who poses a threat. Looking for something to present itself that would allow me to react and get a head start on these people who apparently want to do us harm. I was judging distances and what I had in close proximity that I could use to defend myself. I was thinking, *Who will I hit?* and contemplating how I could do it in a way that would keep innocent people from getting hurt.

My initial move was to get in my vehicle, start it up, and see if there were any indicators—any signs that these men were specifically targeting me.

I waited. Nothing. Reluctantly, and nervously, I pulled away from the building. Driving away, I kept thinking, *Is anyone following me? And should I travel the route I normally take?*

My hyperalertness began to dissipate and my heart rate began to return to normal only after I'd crossed the bridge. Which spanned a waterway. Next to a city. Here in the United States.

The building where all this had happened was a post office. I'd gone there to do some mailing.

Some folks wonder what PTSD looks like. This is one good example.

Even though it had been years since I'd been in any real conflict, I was right back there. Overseas. At war. All my wartime instincts firing. Ready to act. I didn't sleep that night. It took three days to come down off of this experience, and for my senses to fully relax.

There are other men from my former community who say guys like us don't get PTSD. I heard one such claim from a fellow who is most certainly suffering from PTSD. It's dangerous.

Some readers of Action Man memoirs want insights into the cure-alls, the wonder attributes like resiliency. Resiliency happens to be a seriously overused word. It's also inaccurate, in my case, and has nothing to do with my recovery and survival, because resiliency is an individual quality. It doesn't speak to the fact that, for me, nothing would have happened if it weren't for others.

The whole problem with resiliency is that it's self-referential. I referenced myself and saw a failure. I'd screamed. I was not as tough as I thought. I'd become broken and was not an asset.

I think the rah-rah books about the Navy's Action Man crews sometimes cheat the reader of something: the dark places, the brokenness. You might think you don't want to go there. But you do. It's where things happen that have more redemptive power than the rah-rah stuff.

I try to take people there in the talks. After one of my early ones, a big fellow in golf attire walked up to me, embraced me, and broke down in tears, whispering to me, "They just don't know what we've seen." The man was a Vietnam vet, and he was confessing both his pain and the fact that he'd never told anyone about it, because he was sure they would never understand. He'd spent decades scolding himself for not being resilient enough, while constantly mustering the strength to be more so, with the result that he was an island.

Well, guess what? It turns out that it's true that no man is an island—something I understand because I'd tried to be one, and failed. More than that, being one is lethal. None of what we do is a product of ourselves, alone. I could never have taken down a target alone, without my team. Similarly, I couldn't fix myself, heal myself, will myself, anything myself. And that's the point. Nothing happens by ourselves. We need other people.

New Callings

TOSSING VETERANS OUT OF PLANES

Because of the gunshot, I feel pain in my legs and hips when I'm on earth. I don't in the sky, which is something I discovered on my first postinjury skydiving outing. The wind was like Novocain. And I wanted as much of it as possible.

But there was a small problem with my triumphant return to carcass-tossing: I now sucked at it. Just as the psych and my friends had predicted. The issue was my legs. In skydiving, legs are essentially your wings. Their position helps you fly, steer, and stabilize. Thanks to the AK round, my one wing was broken. And because the doctors borrowed so much material from my left leg to reconstruct my mangled right one, both limbs were lacking the musculature and the kind of nerve response needed to control them adequately in free fall.

Imagine a plane with a very wobbly wing and flapping ailerons. That was me.

I'm not fond of sucking at things. So I did something that was groundbreaking for me. I asked for help. Luckily, I happened to be friends with the big-hearted men and women on the Arizona Arsenal vertical formation skydiving team. They were committed to helping me relearn to fly, and they began by taking me back into the wind tunnel to help me regain control of my aerodynamics. It was clearly going to take some time. And it was going to require that I overcome some personal challenges, including pride. I was a teacher who was now shifting back into the role of student. Going backwards.

My friends at Arizona Arsenal helped me ditch my wounded pride and focus on the opportunity to beat the physical damage and get past it. Their spirit was infectious. Two of them are a married couple—Steve and Sara Curtis. He's big. She's tiny. The Curti (which is the appropriate Latinate plural of Curtis) are mold-breakers. World-class skydivers, they compete together at the highest level, as spouses, doing balletic upside-down high-speed vertical free-fall formations in the sky. How many world champion teams have a married couple in the five-person starting lineup? And Sara's not there because of gender quotas. She's there because of skill.

It's ironic, isn't it, that one of the most level playing fields on earth is actually not on the earth at all? It's in the sky.

A habit of the Curti that says a lot about their unusual combination of skill and cheekiness is their curious commuting protocol. On one occasion, when they told me to meet them at their home near the drop zone in Arizona where they work, I arrived by car, only to watch them keep the appointment by coming straight from work and arriving, on time, from the air—screaming in, on a low flyby from above, and landing their parachutes in their driveway.

One true form of love is the refusal to coddle. Steve and Sara have a lot of that kind of love. They told me that, yes, my suspicions were correct: I sucked now. And I needed to face it. But then they showed me how to fix it.

Having received this gift of the Curti—their help—I wanted to pay it forward and help other wounded vets toss themselves out of planes. So I hooked up with some of the charitable organizations that teach vets to skydive. Because I have some experience in aerial video work from my time at Yuma, one of the ways I've been able to help is by filming and photographing the vets in flight.

A favorite picture features Todd Love. Much of the world isn't set up for people in Todd's condition. Including drop zones. When he's in his wheelchair, you have to help him navigate a couple hundred yards of man-made surface before he can get into the airplane. But the moment he enters the aircraft, something happens. He becomes self-sufficient.

I witnessed this on my first lift with him. As we reached jump altitude, I climbed out the plane door and situated myself just past the door frame, holding on to the outside of the fuselage, which is where I normally start when I'm observing jumpers and taking photographs.

Don't slip.

Looking back inside, I saw Todd approach the open door by hopping along the floor, self-propelled. He got to the lip, and then used both arms, one of which is metal and carbon fiber, to pop himself out the door. Sort of like Lieutenant Dan jumping off the shrimp boat into the Gulf.

And from the time he gets out of the airplane to the time he gets on the ground, it's all him. It's a free space. "I'm just another skydiver," he explains. "Essentially, it's a level playing field. Gravity's gravity, and it's going to treat you the same as it's going to treat me."

As Todd falls, he doesn't need help. He doesn't need anyone to do anything for him. This is not true in the rest of his life. You see, he's got 1.3 arms and no legs, both of which were blown off in Afghanistan.

A Marine, Todd started as a SAW gunner in Afghanistan and then became a point man, which made him the odds-on favorite "to step on the IED," as he puts it.

Notice his use of a definite article in front of "IED." *The* IED. Not *an* IED. Before it even happened, that bomb was real to him.

"I almost knew I was going to step on one," he says, "and so I became comfortable with the idea of dying." Still, to avoid doing so, he did an extreme amount of planning, and then was meticulous about evaluating the ground before his crew walked it, en route to target buildings. If he got to a bridge, he'd cross it by getting on his knees—like my friend in Bosnia—and raking the dirt with his hands, as he went.

He knew that the other side's bomb-hiding techniques were getting more sophisticated, to the point that they even used solar panels . . . so that the act of raking dirt exposed the cells to the sun, which was a trigger.

"I tried my best not to step on an IED," he says. "But it just wasn't good enough. Eventually, my luck ran out."

He's been told that the explosion blew him thirty feet. Immediately afterward, his unit was getting shot at from multiple directions. It took his buddies five minutes to find him. When his buddies saw his shredded body, they thought he was already dead. But they decided to work on him anyway. "Faith goes a long way," Todd says. "Despite what they saw, my buddies believed I was going to live, and I did. They kept me alive." His legs were gone, and chunks of one arm were missing. The guys put tourniquets on his churned-up arm and his left leg stump. But when it came to the right leg stump, a tourniquet didn't work. Not enough meat to grab on to. Luckily, his fanny pack strap was still there, and they used it as a kind of cravat bandage to cut off circulation to the right side. As he was telling this story, Todd paused and said, "You didn't know fanny packs were cool again, did you?"

For the first thirty minutes or so that he was in that Afghanistan field, he wasn't bleeding a lot, because of the tourniquets and because his wounds had been mostly cauterized from the explosion's searing heat. After that first half hour, though, some chunks of the seared skin yielded and the bleeding kicked in. This is also around about the time he returned to consciousness. So his guys commenced hitting him with a lot of morphine. As he succumbed, he was asking about his buddy, Thompson, the team leader at the time who worked just behind him in the two-man lead party, which they'd established to ensure that if there were an explosion, the bulk of the platoon would not get hurt. Thompson had gotten hit, too, in the face. He lost an eye, and his teeth were mostly blown out. On the helo that picked them up, Thompson had to lean forward in order to breathe, because he was choking on his own blood.

A week after the incident, Todd remembers emerging from the fog of drugs and feeling a strong urge to assess his injuries. He wanted to sit up in his hospital bed, but he couldn't. He just kept crunching his gut, with no accompanying elevation. Something was missing: the cantilever action typically provided by legs. So he threw the covers back and reached for his thigh, which wasn't there. "It was probably the weirdest sensation in my entire life. Imagine, going to scratch your head, and there's just a whiff of air, because your head's not there. That's what it was like." He looked at his father, who was also in the room, and said, "Wow, it's that high, huh?"

In the bed, when he reached for the thigh that wasn't there, he was worried. About what his life would be like, and whether it would have any quality. But now he feels it was silly to worry. Largely because of his faith, which has deepened. "I was worried that a part of me was gone. My legs. And arm. But that's all they are. Parts. They are not me."

Amazingly, Todd has taken his IED hit in stride, even though he doesn't have one anymore. What he struggles with most is the pressure he feels to help others. "I was glad to be alive, and back home," he says. "But my friends and family took it hard." So, from the beginning, he's felt an obligation "to show them it was going to be OK." He does not see the world getting worse; he sees it getting better.

Thinking about this, you might still nonetheless wince with regret at what happened to Todd. Don't. Todd explains that he volunteered to be the point man. And he feels it was an honor. "I'm proud that it was me who stepped on the IED and not my buddies. I love them. I would do anything for them. And I got to."

Those buddies must love him, too. Because it's a small miracle that they saved him, under fire, like they did. As shredded as he was, I don't think he had a Golden Hour. I think he had a Golden Ten Minutes.

Speaking with Todd at the drop zone, I reflected on how remarkable it is that his body could sustain so much damage and still keep ticking, and how remarkable it is that his head is largely unscathed, and looks as good as it does, despite being right on the X for the blast. He responded, "Yeah, I know. It's crazy. I was born this handsome. It's hard to believe."

This is a guy with an unbreakable spirit who wanted very quickly to get back in the game. Just three months after getting blown up, he was on a mono ski in Pennsylvania. It was infectious, and a few weeks later he was doing black diamonds in Aspen. He says those events were "big confidence builders." Soon after, he was in a wind tunnel at Skydive

Arizona, but he wasn't satisfied with his first performance. He asked if he could get just thirty more minutes in the tunnel, to work on his technique.

The good folks in Arizona gave him much more than that. And in the wind tunnel he made a discovery. Yes, there were things that a guy with two arms and two legs could do that Todd could not. But there were also things Todd could do that the guy with all those appendages could not. "I want to be that guy where, when kids look at me, they say, 'Man, I wish I didn't have legs.'"

In Todd's eyes, his new shape is a refinement, not a loss. Todd doesn't have those bothersome extra control surfaces (legs) to mismanage. As he puts it, "Think of your body like an Xbox controller." People with all their limbs just have more buttons they can incorrectly press.

There's that term "differently abled." But what if we ditched the kid gloves, so that when we look at Todd—and we see that his new shape allows him to do things the rest of us cannot—we actually view him as "enabled."

It's possible in the sky. In that photo I mentioned—the one I like so

Todd Love, USMC, August 2011   I took this photo of Todd exiting an airplane with just one of the limbs he was born with. Todd is an inspiration to many.

much—Todd is perfectly stable in flight. His arms are raked back into a V, and he resembles a truncated swept-wing fighter doing a 45-degree nosedive.

My own challenges are small compared to those of others. I still have my leg, even if it's less responsive, smaller, and missing nerves. Todd Love jumps as a triple amputee—one arm, no legs, a head, a torso, and a fucking huge heart.

Like me, but more so, Todd is in pain on the ground. He rests on his haunches, and he shifts his weight, because the nerve endings in his sheared upper legs are constantly being squeezed by mother earth. In the sky, he does not feel any pain. "It's not the adrenaline," he says. "It's that you jump out, and you're looking at the horizon in every direction, not just one. You can feel the wind. And you're flying. You're not falling. You're actually flying. There's a beauty to it."

I know exactly what he means. Hurtling earthward at high speed gives wounded vets access to something that's become rarer: a place where they can feel everything except their pain, and their limitations. The sky heals in other ways, too. First off, the ground's coming, which I believe provides a pressure and need for action that is therapeutic for people in the military who miss it. On a deeper level, worry, loss, and other kinds of toxicity clog up the psyche, and a good way to flush it is by blasting air in your face at 120 miles per hour. It cleans out the filters.

THE IMPORTANCE OF FINDING THE RIGHT WINTER CAP

Seeing guys like Todd skydive is a gift. And the same goes for Gabby.

That first time she jumped with me, she loved it. And I was hoping that would be the case the second time, too.

In late 2013, Gabby's husband, Mark, called and asked if I'd be there as she jumped on the upcoming third anniversary of the Tucson mass shooting that sent the bullet through her head. She wanted to show the world something.

I, of course, was all for it. There was one small hitch. I explained that, because of my own injuries, I wouldn't feel good about being the actual tandem instructor—i.e., the person she would be strapped to when she jumped—but that I'd find her the best person. And I'd be there as she prepped, and also on the plane, and also in the sky.

The fellow I lined up to attach himself to Gabby for the tandem jump was Matt Gries, an accomplished skydiver with an untold number of tandems under his belt. I also asked the Curti to help me with the jump.

Now, although, generally speaking, being gender-blind is delightful, in this case I was doing a hefty amount of gender-profiling. Sara Curtis is a woman who's highly adept at skydiving, and I thought it would be more appropriate and less obtrusive to have Sara help Gabby get rigged up, because it's a process that involves lots of hands slid in between body and buckles.

And Steve Curtis had a specialized role, too. He's MacGyver. A real-life version. In his garage-cum-engineering-lab, he can rig or build just about anything. Gabby wanted to wear a POV camera for the *Today Show*, so Steve rigged a GoPro to her chest strap the night before. He also worked on another critical piece of equipment—Gabby's headgear. Matt and Steve knew it would be cold at altitude the next day (it was January in the Arizona desert), so Matt gave himself the task of picking out a winter hat for Gabby.

Before I tell you what kind of hat it was, you have to know something: people in Arizona love Gabby. They love her—as in, real love. Everyone involved in that evolution wanted the jump to be awesome for her. So as Matt considered the options for cranial warmth retainers, he wasn't just going for efficacy. He was going for delight. As such, he picked a whimsical gray and red knit winter cap, with a little puffball on top, because he thought Gabby would like it.

The night before, Steve Curtis flicked on the lights in his garage and sewed a custom chin strap onto that hat so it wouldn't come loose in flight. I suspect it's the only high-speed woven winter beanie of its kind.

On the morning of the jump, a number of us helped ready Gabby's gear. Sara was nice enough to let me help a little in getting Gabby rigged up and comfortable. Straps can always use extra checking. What did not need checking was Gabby's level of commitment, which was unwavering. She partook in the hullabaloo—which included sizable TV news crews—with good cheer and smiles.

Once ready, we gathered for a solemn moment, to commemorate the lives lost that day, three years prior. A bell, pendant on a cord beneath some fired clay beads and a yellow sunflower shape, was rung by Gabby. This hanging bell totem had been designed as a redemptive measure and commemorative token by a Tucson mother who'd suddenly lost her two-year-old, and it resonated as a healing symbol with Arizonans, who expanded the applications for its karmic and memorial power. They'd taken to hanging the bells—called Ben's Bells—throughout Arizona and ringing them also for Gabby and the six who were killed that day in 2011.

There was a pretty big group of people in the plane, with at least three guys sporting professional high-end helmet-mounted cameras. Gabby was the least nervous one in the aircraft.

We jumped. The Admiral left the plane first, and then I left with Gabby and Matt. Outside the plane, I flew up to them, on their left. Steve and Sara were on their right.

At this point, you may be expecting something rhapsodic. About the desert below and the glorious empyrean above. About willpower, grit, and spirit. But what was foremost in my mind was simply, *Don't screw this up.*

Because I was not one of the Curti, my flying was not world-class, and so my leg made things difficult for me. Staying safe, in proximity to Gabby and the other jumpers as we made a circle of clasped hands, was paramount. I came in close, and my right hand connected to Gabby's left, in a strong grip, while Matt clutched my forearm. The five of us—Matt, Gabby, the Curti, and I—held hands for a few seconds as we fell.

After we broke off, Matt deployed the big chute, putting himself and Gabby under canopy. This afforded her the opportunity to gaze about. The chest cam that Steve Curtis had rigged caught Gabby summing things up nicely: "So beautiful!"

She still couldn't move her right leg, so the night before Steve had stayed up a bit later in his garage, rigging a suspension device that would ensure her legs were lifted and in the *up* position when she landed. It worked. After touchdown, she remarked on the "gorgeous mountains" and employed two apt syllables to describe the foregoing events: "Good stuff." I said, "Let's make you even prettier," took off her knit cap, and removed her earplugs. Following her lead, I then tried my hand at summing things up in two apt syllables. I looked at her and said, "Rock star."

She echoed the remark, and then looked around, her eyes alive, as folks ran up and the crush of well-wishers crushed.

People talk about the limitations in Gabby's ability to communicate, due to the bullet. But Gabby, through her expressions, deeds, and spirit, says a lot. It's our limitation, not hers, if we can't grasp it all.

BIRTH OF SPIKE'S

The ground coming at you gives you a nice project to deal with—i.e., not impacting it. That's the kind of project I liked. But skydiving was intermittent. I needed the ground coming at me all the time. I needed that military-grade sense of constant mission. Speeches also fit the bill—while I was giving them—but they were sporadic, too.

So, about eighteen months after I'd retired from the military, I went over to the Norfolk, Virginia, Police Department K9 kennel and introduced myself. I'd done a course a few years earlier with one of their K9 officers. It was a decoy course, and I had a knack for it. (I may not be well suited to boardroom schmooze-fests, but I am gifted when it comes to wearing padded suits and being a bite-magnet for dogs.) Having found this cop that I'd done the training with, I asked if I could take pictures for his K9 unit and help out with the decoying. He said he'd confer with the guys. Remember, this was the same Norfolk PD that had dispatched those two officers to my home—the gents who would have been well within their rights to shoot me. So these Norfolk K9 cops knew about me, and my prior episode. To their credit, they didn't hold it against me. They agreed to let me visit them, take pictures, and get bitten once in a while.

This simple gesture of theirs—allowing me to work with them a little—meant more to me than they could have known. Even though

I was technically on the upswing, I was still at a relatively low point in my life. I viewed myself as a malfunctioning member of society who needed to go to mental hospitals. And yet the Norfolk K9 cops were giving me a chance to help their dogs, in a small but meaningful way. By doing so, they allowed me to discover (and demonstrate) that I could still offer something, in a sphere of activity that I valued.

They also gave me another gift—the opportunity to begin paying back some debts, and atone for some things.

One of the big debts I owed was to the dogs. And not just because they'd saved my life repeatedly.

In the world of fighting that we inhabited, I'm sure the dogs often felt something along the lines of *You're sending me into the room with them? I see. That's how this works. Oh, and I get a tennis ball and some dog food for my trouble? That's fucked.*

I knew what we were into. When I got shot, that was fine, because I'd volunteered. But my dogs hadn't. They just happened to be born with some traits that made them candidates for war—like a fearlessness when it came to running full-on into men who were three times their weight.

I've seen them jump off roofs to catch bad guys and then punish them once caught. I've seen rocket fire detonate right next to them. They were like me and the men I went into the mixer with. They had been given, through genetics, the desire to fight. They had been trained and vetted. They struck serious fear into our enemies. They were relentless. And they were not the pretty picture of comfort and warmth that you commonly see in news spots or movies featuring military dogs.

All the dogs I worked with had the traits. They were well suited to the work. They just didn't volunteer for it. Which is why I knew in my heart that it was my job to protect them—something I ultimately failed to do. The pain of that failure accrued. And accrued. And that's why, the night I was shot, after I got the obligatory "I'm hit" out of the way, I switched to screaming something else, something closer to the deeper source of pain: I was screaming Remco's name.

One day, five years after that scream, I was told about a situation involving one of the Norfolk police dogs, K9 Rooster. It seemed K9 Rooster needed some help with his windpipe. He had a damaged trachea, and when it was hot and he was working hard, his throat would close up and he'd have difficulty breathing. His handler had taken him to the city's veterinarian, who told him that the surgery to fix Rooster's trachea would be experimental, and experimental procedures were not something the city was interested in funding. The officer was despondent. He was also determined. You see, Rooster had proven himself on the street and served the community. He'd apprehended some dangerous, armed suspects in his time and shown himself to be a special kind of asset by doing things like finding a not-good person hiding under a pile of clothes in a woman's home after it had been searched by human officers.

So the officer did some research, which included calling North Carolina State University to see what they might be able to do. They had a highly regarded veterinary program, and they surprised him with the news that the surgery would be relatively simple and cost only around $1,800.

I wanted to help out. So I sat down, did a little online research of my own, and ran across a custom T-shirt company that allowed you to raise money selling products they printed featuring designs you provided.

I went looking through some of my pictures, in hopes of finding something that might serve as the basis for a logo. In 2006, about a week before Spike was killed, someone took a photo of us right before a mission. I loved that photo, and so I tried to make it work. With a little help from a buddy and Photoshop, I came up with a design that I then put on some hoodies. White hoodies. Which seemed to make sense to me, and which I went with, over the objection of Kelley, who thought my color scheme was idiocy. She may have been right, but I lucked into a receptive enough audience, and my poor color choices were not a hindrance. I shared the hoodie fundraiser on social media and made a little over $3,000. Enough cash for the surgery, and enough to allow the officer to drive a few hours to the university for the procedure, stay at a hotel, and get back without spending any of his own money. So we helped that dog—and he soon went back to work for the city that wouldn't spring for a workable throat.

After covering K9 Rooster's costs, I still had money left over, and that's when it hit me. This was something I could get my heart into. If done right, I could make a career out of paying back Spike, the Lion, and Remco, as well as the police—the ones who prevented my life from taking a far more negative course after the pathetic, drunken terrorizing-my-wife episode.

And that's how I stumbled into my new, full-time mission. Which I very much needed. I dubbed the venture Spike's K9 Fund, and after some friends helped me get legal assistance in setting up the 501(c)(3), I was off and running. Since that first fundraiser in 2014, we've gone on to do things that I would never have thought possible at the outset, including raising several hundred thousand dollars and helping over 500 K9s.

We keep things small and focused on the dogs and their handlers. We have one employee, and she is a machine. I've seen where other charities get dinged and critiqued for putting a lot of the money they raise into overhead instead of help. I'm proud that we put 87.5 percent of all money raised directly into the dogs—in the form of either equipment or assistance with medical care.*

Those are the two core elements of our mission:

- Provide equipment to working K9s
- Provide medical assistance to active or retired working K9s

And here we are: www.SpikesK9Fund.org.

---

* Two staff salaries are allowed to be counted in this "programs" percentage. I make $300 a month. My director of operations makes $42K annually, before taxes.

With Spike in 2006, prior to a mission in western Iraq. This is the photo I chose to be the logo for Spike's K9 Fund.

Spike's K9 Fund logo

ROSE GARDEN INVITATIONS

Spike's K9 Fund was helping me make amends with some ghosts, but that didn't mean the past was done haunting me.

In May of 2014, I was at a skydiving event with a dozen other wounded veterans, when I got a text from a friend who had been with me the night I was hurt.

He asked, *Hey, have you seen the news?*

No, I hadn't seen the news.

Shithead has been traded, and his parents are in the Rose Garden with the president.

Traded for what? I inquired.

A bunch of Taliban.

Earthbound and waiting for our lift, I checked out a video of this unfolding story on my laptop. I was blown away. Riled up, I turned to an E-4 sitting next to me named Joseph Grabianowski, who'd been cut in half when his Stryker got hit by a bomb, and I asked him, "Hey, man, did your parents get to go to the Rose Garden when you got home?"

"No," he replied.

"Well, apparently Bergdahl's parents were just there. Getting hugs from the president."

The narrative was toxic. I felt the bile rising.

Not Joseph. Seemingly unaware that indignation and anger were the appropriate feelings in such a moment as this, Joseph remained unruffled, doing some casual memory-lane meandering on how American forces were still "looking for that guy" when he'd arrived in Afghanistan in 2010.

For me at least, one thing was clear: the filters definitely needed cleaning. The plane pulled in, and up we went.

It was not on my laptop, but rather up in the sky, falling with Joseph, that I saw what was important. His drive. His temerity to air it out and overcome a battle-damaged body. Up there, in spite of all the silliness unfolding on the national stage, thanks to Joseph we were, in a way, plugging meaning back into our lives. Yes, there was plenty of damage. But having the ground come at us at 120 mph repaired us both.

A photo I took of a young Army specialist, Joseph Grabianowski, who was jumping with me at one of Jason Redman's "Jump for a Purpose" events. This was the same day that the release of Sergeant Bowe Bergdahl was announced.

I took a photo of him in flight, in free fall, as he looked left at his altimeter. Clouds to his right. Arms out. Stable. Poised. No legs. Beautiful.

And then we came back to earth.

When the story broke that the administration had swapped prisoners for Bergdahl, it hit me hard. Susan Rice, then the national security advisor, made the claim that Bergdahl had served with honor and distinction, while the news circus sandwiched its discussion of the issue in between ads for erectile dysfunction remedies, all of which seemed to be diluting the core issue. The core issue, as I saw it, was that I was told before the mission that Mr. Bergdahl had deserted his duty in a time of war. So my spirits sank.

The Mechanic called when he heard the news, to ask how I was doing. That's the much more interesting story to me, much bigger than the prisoner-swap fiasco. I was hurting, and the Mechanic knew it. I was reliving the evening that changed me so significantly. I was stuck there. And then, like he has many times over, he rushed in to stop my bleeding.

And so did my wife. One day she came home from work and saw me looking at photos of Remco, the working dog who'd died on the Bergdahl mission. She hugged me until she knew it was over. And I guess it's a choice we all have, isn't it? To succumb to the injuries we sustain from the combat in our lives, or—with a push from a friend, or a stranger—get back in the fight.

THE NAPKIN

I think it was the napkin that affected the woman most, even more than my speech. But I'll get to that. That came later.

Addressing a banquet hall full of young Navy folks, I began by saying, "This is a special thing for me, and I'm honored to be in your presence." All of them were clad in the Navy's version of a tux, the distinguishing feature of which is those smart, short, navy-blue formal dress jackets. I was wearing a suit, in which I never feel comfortable.

For my speech, I recapped key parts of what you've already read, but with a slightly different spin. Here are the highlights of the talk, which was accompanied by slides:

I've been in the military twenty-five years, which is more than many of the people in this room have been alive.

Here's the best way to sum up those twenty-five years: I went from being a team leader in a gunfight trying to save an American, to being in a mental hospital with a hand towel so I didn't hang myself. This shocking turn of events was largely driven by my decision to put a gun in my mouth.

Entering a second mental hospital (this one down south), a woman went through my bag. I told my buddy I was going to run. He said no I wasn't, because I was doing the advance work for the rest who were coming after. This was a man who had covered ground to get to me.

Who covers ground to get to you? Generally speaking, that's a good thing to know in life. Try to have someone who will. I don't just mean literally.

What changed me in that southern hospital full of civilians, including engineers and other professionals, was the young woman who explained that she had been raped by her uncles in front of her dad on Christmas Eve when she was eleven. I volunteered to get shot at. And then there was this woman. I couldn't even comprehend what she had endured. I was a tough-guy commando? Whatever. That woman was really tough.

I think about our country. I was lucky to fight, because I had a mission. Collectively, we need a mission. We all have personality conflicts. But not when a ship is on fire. Or in a gunfight. When things are serious, not trite, that's when we rely on each other. And that's when silly social differences evaporate. We need to get away from agenda. Agenda is less than mission.

What's my mission these days? Helping dogs. And trying to help people, by telling them my tale. Yes, the structure of the person I used to be has been dismantled, but it turns out there's still a foundation, and although it's awkward for me to admit, parts of that foundation are solid.

Hearing my rapid-fire presentation, the young Navy folks may have felt a bit like they were speed-dating my soul. I wrapped up, and then the Q&A portion of the evening began.

Someone asked about our interventions overseas, and whether we were helping. I replied by saying that an equally valid question is, *How do we intervene and help here at home?* One good method for that is creating an environment where a neighbor or friend or member of your community is OK with saying she is having problems.

Some folks won't admit they're struggling. So watch for signs. Is a friend breathing zoo at work, because he was hammered a few hours earlier? Watch. Speak.

But we don't, because of Stigma. Which I call cowardice. And I was subject to it. In recovery, it was hard. I didn't feel that normal people understood what people like me were going through, and I used that to stay silent and haughty, when what I really was, was afraid.

Whom do I admire? I look at the people I rolled with, and the discretion they showed, and the value they placed on the lives of noncombatants.

What to watch out for? There are two kinds of people in the military who will get you killed. First are the "Status Quoians." They don't have to think, and they like it that way. Their bread and butter is doing things "the way they've always been done." They don't care about evolving threats or efficiency. They love to languish in the illusory comfort of stagnation. The second type of people that will get you killed are the "Ambiguians." They have no spine, so they waffle and wait to make a decision until after they get an indicator from someone who can impact their career, and then they decide. They get people killed.

What's a tool I use in my new struggles? They call it "cognitive behavioral therapy." I call it *touching the dragon*. I have tattoos on my arms of the names of dogs that got killed saving me, and I saw other things that were hard, too. They don't go away. But the key is being able to be comfortable with them if they don't go away.

What's more powerful than cognitive behavioral therapy? Love.

What is the best way to get close to war? Read *Forgotten Soldier*. And chapter 26 of *For Whom the Bell Tolls*. And then go to the Korean War Memorial in D.C., but do it on a very rainy day, in the cold, so that when you stand amidst the poncho-clad figures, you can let your clothes soak through, while you try to feel the weight they carried.

Books that inspired me? In combat, I read Marcus Aurelius, the emperor running the show in a place called Rome. The observations he had about getting real with himself resonated. I also love *Othello*. Shakespeare understands me. But I wonder how the hell he knew what he knew about me. He was never in a gunfight.

I reminded the audience to be careful, and not think for a second that I'm heroic. I've done all these bad things. But don't forget, I served my country, and for the most part, I did a good job.

When I give these speeches, where I throw my guts on the floor for everyone to look at, the "after party" tends to be really interesting. This speech to the young Navy folks was no different. In the scrum that formed afterward, many came up to ask questions, some occasionally pulling me aside so they could tell me very personal things. In those moments, I feel lucky to be able to have an impact. I also feel a responsibility. People come at me with their rawness, and it's heavy. But it's good. I prefer to be in that real world.

This time, the member of the audience who brought the most rawness afterward was not the one you would have picked as the prime candidate for suffering, based on appearances. They rarely are.

A junior sailor on the cusp of being put in charge of other sailors, and looking like the picture of someone with a bright military future, this young woman waited until all of the others had moved on. She then approached me, looked me square in the eye, and said, "Can I meet with you later? I'd like to talk to you about something." And I said, "Well, I'm leaving in the morning, so maybe we can do it via phone or email." She said, "No, I want to talk to you face-to-face." I didn't know what was up, but I could tell it was significant. I said, "OK, let's meet early tomorrow morning, before my wife and I grab breakfast and head home. How about 7 a.m.?" She said, "Cool," and then, being local, told me where we would meet, at a coffee shop in town.

That night, in my hotel room, I began to wonder what it could be that was so important that she wanted to get up early on a weekend to discuss it. I'd had dramatic discussions in the past, but I'd never met anyone as adamant as she was about a rendezvous.

The next morning, I woke up, practiced hygiene, and waddled briskly along quaint small-town streets to the coffee shop, which was not crowded at that hour. I was the first person in. It wasn't yet seven. I'm always early. She was punctual, too. Right on time, she came in with a notebook and sat down. Without much in the way of preamble, she dove in and started to tell the story about her issues with self-destructive behavior. She was recovering from substance abuse and going to CDA meetings, which are like AA meetings, but for the chemically dependent. She talked about how she didn't really like many people in her orbit, and didn't feel comfortable where she was. I could tell that, as with me, there was an underlying issue she didn't feel comfortable talking about, although with her it was deeper, and also somehow tied to the sensitivities of being female.

So I picked up her pen and started writing something on a napkin.

Before showing her the written message, I prefaced it by saying, "This is the most important thing, I think." What I scrawled on the napkin was, *Forgive yourself.* I turned it around and slid it in front of her. Her eyes welled up.

The gates opened a little bit, and she revealed what was troubling her. It turned out to be an issue that comes up far too frequently when I do speaking events with military audiences.

It was sexual assault.

In today's military, sexual assault training is so prevalent that not a week goes by without a new mandatory class or a new flyer posted on a bulletin board talking about zero tolerance and other bold statements. And yet this person had experienced it, and, what's more, she'd been forced to stay in the same organization as the person she'd accused of committing the sexual assault.

She explained what had happened. They were at a remote location, in a hotel, with no real senior guidance. These were people in their early twenties, and there was heavy drinking, which is typical, and risky. She doesn't remember it, but a man had sex with her. He says it was consensual. They were both drunk. She didn't want to talk about it with her family because she was ashamed, and she didn't want them to feel that way, too. She had reported it through the proper channels, but the events weren't significant enough for action, and there was no real verdict in the case. Actually, that's not quite accurate. There was a verdict. The verdict was, *Sorry, you have to live in close proximity to this guy. We are not changing his location or day-to-day life.* The military review panel couldn't determine guilt or fault; it was his word versus hers.

That's why she blames herself. Because it is hazy. And booze had been a key factor. In fact, it still was. She had been abusing alcohol recently. And in the psychological blender of her mind, the alcohol abuse was getting jumbled up with the other unhealthy ingredients that kept piling in: cultural taboos, unwilling witnesses, managerial hypocrisy, shame, guilt, regret, self-hate, and anger.

She was angry that someone had done something wrong and not been held accountable. Making matters worse, "I still have to be around him, every day," she said. "And, if nothing else, I wish the leadership would get involved and at least make him avoid me. Why am I the one who has to avoid him? Why is it my job?" I said, "Why should you be uncomfortable around him? You did nothing wrong. Do you ever stand there and stare at him and make HIM uncomfortable?" I don't know if I should have suggested that.

Complicating everything was the fact that it was all happening in a military environment, which inadvertently intensifies certain pressures, especially self-loathing. I could relate. I did not experience anything even remotely close to what she had, but I was also disgusted with myself for not suffering well, just like she was. It's often the case in the military, when bad things happen: people hold themselves to a standard that is unrealistic. I was one of those people. So was she.

Her situation was different from mine, in this regard: I felt like everything that occurred was my fault. Everything was a result of decisions I'd made that were wrong. All of my dragons were my own errors. With her, I don't believe it was that way. Yes, there was a significant amount of regret on her part, I could tell. But she was not the only one at fault. There was the guy, of course. But there was also the system. Based on the message that was being communicated to her in the weekly sexual assault training fiestas, she was, ironically, put in a very vulnerable position. If, instead, she'd just been told, "You are at risk, so watch out," well, then, OK, that's different. But the amount of (mostly cosmetic) seminars and posters in the military ecosystem suggesting there is a way to handle sexual assault, and that it *was* being handled, and that everyone was in sync on the issue, misled her. She was hurt that her expectations had been so wrong. And I think she also felt guilty, and stupid, like she'd fallen for something.

So she was on her island.

I sipped my coffee, not so much for the caffeine hit, but more to give myself a moment to think. *I do not have adequate tools for this girl,* I thought to myself. *I'm not a professional therapist.* Seeing her pain, I was emotional and sad. And then I remembered where that pain can lead, based on my personal experience. A bad place. But before I could ask about that bad place, she broached the subject herself and volunteered that she'd thought about suicide. We discussed it. She had been thinking about it because she didn't have any hope that things would get better. I wasn't surprised. I knew what it was like to not see hope, because you feel like a pathetic, worthless waste of oxygen.

The coffee shop was more crowded at this point. And because we were now talking about things that were sensitive, we stepped outside and started walking.

I decided to use some of the mental judo that had been used on me. I said, "If you take yourself out of the world, you will leave a gap where you can't help people who aren't as strong as you. You won't be able to help people who will be going through something similar, people who are coming down the pike, because you have to realize that you're not the last one who's going to go through this kind of thing." She was shocked; it seemed she'd never considered that. Which I fully understood, because I'd never considered it either, until the Fly Fisherman hit me over the head with it.

It's amazing to me how prone we are to this error. This woman was a very intelligent human. And I'm not a complete moron. And yet the two of us—and a lot of other very smart folks I know—suffer in this way, thinking we should be able to heal ourselves. The truth is, you just simply cannot apply your own intelligence to the emotions going on inside your body. I don't believe there's a way out of it on your own. I had this idea that *I'm a fucking commando, and I'll straighten my shit out.* But I didn't have a clue how. She didn't either. She was so overwhelmed with so many things that were so far out of her control that she only saw reasons for ending her own life. This only supports my idea that smart people can disproportionately add to their woes by dwelling on the fact that they are unable to fix themselves.

The pick-yourself-up-by-your-bootstraps idea is a fallacy. That might apply to a hike, but not to self-destructive things you don't understand. When you employ that mistaken rallying cry, you end up stranded on an island, blaming yourself.

We talked more, then stopped. I gave her a hug and said, "I'll be in touch." She went back to her life. I went to breakfast. I then made a call to a friend at the Marcus Luttrell Lone Survivor Foundation, which had created a dedicated retreat staffed by professional female therapists whose focus was helping military sexual assault victims. I requested access to a therapist for this young woman. My friend obliged, and then some.

Within thirty minutes, the young woman was on the phone with someone. Within three hours, she was offered an all-expenses-paid five-day retreat.

I was impressed that she'd jumped on the phone to talk to a stranger. Later that day, I texted her: *You're a very strong woman, and the world needs more of those.* She texted back: *Coming from you, that's incredible.*

That struck me, and I marveled at where I was in life. If you'd told me several years ago that I'd be talking to a woman about suicide and her options, after having met her at a military event where I told a crowd about putting a gun in my mouth in front of my wife, I'd have said you were batshit crazy. And yet here I was.

I feel like I gave the woman a few things. (1) I revealed some of my dragons in the speech, which allowed her to feel comfortable offering me a glimpse of hers. (2) I did her the service of not judging her, but also not kissing her ass. (3) I told her to forgive herself and to think about her ability and obligation to help someone else in the future—two ideas that really took hold. (4) Through my friend at the Lone Survivor Foundation, I gave her a ladder to climb out of the hole she was in.

But there was nothing I gave to that woman that had not been given to me.

I'd had a moment's doubt, sitting with her in that coffee shop, about whether I possessed adequate tools to help. That fear wasn't well founded. Looking back on it, I see that I was, in fact, carrying some equipment: a wrench in my hand, and a pole over my shoulder.

Some Christenings

HER LEFT ARM AGAIN

It took a lot of courage for that young sailor to confess her trauma to me. And when I told her that she was a strong woman, I felt authorized to speak on the subject, because I'd been lucky enough to know a few. Some of the strongest links in the Chain were women. Her Highness. The Machine. The fighter down south. And also the one who was about to get her own warship.

Gabby's staff was actually nice enough to invite me to attend the christening of said warship—the USS *Gabrielle Giffords*. I RSVP'd in the affirmative—*Heck yeah, I'd be honored*—and flew to Mobile, Alabama. At a dinner given the night prior to the event, I learned there were going to be speakers, so I approached Mark and mentioned that I felt compelled to tell a story about Gabby. Could I be added to the docket? Even though it probably meant upsetting the schedule, and probably also the protocol, Mark was gracious, and he gave the idea his blessing.

At the appropriate moment, I got up from my table and told the Emissary of Embraces story—how I'd asked Gabby to deliver bear hugs to my friends on the other side of the planet, and how she'd made good on her promise to do so. After recounting the tale, I surveyed the room full of admirals and corporate titans—many of whom I admired—and then looked directly at the CO and master chief of this new warship. These were the guys who'd be operating it. Addressing them, I described how Gabby's act of hugging my friends overseas had touched those hard individuals, and then said, "That is the character of the namesake of your ship."

The christening was the next day, and I was impressed—with the woman, even more than the vessel. There was an army of shipbuilders putting the event together, having already put together the epic boat. Dignitaries spoke. The national anthem was sung. And nobody could have faulted Gabby if during the proceedings she'd just sat there and smiled.

But no. The easy route is not something Gabby's interested in taking. Ever. In spite of all the challenges inherent in having had a bullet pass through her brain, she had nonetheless worked diligently in preparing herself to be able to get up and say a few words. Not only that, what was truly astonishing was that she'd incorporated gestures into her presentation, with her left arm. Watching her do this, I was hoping that the people in attendance realized what a big deal it was—those little movements of her left arm accompanying remarks she didn't have to make. It was extremely difficult for me to maintain my composure during those remarks.

I had served on ships, and so I knew from experience how big this christening day was in the life of this ship. You've seen folks smash bottles of champagne against hulls, but a gesture just as sacred, if not more so, especially in the U.S. Navy, is the entombment within those hulls of symbolic things important to the namesake. One of the things that had been embedded in the keel of the USS *Gabrielle Giffords* was a Purple Heart. Mark explained that they didn't know if it was mine or the other fellow's. But he did tell the crowd about the award citation letter I'd written for Gabby, saying that if he were to breach confidentiality and read it, it might put some people to tears.

The letter is best kept a secret. The more fitting tribute is the boat. The USS *Gabrielle Giffords* is an Independence-class aluminum trimaran littoral combat ship. Although a relatively small vessel in the Navy fleet, it's potent, and capable of quite a bit. Just like Gabby.

BULLET-PROOFING DOGS, AND GIVING THEM NAMES

It was January 11, 2016, and it had been a long standoff. Almost seven hours long.

I wasn't there for its fatal conclusion, but I did get invited to be a part of its aftermath, a few hours later.

Norfolk police had responded to a call about a domestic dispute between a husband and wife involving a possible firearm. When the police arrived at the scene, the wife had escaped, but the man had barricaded himself inside the home. After some fruitless negotiations, the suspect emerged, armed, and refused to disarm. The decision to act, or not, rested on the shoulders of all the police on scene, but maybe on the shoulders of one of those officers just a little bit more than the rest.

And he chose to act.

"I knew the bad outcome was possible when I sent my partner in," recalls the officer, whose name is Ryan. "And I deal with that every day. Our job is to resolve situations as safely as we can, even for the perpetrator or suspect. I did what I did because I truly believed that if I didn't send him, there was no other way to end it any less violently, or peacefully. I had to make a split-second decision, and I decided that it was the safest way to prevent a possibly deadly situation."

The partner he sent in was a Belgian Malinois police K9.

Prior to being a K9 officer, Ryan had been a plainclothes in the gang unit. One of the highlights of his tenure with that crew was working a federal case with the FBI, during which he bought enough guns and drugs to help assemble a RICO case against a local gang that was on a murder spree.

After that, Ryan transitioned to the K9 unit, where he was assigned his first K9, and he basically learned the ropes of this specialty discipline at the same time that his new dog was learning them. The dog was eleven months old, and his name was Kali. But that would eventually change. One of the things K9 officers are able to do with new dogs is rename them, if they choose. Typically, the rechristening only happens after the dog makes it through the specialized K9 training. It's considered a bad omen if a handler renames a dog while he's still in training, and that dog then washes out. Better to wait. So Ryan did.

The police department's master K9 instructor oversaw the training, and Ryan was under his tutelage. As he worked the leash, Ryan looked closely to be sure Kali was proficient in certain drives—especially a good prey drive and the ability to track. Kali had to be able to use his nose to sense ground disturbance and also to follow wind-borne scents, both outside and inside structures—what's called "air scenting." He also had to show evidence of being environmentally sound, able to handle and not get rattled by virtually any condition one could think of—water, slick floors, transitions from dark to light, and light to dark. It takes a lot of training to make sure a dog has no deficiencies in these areas. If a dog does display a deficiency that might cause him to be a risk to himself or other officers, then he goes back to the vendor and the process starts over.

These are hard dogs. They have to be. So in addition to passing through all the skill-set wickets, the larger question was, *Is Kali hard enough?* Hard enough that if there's a mishap in training, or if he attempts to clear a hurdle and fails, or if something else goes wrong, he won't freak out? He needed to be able to overcome almost any bad experience. And Kali showed promise in that department.

At the end of the training certification period, when it had become clear that Kali would make it through, Ryan was feeling confident, and he decided to exercise his naming privilege.

While evaluating different names, Ryan came across "Krijger," which means "warrior" in Dutch. Ryan's wife, Julie, didn't like it, because it made her think of Freddy Krueger, the fictional razor-wielding specter who was less than cuddly. Julie's vote mattered, as she'd be welcoming this dog into her life, too.

But Ryan pushed for it. First of all, he thought it was an original name. And he pressed that point, until someone at the K9 range burst his bubble and told him there was another dog in the area named Krijger. This only added to Julie's hesitation, dovetailing as it did with her sense that the name should be special, so that it would have a special meaning for Ryan. Still attached to the word for "soldier" in the Netherlands, Ryan fixed on it, and then soft-pedaled the whole issue, reasoning that it really wasn't such a big deal. Everything the dog does is based on a command, anyway. "They respond to the tone of voice and body language more than any word or phrase you're giving them," Ryan pointed out. "For us, the name is just an identifier. The name itself doesn't mean much to the dog."

But the name came to mean a lot to Ryan. And his wife. For both of them, Kali would quickly become "our beloved Krijger."

He was mostly tan, with a few handsome chromatic highlights—short black ankle socks, pointed black ears, and a black snout. Ninety-two pounds and tall, he was a beast. But he was also a love hound. In order to get a pet, he'd trap Julie against a wall and lean his head in under her hands, nudging them. "Yeah, he was a leaner," says Julie.

"If you just knew him from home life, you'd never believe he could do the things at work that he did, on a day-to-day basis," says Ryan. Julie would sometimes meet up with Ryan during the day, and see Krijger jerking around and barking in the back of the car—a fission-able reactor of fierceness—and she'd barely recognize the loving dog she knew. At work, Krijger was intense. But at home "he was just a big baby," says Julie.

Krijger lived in a roomy complex that Ryan had built in his back-yard. It consisted of a cozy wooden domicile surrounded by chain-link fencing and covered by a gabled roof. One night, early in Ryan's career with Krijger, Ryan and Julie were in bed in their first-floor bedroom, when they heard loud noises coming from Krijger's swank custom ken-nel out back. Usually, when he was ensconced in these digs, he was not a barker. Maybe he'd bay at a lawn mower once in a while, but for the most part, he was quiet at home. That night, Krijger suddenly started growling, snarling, and barking. Julie immediately thought someone was outside, a prowler. Ryan got out of bed to see what was going on and to ensure nobody was afoot. "I went over to the kennel, and I saw Krijger repeatedly moving his head down toward the ground, and then jerking it away, backing himself up a foot or two each time. Barking madly."

There was indeed an intruder. A frog. It had entered the sacred pre-cincts of Krijger's kennel, and Krijger was losing his mind. Ryan liber-ated the offending frog, went back inside, and told Julie, "It turns out we *do* need to call the police . . . and report that my badass police dog is freaking out over a frog."

The frog was lucky. Remember, Krijger was a hard dog. In fact, when Julie would play or roughhouse with Krijger at home, Ryan would be okay with it, but he would also make one thing clear: "Just be careful if he gets you on the ground."

Ryan and Krijger were partners, and their love for each other was equal, but their positions were not. Ryan thought of himself as dad, and during training, he'd often tell Krijger, "Good job, son." "The dogs work under the pack mentality," explains Ryan. "And we need to let them know their role in the pack. Yes, they are alpha dogs. But they have to think we are the pack leader."

And that's why, when they decoy, Ryan and his Norfolk police colleagues only get bitten by other officers' dogs, never by their own. "Your own dog should not bite you on purpose," Ryan explains. "We don't teach them that it's ever OK to bite us, even out of frustration. It's never OK to bite dad. If you don't handle it right, you risk letting the dog think he is alpha."

With me, it was different. My own dogs did bite me. In training, I allowed it. But even outside training, they'd occasionally indulge in the privilege, with or without my permission.

On one deployment, the Lion and I had been on a tear, going out on the regular, hitting targets. The Lion had gotten used to a certain pace of life, and death. He'd been quite busy engaging enemies, and he'd hit a flow state, just as humans do. Flow state is great when it's in effect, but when it's disrupted, you have to handle the fallout. And that's what I found myself faced with one evening.

After two busy weeks of missions every night putting bad people down, we went out yet again, and this time our target turned out to be a "dry hole"—nobody there. When we got back to our small base in northern Iraq, it was still dark, which presented an opportunity for some fitness. It was so hot in this region that there was realistically no way to exercise during the day, so I seized the opportunity and took the Lion for a pre-dawn run.

And I made a foolish decision. I didn't take the leash. I opted to just use the electronic collar, which I operated (when and if necessary) by using a remote control that I held in my right hand.

The Lion was charged up. He had not turned off. He had not gone from green to red. He was in a certain frame of mind, still thinking we were on a mission. As a result, about halfway through our run, he decided he wanted to get it on, with friendlies. It occurred when we ran past a zone where the local Iraqis who worked on the base (driving trucks and such) slept outside in the open air. The Lion smelled them and unilaterally decided it was time to go to work. He started spinning, and it was clear he wanted to fight. But instead I gave him a little juice from the electronic collar and said, "No." To this the Lion reacted in a manner I'm sure he deemed reasonable: he decided that the best course of action—the best way to find an outlet for his energies—was to fight me, mostly because I would not let him go bite the locals. So he jumped up on me, hit my chest, and tore my T-shirt off.

Believing strongly in the childish principle of tit-for-tat, I kicked him in the chest.

Demonstrating the benefits of the exceptional training I'd provided him, the Lion responded by hitting me in the arm. It's important to point out that he knew damn good and well what he was doing. He knew my right arm held the controller for the electronic collar, and his strike knocked it out of my hand, sending it to the ground. But that wasn't the full extent of the very bad situation I was suddenly in. The Lion's jaws were unusually strong, and after they'd split the flesh wide open in a clean five-inch gash, like raw tuna being filleted, I felt his teeth hit the bone in my forearm.

I had to fix this problem ASAP.

I used a technique to temporarily dampen his enthusiasm. It worked. But as he let go of my arm, he regained sufficient vigor to regroup and launch another attack. His jaws successfully sank into my ass. It took all of my superior human intellect to figure out how to remove those jaws from my backside and then return to my camp, accompanied by this psycho, without getting bitten by him again. So I made my way back gingerly, holding my newly injured right arm over my head to slow the bleeding, and holding the Lion's collar with the other hand, giving him enough leeway to walk, but not enough to mount a re-attack.

The results of this little melee were some stitches for me, and my leadership deciding that the dog was unstable. Per that verdict, the Lion was suspended from going on any further missions for a while, and sent away. But I was to blame, not the Lion. He was not unstable. I'd riled him up. I'd made a very poor choice that caused the situation. It was on me.

And the result was that I had my dog taken away from me. That's the worst kind of fired you can be. It's why I don't have a tattoo on my right arm, just the scar. To remind me that I'm not nearly as smart as I sometimes think I am.

But it's not just the Lion that comes to mind when I look at my right forearm. I think of someone else's forearm, too.

About a year later in southern Afghanistan, while out with another handler after being cleared to work again, the Lion rushed ahead of the men he was with (my friends), entered a dirt-walled structure, and found a hiding enemy who was wearing a suicide vest. The man detonated his outfit, blowing himself up, and also the Lion, who was locked onto the man's forearm when the vest exploded.

More than a few men were saved that day because of the Lion.

It was that seventh hour of the Norfolk standoff.

The man's wife had escaped, but the man was still there, in front of his house, brandishing a firearm, with police all around.

That's when Ryan made the call to release Krijger, and sent him running toward the man. The plan was to have Krijger apprehend and subdue him. What that was supposed to involve, most likely, was that Krijger would target a part of the man's body that people (like us) train dogs to hit—a bite spot less likely to result in a mouthful of clothing, which can tear away.

And Krijger did hit the man. He got purchase on the left side of his body, but the guy didn't go to the ground. The man was big. They both struggled, and the man stayed on his feet. Krijger was trying to get him down. That's when the man raised his small firearm, put it against Krijger, and pulled the trigger twice. Both bullets found their mark.

Although shot twice, Krijger stayed on him, still fighting. Ryan yelled, "He's shooting my dog!" and then tried to move into position to take action, but there were officers on the opposite side of the man and the dog, so he couldn't do much, and he was pulled back into the stack by a team member.

Quickly another dog was deployed, and the bad guy ended up on the ground. To furnish details about how that happened would be speculative on my part. What's fact is that the man later died in the hospital.

But he wasn't dead yet, as he lay there on the ground in front of his house. And once that new dog had gotten ahold of him, Ryan was finally able to head toward his own wounded dog. The other officers also moved in and took control of the man, while Ryan tried to manage Krijger's wounds. Ryan located the holes and applied pressure to them, as colleagues from the K9 unit pulled up in a vehicle and yelled, "Jump in." Under way, Ryan told the guys to notify the animal hospital personnel that they were coming. As Krijger's blood poured out through Ryan's hands, Ryan kept talking to him, saying, "Hang on, it'll be OK," just like he would to a human partner. Or son.

They raced. Against a few things. And lost.

"Krijger ended up bleeding out and dying en route," recalls Ryan. At the hospital, they got him inside, on a table, where a huddle of vets tried to resuscitate him, assessing the wounds and putting a tube down his throat to get him breathing. But it was too late. He was dead.

Shortly afterward, I was texted by a Norfolk PD officer, who told me about what had happened and asked if I could come down and visit Ryan in the hospital, adding, "He could use it."

Because of the training I'd done with the Norfolk police K9 crew, I knew Ryan. So I went to the veterinary hospital and was directed to an examination room, where Krijger lay on a steel table, on his left side, dead, with his black-socked feet protruding out from under the American flag that was draped over him. A familiar sight. I wouldn't touch the flag, or the dog, out of respect. I knew the only person who should be able to do anything to that dog was the guy who lost him. Ryan.

And Ryan was there in the room, sitting next to Krijger, looking like he was still in shock. I hugged him and listened to him talk a bit. He said, "It's probably hard to understand . . . but I spent more time with Krijger on a daily basis than my own human family. Every minute of every day." I did understand. Because I'd done the same, and I'd lost dogs. He was devastated, and I felt bad for him. I was also concerned for him, because he'd stood there and watched someone kill his dog. That loss was personal, and hard. It was like losing a human with whom you'd worked and risked things. It's no less punishing. And that's not meant to be a diminishment of the human bond; it's meant to be an elevation of the canine one.

Krijger's X-rays were up on the wall, backlit. I could see two small projectiles in Krijger's midsection, behind the shoulder area. What had probably killed him was the blood loss, but also, I think, the energy pulse of the bullets hitting his mass. All of his vitals were right next

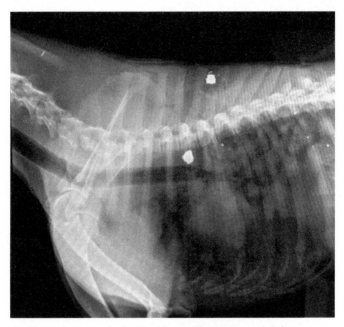

An X-ray showing the bullets that took K9 Krijger's life

to where the projectiles had lodged. That energy pulse sometimes gets short shrift in casualty analysis, because blood loss is more evident. But it doesn't get short shrift in my lexicon of real-world kinetics: the energy from one shitty bullet had disintegrated my femur, the biggest bone in my body.

Later that night, I realized the day's events had peeled back the scab on the hurt I felt about the dogs I'd lost. I talked to Kelley about it, and cried a bit. No matter how valuable I think the human-K9 partnership is—in both war and law enforcement—I guess I'll always struggle with the brutality of humanity, and how the dogs are just innocent players in our savagery and our drama. And how un-fucking-fair it is.

I hate sitting around feeling glum. Not taking action is like reclining in a warm bath of toxins and refusing to get out. I had to do something. So, shortly thereafter, I sent a text message about the whole episode to Anderson Cooper (whom I'd met because of a Bergdahl-related piece he did). Anderson said he felt like he should help, and he said he'd take his speaking fee from an upcoming event and donate it to Spike's K9 Fund.

I was shocked, and very appreciative.

It had become clear to me that what the dogs needed were tactical bulletproof vests, the best I could provide. Based on the caliber of handgun used on Krijger and the locations of the wounds, I believe the material in a ballistic vest would have stopped the bullets and saved him. The thing is, the best vests are expensive. Level 2 vests are light enough that dogs can wear them for a whole shift, but they're still hefty enough to be able to stop smaller-caliber ammunition and knives. And most police dogs that get killed by guns are killed by handguns. I favor vests made by K9 Storm, because I used them in combat (the even-lighter Level 1 variant), and because the company that makes them is a family-run affair. The creator of K9 Storm, Jim Slater, was a former K9 officer who was shot in the face and is now blind in one eye. It is clear, however, that, like Jason Redman, bullets pumped into his eye socket have failed to hinder him.

His top-notch vests cost $2,500 each, and buying them for the Norfolk dogs was a tall order. But Anderson's gesture was the needed catalyst. And as a result, the K9 Krijger Campaign was born. Anderson did not want me to mention his donation, but I did anyway, without disclosing the amount (which was considerable). And his gesture had a cascading effect. When folks found out about his generosity, they also chipped in. There was an overwhelming response. Pooling Anderson's contribution with subsequent ones, we started purchasing ballistic vests to cover all the working police K9s not just in Norfolk, but also in the other municipal police departments in Hampton Roads.

The K9 Krijger Campaign thrived. Right off the bat, we raised money for sixty-five K9s. And every one of those sixty-five ballistic vests that we provided was embroidered with Krijger's service number, K-148.

When I put police K9s into their ballistic vests, I feel like I'm making some progress on the project of trying to pay the dogs back.

The funny thing is, the K9s don't necessarily know that. Dogs don't always know that you're trying to help them. When they're in pain, you need to muzzle them, or tape their mouths for a second, while you apply bandages or tourniquets from your first aid kit. The same holds true when you first put them into a ballistic vest that cost you a pretty penny; they resist it.

In that regard, they're just like us. Sometimes we fight the ones trying to help us.

Krijger is now buried just down the road from Ryan and Julie, at a gravesite surrounded by ponds and trees, with other K9 dogs beside him. Ryan visits him all the time.

The funeral for Krijger took place on a day that was probably the coldest of the year, but also sunny. During the service, all of a sudden, in the quiet, a jet flew right overhead, low and loud. An accompanying gust of wind shook all the pine trees at once. Coming as it did right after the twenty-one-gun salute, Ryan thinks of it as a final tribute to his dog. "It was very moving," he says.

Before he was laid to rest that day, Krijger was awarded a posthumous Medal of Valor. At the ceremony, and in subsequent days, it was recounted how Ryan and Krijger had earned "K9 Officer of the Year" honors in the last two years of their four together. It was also recounted how every time Krijger helped with an arrest or apprehension, he was rewarded with a fine Angus steak, his favorite. Well-meaning people poured out praise on Ryan and Krijger. And it ran off Ryan like he'd been wearing emotional Gore-Tex. He didn't feel heroic. Not at all.

All he could think about was one thing. "Krijger was family. I didn't bring him home that night. It was my job to bring him home, and I failed him." Julie heard Ryan say these very words some months after the event, while sitting with Ryan at a restaurant near their home. She disagreed. "Ryan, you did not fail. You did exactly what you were trained to do."

This well-intentioned and fair-minded observation elicited the very response that I myself am familiar with: nothing. It means almost nothing. Ryan feels at fault. Just as I do, for my dogs. That's why my being there, at the hospital that night, was perhaps helpful. Not to alleviate or temper the pain. But just to understand.

Because he is a loving husband, when Julie said those nice things, Ryan looked up, nodded at his wife, and replied, "Yes, I saved lives, but at the same time, it feels terrible. It's a dichotomy. All I can think about is what I could have done differently."

Yup.

Ryan has a new dog. His initial name was Igor. During Igor's training, Ryan was thinking about what to name him, once the training was done.

Julie hoped that this time Ryan wouldn't go for anything severe or tough-guy, like "warrior," because that's just karmically attaching the dog too closely to the concept of people who go into battle to die. She provided some alternative options: Bob, Joe, or Barry. Something nice.

But Ryan already knew the name he was going to give to Igor.

"AC."

TEAL VESTS AND HANDCUFFS

I've worked alongside some of the world's top specialized units. Famous ones, like our counterparts in the Army, and a few of the sexy ones from Australia, Germany, and France. All these crews consist of formidable folks. But there was one member of a particular unit—a group called Troop 5450—who stands out in my memory, because this person did something for working dogs (including AC) that I'd never seen before.

When I first met the 5450 crew, its members were in uniform, which featured some of the standard insignia, like American flag patches, but also had some noticeable oddities.

In general, I am no stranger to non-standard clothing. My former Navy unit had some discretion as to what we wore when we operated. In fact, our uniforms were not technically "uniform," at all. We were not bound by standard NAVPERS 156651 clothing and insignia regulations. For us, it was about optimizing performance and efficiency, with each guy making the decisions about what made him effective and functional. The outermost part of my "uniform" when I suited up was often a tactical vest with pockets, each packed with various kinds of equipment. I noticed that the same was partially true of the members of 5450; their outer kit was also a vest, but the color schemes were a tad atypical, and their patches seemed to place a premium on meritorious conduct. Most of them wore a brown vest, but one of them had a teal green one. And they were more like cowboy vests.

When I was briefed on what the unit member in the teal vest had done, I was amazed. Ever since, I've looked up to that person in the teal vest. But I say that figuratively, because in fact I looked down at that person. And that's because this member of Troop 5450 was about four and a half feet tall.

She was a Girl Scout, and she was ten years old.

Her name was Selene Parks. I met her at a tactical-vest-fitting event that Spike's was hosting as part of the K9 Krijger Campaign. (Outfitting dogs with ballistic vests involves two sessions with the animals—an initial day when you fit and measure the canines, and a second day when you deliver the finished vests.) Selene and her troop had been invited to the event by Brian Ingram, a warm and highly capable police officer with the Portsmouth, Virginia, Police Department Canine Section, whose dog was being fitted that day, too.

Some of the day's festivities were geared toward community outreach, and that involved us giving Selene and her troop a little class on working dogs, and letting them meet one of the animals—in this case, Mina (aka the Machina). To me, Mina is beautiful. But I recognize that to many, she can seem menacing. Sensitive to that fact, I asked if any of the girls were afraid of dogs. A good third of them raised their hands. Got it. This was going to be a challenge. Fully 33 percent of the audience was uncomfortable being in close proximity to the star of the show. To manage this situation, I began by listing some of the more palatable things dogs help us do. For example, they use their superior sense of smell to help us find people lost in the woods. The girls liked the idea of missing folks being found. Next, I staged a little demo.

Oftentimes people who are afraid of dogs don't understand how dogs think, and they inadvertently create a situation that's more dangerous for themselves than it needs to be. In order to demonstrate this and give the girls an insight into dog management, I asked one of the girls who'd said she was afraid of dogs to stand in a certain location. Having already done some assessing of who's who in the zoo (an old habit), I'd identified the confident, ebullient scouts in the mix. I asked one of these confident girls to stand twenty meters from the girl who was scared. Then I had Mina situate herself in between them, but ten meters off their axis, making a triangle. Mina was perfectly calm, but the somewhat-uncomfortable girl regarded her nervously nonetheless. "Now," I said, "let's pretend you're at a park and you see a strange dog enter that same park." I addressed the confident girl: "Jump up and down and watch what happens." The girl indulged me, and did a fair amount of leaping and kicking, accompanied by some expert hooting and hollering. Mina turned her head and focused on this active girl. I addressed the rest of the girls: "Now, notice where the dog didn't look." Mina did not look at the motionless, scared girl. "If you're quiet and stand still, you're not going to be interesting to the dog. But if you yell and run, the dog will think you want to play, and she will come to you." I think I saw the face of the worried girl in the triangle relax a bit.

Afterward, Officer Ingram introduced us to Selene, who had been one of the confident girls. We chatted, and she told us about a project she was undertaking as partial fulfillment of a requirement for an achievement badge. On her own initiative, and under her own power, she was raising funds so she could provide emergency medical kits for the K9s in the Portsmouth PD, because they didn't have them. Selene's family was friendly with Officer Ingram, and Selene had grown up knowing one of his longtime K9 partners, Tyro. Through conversations with Ingram, she'd identified a need, and she was moving swiftly to address it.

Ingram was giving Selene guidance on which materials would be best in the kits. Dogs need the same things we do when it comes to first aid. At the top of the list are Airway, Breathing, and Circulation fixes—the ABCs. Just like us. So the kits Selene was assembling included the basics—gauze bandages, waterproof tape, disinfectants, scissors—plus some non-essentials, like shampoo, "because," as Selene explained, "every dog likes shampoo."

She'd go on to make and donate a total of twenty-six kits—six to the Portsmouth PD and twenty to the Norfolk PD. It just so happened that she ended up delivering these kits a little while later, at the same event where we delivered our finished ballistic vests. Bearing a resemblance to a bunch of smaller Santa sacks, her custom red nylon bags were each tagged with a specific dog's name, and they were accompanied by a framed set of photos of the dogs, with this inscription: "Thank you for everything you do to keep us safe. I hope you enjoy your K9 first aid kits. Love, Selene Parks."

Sometimes, when I think about assets, I think about this little girl.

I also think about Officer Ingram. His good nature, dedication, and community involvement are a marvel to me, especially given the sorry state of the municipal government for which he works. News of yet another corruption probe targeting Portsmouth's vice mayor or city treasurer is not news at all. It's expected. And this mismanagement has consequences. The city now experiences over 600 violent crimes a year, which amounts to 6 violent crimes for every 1,000 residents. It's often rated Virginia's most dangerous city.

Compounding the crisis, the Portsmouth Police Department is critically under-resourced as a whole, and at the bottom of the list are the dogs. So I help where I can. As do girls in teal vests.

Seeing an opportunity to further repay the dogs and also get to know the officers and their families, I started training with the Portsmouth PD. I see how hard they work, and what they have to work with. The guys put a lot of their own money into the dogs' equipment. When I'm with them, I find myself comparing their experiences to mine. I notice the similarities: their commitment to protecting the innocent, their love for the dogs. But I also note the differences, which are major.

My unit had the resources and time to be truly proficient. As I've mentioned previously, each man shot about 3,500 rounds a week, at minimum. We could go into our well-maintained indoor range at any time of day or night, and fire away on complex targets, working on our craft, maintaining muscle memory. Most cops don't shoot 3,500 rounds in a year. Also, our missions are more specific than the vast array of scenarios a police officer may face. But perhaps most striking is the handcuffs they volunteer to wear. Handcuffs of civility. When I was overseas, doing what I was doing, I knew I would capture or kill the people who would try to kill me. In a way, I had the curious luxury of always entertaining the worst-case scenario in my mind—anticipating it, being prepared for it, and being authorized to address it. But a police officer does not have that luxury. He pulls someone over, and he just simply does not know what's going to happen. He goes in hamstrung, because first and foremost, cops have to be polite and respectful. And *then* they have to deal with the cards they're dealt. If the situation deteriorates and someone starts to exhibit threatening behavior, the cops are still obligated to be on their best behavior. They have to be the good guys, while ensuring that the bad guy's rights aren't trampled.

Those handcuffs of civility? They are an operational impediment that endangers cops' lives. But the fact that men and women volunteer to wear them is one of the things that makes us us.

Nonetheless, a climate of hostility toward cops has sprung up. It's wrong. If there is a bad apple on a police force, he or she is the anomaly. I truly believe that. Hell, I know it. I work with lots of cops. And I can see that the fallout from this trend of flawed, misdirected cop-hate is dangerous for everyone—cops, especially, but also the communities they serve.

Sometimes, those handcuffs of civility need to come off.

Recently, eleven or twelve police K9s have been dying every year from heat exhaustion, and some of those fatalities are the result of being left in sweltering police cars. If the vehicle's A/C unit fails while the officer is away—while he or she is down the street serving a warrant, for example—then the dog's in trouble.

To help out, Spike's K9 Fund has donated some in-vehicle temperature sensors, synced to key fobs that alert the human officer if the interior of the car is getting too hot, and allow him or her to push a button and remotely pop the doors, releasing the K9.

We gave one such sensor-and-key-fob unit to a Virginia police officer. It quickly came in handy, in a way we hadn't anticipated.

The officer was talking to two suspicious men, who quickly lost interest in further dialogue and switched to pummeling the cop instead. They had the upper hand, and they were severely beating the officer. But he had that door-popper. So, with blows raining down on him, he hit the key fob, and his K9 bolted out of the car, and came running. Quickly sensing what was up, the dog put some hurt on the assailants. The officer told me he's sure the dog saved his life.

That was interesting to hear, and satisfying. But more remarkable to me was the fact that after recovering from this incident, the officer went right out and put those handcuffs back on.

PATCHES AND VELCRO

Word of mouth, the contributions of genuinely decent citizens, and some extremely resourceful volunteers have driven the expansion of Spike's beyond both (a) the borders of Virginia, and (b) my wildest dreams.

I was lucky enough to go to Ohio because Keith Hawk, a business executive, had put me in touch with Wright State University, and they in turn invited me to speak to one of their graduate schools. At the time, Keith's son, A.J., was a pro football player for the Bengals, highly regarded both for his athletic prowess and his citizenship. After the speech, which was in September, I was invited to attend a pre-season football game at Paul Brown Stadium. Indicative of the kind of goodwill that is extended toward me a lot these days, I found myself again in that delightful piece of elevated stadium geography—the skybox.

There, I met a woman named Jill, who struck up a conversation after her curiosity was piqued by my Spike's K9 Fund T-shirt, with its silhouette of me and the charity's four-legged namesake. Medium-length story short, that conversation quickly led to her donating money, generously, and becoming a fairly active follower of our activities.

Not long afterward, she made the eleven-hour drive with her teenage daughter and her daughter's close friend to an event we had in Virginia, just to show her support and provide three new and able persons to help out as volunteers. I let them take Mina for a walk, which was a big deal. Dogs are good judges of character, and the Ohio trio passed muster. After the event, Jill asked for a meeting with the brass, and—given that I was nominally, and Kelley was actually, the brass—the two of us sat down with Jill and her crew. I was prepared to educate them on the subjects of charities and passion, but instead found myself receiving lessons. Jill produced some objects from a bag—dog chew toys that they'd made out of a fleece-type fabric and customized with the Spike's K9 Fund logo. She then launched into what was essentially a pitch for her and the teenage girls to be our reps in Ohio.

Partially to demonstrate her chops and give us a sense of how she rolls, Jill helped set up a weekend cavalcade of events in which we'd get to participate, back in Cincinnati. On the first day, a Friday, she organized a press event, the early part of which involved a news channel coming to the Cincinnati Police Department's AstroTurf dog training space and interviewing a local Cincinnati K9 officer, John Neal, and me.

Cincinnati is one of the more dangerous towns in America. It sees 2,600 violent crimes a year. That's 7 violent crimes a day. Neal made the point that officers like him stay alive by wearing bulletproof vests, and yet they're forced to send dogs in without them. I'd never heard a cop speak so openly about the poor equipment his department had.

It's not politic to implicitly refer to a city government's shortfalls when you're employed by said city. But I'm glad Neal did. Predicaments like his were our specialty, and one of the reasons we'd come to his city was to pledge our help, while also kicking off the fund-raising that would allow us to make good on that pledge.

With the cameras still rolling, Neal and I did some K9 demonstrations with a SWAT dog named Jones, who was sporting a model Spike's K9 Fund ballistic vest. We had Jones make some runs and execute a mini-drill of police dog acrobatics—jumping onto a car and into its trunk and windows. I also spoke a little Dutch to him, and let him bite me for the cameras.

Getting bitten is a favorite pastime of mine. In fact, decoying is what I mostly do when I train with dogs.

On the face of it, the decoy is the guy who runs and evades and then gets bitten. The human chew toy. But it's also much more than that. The decoy is an important part of the dog's development and

This was taken in 2017 at a demonstration in Virginia Beach, Virginia. The K9 is named Boru, and he has quite a bite.

upkeep. The decoy is in charge of much of the behavioral feedback a dog receives during patrol training. Accordingly, there's real craft involved in being a good decoy. You have to be able to "read" the dog. For example, dogs need confidence to attack a full-grown human. If you as the decoy put too much pressure on the dog by being too aggressive in his initial bite training, you'll ruin him. In a strange inversion, you have to be appropriately sensitive early on, so the dog can grow to be appropriately aggressive later.

When you've done some of these things well, and consistently, the least you can do is reward the dog with an opportunity for a good grip. On you. And there are basic guidelines involved in this kind of activity. Sometimes you're bitten in the back as you simulate a running perp. Sometimes, though, you're bitten in the front, because certain folks, like the Norfolk shooter, will engage dogs that way. It's also up to you to make sure the dog releases when told to, or resists the urge to engage at all, on a recalled attack.

The training is no-nonsense, governed almost entirely by practical necessity. But there are also some deeply meaningful things wrapped up in the act of allowing a bite. To begin with, there is care and concern. When the dog bites you, for example, it's important to be able to position yourself properly so that you don't break his teeth.

And for me, there's something else. When I decoy and welcome their bite, it's intimate. I can feel their strength and drive, as though I'm in tune with their spirit.

With Jones, I could definitely feel his strength as he hung from my arm, writhing in the air. His jaws were clamped down on the heavy braided burlap bite sleeve covering my left forearm, just a few inches beneath the tattooed names of Spike and Remco.

By performing all of these exercises, Jones was helping us demonstrate how light the ballistic vest was, how well it was made, and how the handles worked. Handles are helpful when hefting dogs through windows of cars or inside blacked-out buildings. Handles are also useful when your intent is to smoothly remove a biting dog from your forearm at the conclusion of a media event.

Which I did. As the media event wrapped up, we were quite happy with how it had gone, and some of us felt that perhaps it was a good time to bring out our laurels so that we could do some conspicuous resting upon them. But it became clear, quickly, that this was not the capstone moment for our Introduction to Ohio weekend. Jill had more in store.

The following day we set up a Spike's tent at the St. Patrick's Day parade, which was geared toward honoring veterans. Jill was prolific. She sold Spike's K9 Fund swag, T-shirts, and custom fleece dog chews. She answered questions and pressed the flesh deftly. After the parade, she brought us to a Cincinnati Cyclones hockey game, where her hard-charging triumvirate (of mother and daughter and daughter's friend) set up another Spike's table. Beforehand, she'd warned me about a little surprise she had planned. She'd arranged for me to receive some recognition on the ice between the second and third periods of the game, during a veterans appreciation interlude. I was not looking forward to it—a state of mind that my director of operations, Emily, had anticipated. She was ready with the rationalization, and cajolery. She explained that it would be a good way to generate attention for Spike's K9 Fund, which of course was a tough point to argue with, so I agreed to do it.

When it actually came time to walk out on the ice, I was somewhat sick to my stomach. Emily walked with me to the boards and said, "Just think about the organization." Walking out on the freshly slicked ice, I was passed by the returning Zamboni. The crowded arena stands were dark, but the ice was well lit by spotlights. The only two people in the glare of those spotlights were the talented announcer with the mic and me. Mercifully, his praise was abbreviated and his tribute was quick. He talked about my deployments and medals. There was applause. I felt cheesy.

Those moments, when folks thank me for my service, are hard. There are people who have done much more than I have, who genuinely deserve those kinds of accolades, and deserve to have their service recognized. For my part, I feel I could have done more. It's probably a bit self-indulgent, and unkind, to self-critique when being praised. But I am skilled at it now, and I don't intend to abandon the habit.

However, as sheepish as I was with the spotlights and cheering citizens, I also understood that I was now in a new role, with new priorities. Employing the ethical calculus required of an aspiring nonprofit chieftain, I knew that the attention (generated by me being on the ice, and by tents at parades) was going to serve a larger goal. Thanks to the events we'd already done that weekend, small bills and heftier checks were starting to arrive, and we were well on our way to raising the $2,500 required to buy a custom-made ballistic vest for Jones. But we needed more, because we wanted to outfit all the other dogs in the Cincinnati PD, too.

So, while focusing on not slipping and falling on the ice, I put on that most useful of expressions—the smile that implies "I belong here and your praise is well directed." I guess it's the emotional equivalent of a white lie.

Which is what I'm pretty much guilty of anytime someone praises me, because when people praise me, I feel like they're approving of me. And it churns my stomach, because I don't think they know what they're praising. "Veteran." And "my service." That's great. But do they really know what my service entailed? The death and savagery? Do they even want to know? I doubt it.

As for Jill's audition to be our rep in Ohio . . . Suffice it to say that we now refer to her and the teenagers and the other motivated Ohio volunteers as the Ohio Crew. And over the next couple of months, as we added to the tally of vests secured for Ohio dogs, I admired how Jill went all-in. Widowed for fourteen years, she was raising her kids on her own, working a full-time job, and advocating on behalf of Spike's K9 Fund the rest of the time. In addition to limitless energy, another attribute of hers that revealed itself was fearlessness. I could tell, because there's a certain facet of Spike's K9 Fund volunteer work that serves as a pretty good barometer of courage: the vest fittings for the dogs. They can be tricky. And I noticed that Jill didn't leave them to someone else.

Each ballistic vest is custom-tailored, because a bad fit impedes the dog and creates opportunities for bullets. The sizing pattern that we use was developed by the folks who make the vests—K9 Storm. The pattern consists of interlocking canvas swatches of material that you lay over the top of the dog and tighten using Velcro edge fittings. There are lines at special points, like the shoulders, where you actually cut the pattern, so that the finished vest is sure to allow the dog freedom of movement in the shoulders and back by the ribs.

Patches and Velcro. Sounds easy. But it's not. These dogs are tough dogs. They don't like people fidgeting with sharp things such as scissors around them, or being confined, even in something designed to protect them. As a result, when you're fitting them, you have to muzzle them.

When Jill manipulates the canvas and Velcro on the dogs, it can be iffy. Wearing a leather muzzle and a poke collar, the dog often growls for the duration of the fifteen-minute fitting, with one eye on her and the other eye forward—an ocular trick that denotes a predator. If the dog bucks, it can knock her over. Jill is not a large person. But Jill sticks it out, even though she admits the dogs are menacing.

And that's the way they're supposed to be. Jill gets it. But not everyone does. In this regard, there's a bit of a parallel between the dogs and me. During these fittings, we take pictures of the dogs, who are, let's remember, trained to bite human beings. That's why most of them have to wear a muzzle—for Jill's sake, and sometimes even mine. Often, we put those photos on social media.

And while almost all of our other Spike's K9 Fund efforts are incontrovertible evidence that good deeds can, in fact, go unpunished, these pictures are not. There is always—only every time—a handful of people who just can't help themselves and have to remark on what a horrible thing the muzzle is. Condemnation of the muzzle is just the beginning. Next, they train their fire on us, the muzzlers, expounding on what monsters we are. The poor sweet canines! What an outrage! My dog would never be in a muzzle!

From this digital hemorrhaging of bleeding hearts, one thing is very clear: many people don't understand what working dogs do. They don't understand that we send them to fight and bite. Well, let me amend that statement a bit. I think they do know the dogs have been trained to bite people. They just don't want to believe it.

And what does this reveal about humankind—first-world humankind, specifically? It reveals that many people don't understand the world they live in. They don't understand that some dogs are OK with violence. Some dogs want to hurt people. Some dogs need to hurt people. The outraged commentators would never muzzle their dogs, because their dogs don't get exposed to the ugliness of humanity on a regular basis.

Not muzzling your dog does not mean that the ugliness goes away.

Would it be nicer if the world were such that I never had to gun people down? Sure. But I was ready for it, and I had the equipment in my head to do it well. Because sometimes it's necessary.

But I also realize that calibrating the precise amount of violence that causes the greatest amount of peace is a tricky thing. It's the great puzzle: When you practice violence in the name of establishing peace, how much violence is OK? And who decides?

Well, I did, for a while. And I tried to decide well. But I didn't always get it right. I'm haunted by some of the dark things I've done. Then again, you asked me to do them. You asked me to spend decades honing that side of me. And when a man spends two decades honing that part of his instinct—the dark and violent part—it changes him.

It changed me.

Hoping to run some diagnostics on the hauntedness I often feel, I once sat down with John Langan, the distinguished Georgetown professor and Jesuit whose specialty is just-war theory. In black, and a collar, he sat in his simple and humble wood-paneled office lined with books, exuding what I'll call a quiet power. Quiet, because it wasn't outfitted with any bells or whistles. I recounted some of my exploits to him, and was surprised to hear him assert that God was there, present, on all of those occasions. I respected this man, but I'm also someone who can only learn if I feel I've strained against the limits of something, so I decided to push this conversational envelope a bit, too. I told him about a dark and violent night that I'd been a part of—where, due to the confusion, I'd killed some guys in a way that was particularly brutal, even for me, and even though they certainly merited punishment. I then asked him, "Do you really believe God was there with me that night?" God would not have liked what He saw. But the professor said, calmly, without hesitation, "Yes, He was there."

I got the impression that I had not shocked him, which is what I thought I'd do, with my gory tale. And I don't want to say the man was wrong, but I'm still doubtful that God was there in the darkness that particular night. Nothing godly occurred.

Frankly, I doubt that a God could create a human like me, someone who loved his work of punishing other humans—let alone stand next to me while I did it.

Luckily, I read Rumi from time to time. And Rumi, in some ways, echoes the professor.

Be silent,
Only the hand of God
Can remove
The burdens of your heart.

That may be true. But if it is, apparently He isn't quite ready to remove mine.

The reason I struggle to embrace the idea of finding peace through God is that, given the opportunity, I would go overseas and wade back into the violence. Enthusiastically.

You see . . . in polite society, I wear a bit of a muzzle, too.

UNDERSTANDING BURNT BODIES

If you want to be good in a close-quarters gunfight, you need to spend thousands of hours perfecting your craft. You fight like you train. It's a maxim that applies to the rest of life, too. In the mental health battle space, you don't just arrive at victory one day, fit as a fiddle, because you've notched a breakthrough or two. If you want to heal your mind and spirit, you need to be disciplined about your practices. Every day.

When sadness comes and Stigma threatens to silence you, or someone else, you need to smash it.

When fate throws folks in your path, love them relentlessly, like Aurelius recommends.

Try to have a Chain in your life. Even better, try to be part of one.

When the dragons hiss, every single time, don't cower. Run at them and touch them and destroy the illusion of their fierceness.

Over and over and over.

And never make the mistake of thinking you've defeated—or even know—all your dragons. In my life, every now and then, the mists enshrouding some past event will thin a bit, and lo and behold, there stands another beast.

This happened to me recently, with the Red Wings disaster. I thought I'd assigned appropriate emotions to that tough episode and successfully moved on. Eleven years later, I realized I was wrong.

2005. Afghanistan.

When the sun came up on our second day near the remains of the CH-47 that had gone in to rescue the four embattled Americans, I was sitting on the side of a muddy, freshly rained-on mountain. We'd been working for about twenty-four hours at our grim task of looking for survivors. But because there were none, most of our efforts involved retrieving bodies and putting them in body bags. Taking a breather, I kept looking up at the trees on the hillsides above me, saying over and over to myself, "It's stunningly pretty up here." The forested mountains, in their immensity, were a safe place for my mind to go while I waded knee-deep in horrors. Like the shoelaces in Bosnia.

Yankee came over and sat down next to me. He swung his gaze to where the remains of the helicopter were still smoldering and said, "God damn, Jimmy, I would never want to die like that. You don't even get a chance to fight. It's like being in a car wreck." Then he smacked me on the shoulder, shook his head, and walked off.

Six years later, Yankee would die the same way, when a Taliban RPG downed Extortion 17 in Wardak Province.

Two days prior, we'd received information that four men had fallen under attack during a recon mission in the Korengal and that the helo trying to rescue them had been shot down. So we planned quickly and flew in, our job being essentially to find the dead bodies, and if there happened to be anyone alive, which we hoped for but doubted, then we were to find and help them, too.

We roped in at night, with the Rangers, and walked in several kilometers, at about 10,000 feet. As the sun came up, we arrived at the crash site. When I saw the shards of metal that had been the helicopter, I knew nobody had survived. There wasn't much left—part of a rotor blade and an engine cowling, scattered among some charred, severed tree stumps. The whole side of the mountain near it was black and burnt. The Rangers immediately set up a security perimeter and went to work scaling down the mountainside to get the remains of the men who had been blown out of the helo.

There had been eight Army guys flying the helo, strapped in, who went down with the ball of fire. They were burnt bones.

There had also been eight Navy guys getting ready to fast-rope, which probably meant they were perched at the open back of the helo when it was hit. That would explain why they were ejected into the ravine. The Rangers went 1,400 feet down into that seriously steep and rocky ravine, retrieved those burned bodies, put them in body bags, and hauled them back up the mountain to a grassy clearing where they arrayed them in a line. I can't emphasize enough how steep it was, and how hard it was to drag those burned bodies up that hill. What those Rangers did was significant.

Meanwhile, we patrolled, looking for any signs or clues as to what had happened, and where the missing four-man team might be. We didn't know much. All we knew was that a member of the four-man team had called in using a sat phone to say they were being ambushed and overrun, that this communiqué had been drowned out by sounds of gunfire and explosions, and that it had then gone quiet. The quick reaction force (QRF) went in by helicopter to the exact same spot where the four-man team had been deposited, and then made a last radio transmission before being shot out of the sky by a member of the local militia waiting with an RPG. The two other helicopters that were nearby, in the air, watched their buddies die, and then peeled out and flew back down into the valley.

This is all we knew when we got summoned. There'd been a sat phone call, a last radio transmission from the downed QRF helo, and some eyewitness accounts from the other helos.

Ranging over the beautiful, rocky, grass-patched, pine-forested terrain that at times resembled the Utah of my boyhood, we found one of the ambush sites where the enemy had been shooting at the original four-man team. From the little hills of brass stacked up, you could tell there'd been a lot of shooting.

We also ran across a herd of goats and a goat-herder and a little boy wearing a belt with a canteen on it. When we did, the man and the boy turned white. We walked right by them and kept going. Nobody had read Marcus Luttrell's book at that point, so we didn't know his team and the goat-herder had crossed paths, too.

At the end of that first day, the four original guys were still missing. There was no sign of them. As for the helicopter, it was confirmed there were no survivors. We waited for the sun to go down, and then we loaded the body bags onto another helicopter, which flew in after we'd blown down some trees with explosives in order to make a space where it could land. I remember the body I loaded. I knew him, because he was the biggest guy in the group and I recognized the heft. It was gut-wrenching, seeing those bags. Every one of them was a good, committed man. Gone. In a flash.

There is a certain smell to that kind of work. It, too, paralleled the pit in Bosnia. It was horrible.

It was also somewhat insane . . . to fly that body-retrieval helo back in there, to almost the same spot, a third time. Flying a helicopter into the Korengal Valley Echo Chamber is, as I see it, somewhat akin to staging a Who concert in a bowl with sharp, 11,000-foot-high walls on both sides. When we'd flown in, yes, it was also a little crazy, but at least we were able to take some precautions, land elsewhere, and do some other things that neither the QRF nor this body-retrieval helo had the luxury to do.

When the helicopter picking up the bodies was landing, there was a terp monitoring the local Taliban radio chatter, and he could hear a senior guy angrily commanding a lackey to shoot down the helo, peppering his injunctions with some incentive-builders along the lines of "your mother is a whore." But the lackey was balking, saying he was afraid to shoot the helo, because if he shot it, the Americans would know where he was and they'd kill him. To which the more senior Taliban leader replied, in a nutshell, "I don't care. . . . If you don't shoot them, *I'll* kill you." We didn't know where this nervous triggerman was. He could have been anywhere on that mountain.

Luckily, his fear of us outweighed his fear of his own. He never took a shot.

The helo filled up with the dead . . . plus one of my living friends, who had learned a few hours earlier that his wife was about to give birth. The command sent word that he was authorized to go home to be with her. So he boarded the body-retrieval helo and flew home with those bodies. I think it was a bad thing, flying alone with the corpses. It wrecked him a little.

A couple days in, while we were sitting on the side of a hill right by a small and uneven dirt road, a man walked up with his son and started speaking loudly. He looked a bit agitated. The terp approached him, to see what was up. To our surprise, it turned out the man was inviting every one of us to his home for dinner. It was striking, to me, that this was the norm there: When people come to your town, you treat them as guests . . . even when they're not really in your town but are adjacent to it, high up, on a mountainside, as part of a foreign fighting force.

Some folks suggest Afghans are savages, but it's just not true. This man wasn't just saying "please come in" to some harmless vagabonds appearing at his door, which would have been easy. No, he walked all the way up a mountain, on which there had just been a big gunfight, with explosions that scorched the earth, to approach armed Americans and extend an invitation.

As gracious as it was, we declined.

During those first few days, we got shot at from a couple of tiny pockets on neighboring mountain ridges, which were actually fairly close in terms of measured space. But between us were those ravines, and they were so steep that hiking to the attackers would have taken hours. Furthermore, theirs was not effective fire. You really just heard it, and then you'd point your gun in their direction and try to keep eyes on them, but there was nothing to shoot at, and therefore no reason to waste bullets.

A few days after we'd arrived, we got word through various channels that someone in the village situated at the bottom of the mountain was claiming they had an American who was alive—an American to whom that unique brand of local hospitality had also been extended. And unlike us, this other American had accepted it.

The Rangers were on a different part of the mountain at that point, and their group and our group tried to get down to that location as fast as possible. It was a bit of a race. And because the Rangers are really, really good at marching while carrying heavy gear, they beat us to the location. Capable pricks. They got to the American before we did. We arrived in time to see the helicopters swoop in and get him, and as they did, I said to one of my buddies, "That guy is going to write a book and make a million dollars."

We ended up spending a week on that mountain in the Korengal Valley, mopping up after Red Wings. All of us slept on the side of the mountain. No sleeping bags. And even though they'd fly overhead and push parachute-rigged bundles of food out the back of the airplane, supplies nonetheless ran so low at one point that I was down to my last Soldier Fuel bar and the Rangers had to drink their IVs because they were out of water. People talk about Hell Week. Hell Week was a cakewalk compared to this week. And it had nothing to do with the physical challenges, which were minimal. In Hell Week, you get wet and cold. Here, we'd begun the week by picking up our buddies who were dead and burnt, and spent the balance of it scouring mountains looking for more dead. It was grim.

And that was really the entirety of the objective for the duration of my team's time there: find the first four guys. After Marcus was picked up, we weren't having much luck with the three who were still missing, even though we were covering a lot of ground. When we got pulled out of there, I wasn't sad about leaving. But I was a little scared, due to the manner in which we left. The helicopters picked us up down below, in the valley, landing in a field next to a river. Imagine the bottom point of a very narrow V, and that's where we were, about to board two loud school buses that any amateur with an RPG had a pretty good chance of hitting. Easy pickings. I thought of what was left of that big machine that had gotten vaporized up on the mountain, and I imagined that somewhere nearby there was another angry man calling another young shooter's mother a whore.

It's possible that I may have been alone in being scared, because I noticed that the rest of my crew was much tougher than I was, and unstressed.

After we'd gone, the Green Berets and Marines who'd spelled us started finding the bodies of the other three members of the original four-man reconnaissance team. It began to become clear that they'd essentially been ambushed in a gulley, and it had been like shooting fish in a barrel. After killing those three men, the Taliban then also successfully killed all the men aboard the rescue helicopter that came in to try and save them. In all, it was a horrible day.

Years later, I was helping a group of veterans called Operation Enduring Warrior. They run one of the programs where wounded vets can learn to skydive and get help with equipment costs. We were at Skydive Suffolk, and I was there to take photos of some of the vets who were learning how to jump. The wounded warrior rep from Walter Reed was someone I felt I'd seen before, and he felt like he'd seen me before, too. So we started chatting. And it turns out that he was part of the Ranger group that roped in with us that night in the Korengal. When he saw my leg, his mouth tightened a bit, and he said, "That mission was bad luck." He explained that several of the men in that Ranger group had since been killed and "almost all of us have been wounded." I corroborated his theory about bad luck, mentioning that, from among our small group, we'd had one man killed, two dogs killed, and I'd been injured. And remember that friend of mine who'd flown home with the bodies in the helicopter to see his wife give birth? He ended up divorced.

This Ranger was convinced that the Red Wings event put a cloud over everyone involved. And I happen to think he was probably right.

But the source of that cloud is not just the grim legacy of loss. It also has to do with how the narrative has been managed after the fact.

When we were first briefed on the Red Wings mission, we were surprised at the details and the conclusions that it appeared some of the planners of that mission had drawn. There's no need for specifics here. Just know that some of the decisions and assumptions were criticized.

And I was right in there, doing a good chunk of the criticizing. I was angry, because that's one of my default emotions. Anger. In this case, anger at the deaths of all those men.

You do not sneak into the Korengal Valley in Kunar Province. Especially in a school-bus-sized helicopter that sounds like a Who concert on your front porch.

And that's where I'd stopped on the whole Red Wings event—feeling love and sadness for the lost men, and judgment and critique for parts of the mission that got so many killed. Out of fear, and because the whole thing was so ugly, I simply embraced my anger, and swung the gavel accordingly. For years I never got past that.

It took getting shot to break that pattern and put me in the proper frame of mind to finally do what was needed: touch the Red Wings dragon.

When I did, I came to see that my anger and condemnation were just paltry Band-Aids on a massive soul wound that had been festering for years. I'd seen more American death on that mountain than I did during all the rest of my time overseas. Having taken that emotional hit, I didn't plumb its depths, or address it. I pointed the finger. Somebody being at fault satisfied my craving for some semblance of causality and logic in what was essentially madness.

But by blaming people and getting angry, I was simply using a sidebar issue to mask the real one. The loss and sadness. Which I have now faced. And tried to understand. Here's what I know:

Every one of those men involved in Red Wings is a hero. And, yes, the planning behind the mission is harder to praise. But the horrible outcome is nobody's fault. In believing that it was, I was being hypocritical. I'd looked at it harshly and judged the Red Wings decision-makers, but I had not done the same for myself.

Folks have criticized the helos landing so close to the target the night I got shot. Folks have said it's why I got hurt. They've said this to me, expecting me to roundly endorse their critique. But I've replied, "No, I was one of the people who made that call." I was one of the people who wanted the helos close. Yes, I'd long felt that flying school buses into gunfights was a bad idea, but in this case, it was a hostage rescue mission. The key was being aggressive and denying the enemy time to think and prepare, if possible. So if we were being given a school bus, then that school bus would land close.

And that's what the four men on that reconnaissance mission in the Korengal were doing. They didn't want any of that horrible outcome. They weren't any more at fault than I was. When they were stepping off on that mission, they were just trying to be aggressive Americans. And I now realize it's blind, dumb luck that something as horrible as what happened to them never happened to me.

I finally touched the Red Wings dragon.

The American myth-making machine still needs to.

Certain parts of the Red Wings episode have been chronicled by skillful storytellers with good intentions. But I believe there's a deep pain felt by guys who've been involved in the loss of others—and I'm guessing maybe by some of the families of those lost ones, too—when you take a version of their story and just tell the parts that allow it to be a legendary epic about flawless heroism.

When you uphold only the hero image, you deny those same heroes the ability to admit mistakes. And that, in turn, creates a distorted reality. Which has a tendency to outfit those involved with an emotional straitjacket.

Just as there is no such thing as the perfectly happy wounded vet, there is no such thing as the perfect war hero. The fact is, you hurt yourself when you try to be one, and you hurt others when you force them to.

There's a lingering pain that you don't know what to do with if everyone is saluting you. Being forced to propagate a shiny version of what you experienced exacerbates the pain. Getting to the truth about what you really feel ameliorates it.

That hero riding into the sunset? He's lonely and hurting. But he'll keep riding—right into the grave, by the way—if you keep hinting to him that this romantic sunset view of him is the only one you're interested in.

OMAR

I had only ever visited them at night.

And there was a certain amount of horror inherent in our visits. Especially when we hit the right house. But also when we hit the wrong house, because although we didn't hurt them, we still scared the hell out of a bunch of innocents.

In all those years I spent deployed to the Arab world and Afghanistan, I was never once in a normal civilian area during the day. I never walked around, or shopped, or dined, or chatted. We were always staged in places where if you left for a stroll, you stood a good chance of getting your head cut off. So we'd only leave when we were prepared for violence—delivering it, and receiving it.

I've always been a fan of skydiving, and as an active-duty human whose time was mostly spoken for, I was content to be simply OK at the skill, and not lust after being a super-kid in the sky. But I did admire those who were.

Some years ago—way back in the late twentieth century—a new kind of skydiving emerged called freeflying, and one of its pioneers was a fellow named Omar. I'd watch slick videos of freeflyers doing their thing set to music, and he was one of the stars. He's beautiful in the sky. Famous for high-torque contortions as well as holding motionless lotus positions while falling—and appearing as relaxed mentally as he clearly is physically, mid-flight—his liquid slicing of the air and total body control is something to behold.

In the 2000s, our crew decided to get some professional skydiving coaching out west, and the person who put the course together invited Omar to be a part of it. When I got there, I recognized him from my video fanboy days, and I was happy when we started to get to know each other—even happier when we became fast friends.

Omar, I learned, was the son of a former Saudi ambassador to the U.S. during the Carter and Reagan administrations. As the son of a diplomat, he was strikingly gracious, and it was something I came to admire as much as his skydiving technique, which was considerable.

He'd won several world championships. And while not all of his skills were immediately transferable to our needs (in the military, there isn't a pressing need to be able to plummet in lotus position), during that week-long instruction session, he helped us greatly. The focus of our tuition was on how to fly our bodies at all angles and upgrade our canopy work. Once you get out of a plane, before you get under canopy, your priority in the military is getting stable. So fixing instability is paramount. Because Omar had so much experience flying at all different angles, he could teach us how to recover quickly from virtually any position. And he did.

At the end of the week, we had an informal competition, a kind of accuracy contest, followed by beers, which Omar didn't drink. But he did invite me over to his home, which was nearby. It was a normal home in many ways, with one or two extraordinary attributes—the first of which was his lovely blond and blue-eyed wife from Minnesota, and the second of which was the featured reading material. I was in between deployments to Iraq, so I had never yet, in my life thus far, been inside a house where there was a Koran on the table in a place of prominence without my being there for the express purpose of conducting a combat operation—being there either to kill somebody or get killed.

Although he himself is not a regular mosque-goer, much to the chagrin of his devout father, we talked a bit about religion, and I told him that I wasn't well versed in Islam, or even Christianity for that matter. And that I was, frankly, somewhat turned off by the whole proposition, especially since I struggled with my exposure to what I'd seen of the Muslim faith. Admittedly, my exposure had been of a limited sort, but still and all, I had actually seen practitioners of the faith put their kids in front of themselves in gunfights. Omar said those weren't good representations of Islam. What he could also have said but didn't (remember, he has diplomacy in his genes) was that my sample set, though factual, was perhaps a tad extreme.

Back in Iraq, deployed again, I asked Omar if I could email his father and his mother, who is Syrian, and ask them for some recommendations on good Arab or Middle Eastern writers that I could read, in order to maybe get a different perspective on the world I found myself in. I knew I was not seeing its brightest side, and exposure to some other facets of the culture would do me good. After a quick set of tips on how to address his father—"H.E. Sheikh," followed by his names—I sent the ambassador a note, and was delighted a short while later when his wife wrote me back. She gave me some recommendations, including Kahlil Gibran, who was quite accessible to me, and who provided the beginnings of an opportunity to understand another side of the people in whose midst I found myself.

Omar's mother and I also exchanged some thoughts on current events. For the most part, they were breaking her heart. I've never met her, but just from her missives, which she wrote to me in English (one of the six languages she speaks), I consider her one of the more gracious and beautiful humans I've encountered. And I'm not the only one who feels that way; more than a few Washingtonians had similar feelings about her when she lived in that city in the 1980s. During her D.C. tenure, she apparently drove an orange Fiat around the capital and made the scene accoutered in elegant Western, not Arab, dress. Stately and decorous, she was also not above setting up a tent in Lafayette Park and going on a hunger strike in front of the White House to protest things like Sabra and Shatila.

A few years later, because of his status in the community, Omar moved to Dubai, at the invitation of the crown prince, in order to start up the most prolific skydiving center in the world. He brought his wife, Cheri. One day, the prince was chatting with her, and he asked, innocently, if she and Omar were planning on having children. She explained that they'd tried, but couldn't get pregnant. Fertility doctors and special treatments hadn't helped. Something was wrong. The prince responded by saying he'd like to send them somewhere. *Somewhere* happened to be London, to see one of the best fertility specialists in the world. It worked. Cheri got pregnant. They eventually had a girl. Her name is Dunia. Omar once showed me a picture of the prince holding her.

Omar's brother is another miracle. He owns a sushi restaurant in Chevy Chase called SushiKo, and every few weeks, he travels to Massachusetts General Hospital in Boston to get all of his blood pumped out, and then back in. Even though his heart is a bit frail—he's had congestive heart failure four times—it's very big. After Omar found out I was hurt, his brother showed up at Bethesda, bearing a huge sushi platter that was about as dazzling as a food tray can probably be. (It would remain uncontested Sushi Platter Champ until a few months later, when the Admiral took a shot at the title with his raw fish tray at the Mayo.) Omar's brother stayed awhile, just sitting there, in the hospital, chatting with me and my friends. It was generous, but, of course, after he'd checked in on me, I checked out, not wanting to be in touch with anyone, including Omar, for a long time.

When I started coming out of the darkness a little bit, Omar said I should come visit him and Cheri and meet the baby, in Dubai. I said, "Yeah, I'd love to," but then basically blew him off for several years, making excuses.

Truly, I was afraid.

I didn't want to put myself in a situation where it would be easy for someone with ill will to kill me—a confluence of factors I felt was likely in a place like Dubai. Additionally, I didn't want to bring danger to Omar and his family. Deep down, I think I was afraid to confront a culture toward which I had already made some very concrete stands. Translation: I had brought some pain to their world, the greater Arab one, and I feared retribution.

Eventually, one October day, Omar called me out on my evasions and rickety avoidance philosophies, and said point-blank, "Hey, stop blowing me off. When can you come?" I hemmed and hawed a bit, and then, off the cuff, mumbled something about the coming January maybe affording some potential openings in my schedule.

The next day, I had a plane ticket. Courtesy of Omar.

And so, in January, I went. I was scared. I couldn't sleep, despite the plush seats on the nonstop flight from D.C. to Dubai. When we arrived, even the airport threw me off. It was spotless, with customs people in crisp uniforms, and everyone looking clearly Arab and being very polite. Having retrieved my luggage, I had a happy reunion with Omar, and off we went.

Being at a loss for words when speaking is one thing. Being at a loss for words when writing is another. It's kind of embarrassing. But it's where I find myself. I really don't know how to explain it, arriving in Dubai. The culture shock was overwhelming. The topography. The signs in Arabic. The climate (the hallmark of which is a dawn-to-dusk siege of dust and heat). The fact that there was going to be no gunfire and no IED risk. My circuitry considered shorting. But I trusted Omar.

We went to his home; it was lovely. And then we met his little girl at school. She is a precious soul, naturally radiating love and sweetness.

I asked Omar to bring me to a mosque, which he did. I've had a bit of training, so I can sense when a phone is taking my picture. And there was some of that while I was on the streets in Dubai. Certain eyes were on me, and I suspect some of the security specialists in that emirate knew who I was.

Venturing further afield, Omar took me to the Meydan horse track, where a handful of European expats were sprinkled among the Arab families, who were in traditional dishdashas, enjoying the day. Some owned horses. Some were just there as spectators. All of them were conducting themselves in a surprisingly normal fashion. Up to this point, I still hadn't been exposed to real everyday Arabs. The only times I'd encountered people in this kind of dress was when I'd visited them at night. And now I was rubbing shoulders with them—figuratively speaking, anyway. There is no actual rubbing of shoulders. In Dubai, the occasional jostling of bodies that happens in American crowds would never fly. Contact between strangers is taboo. So is lovers kissing in public.

Still, watching the families just being families, it hit me that we're clearly more alike than we are different. And I felt this way even though, as an American, I was obviously in the minority . . . along with Cheri from Minnesota.

I'm not a horse guy, but it was made clear to me that this Meydan equestrian facility was one of the best in the world, and I believed it. In the stands, there's a royal enclosure under an array of lights that would make Siegfried and Roy's prop master swoon. In some ways, the place looked like someone's glammed-out fantasy vision of the central pavilion at an Arabian World's Fair, where the host nation was proudly exhibiting its two cultural mainstays—horses and royalty.

Omar and I mingled freely, because we were the guests of a man who was both a champion jockey and a farrier who shod horses for the sheikh. He hailed from France and spoke English very well, when he was not speaking French with Omar. The man was committed to his craft. And/or obsessed. He was unable to stop looking at, and evaluating, the shoes of all the horses that went by, even those horses that were not his.

I had the strong sense that I'd gone from one extreme to the other. In stark contrast to my night-shift work in the Middle East, my daylight debut among Arab civilians was happening at a racecourse that cost $2 billion to build.

I kept pretty quiet, and it was noticeable, so I had to explain myself to Omar and Cheri. I told my gracious hosts that I felt as though maybe I didn't deserve to be there, because previously I'd brought some violence into this part of the world. The diplomat's son told me he didn't agree with war, or with what my job had been, but then he also said, "I love you, and you're my friend, and we all have our own path, so I'm glad we could bring you to a part of this world where the people are good, and you can see it."

Omar was doing the same thing he'd done back when I met him. Since coming out of the plane at the airport, my mind had been in the wrong position. Omar was now trying to fix it—trying to lessen my instability.

Having inadvertently won a temporary membership to the horse set, I found myself milling about at an endurance race a few days later, when Dubai's crown prince walked by and looked straight at me. He was alone, with no visible protection. That amazed me.

And he wasn't my only high-profile ambulatory encounter that day. The prince's father, Sheikh Mohammed bin Rashid Al Maktoum, was at the endurance race, too. He walked up, paused, stood within a few feet of me, and began talking with some foreign workers at the prep stable who supported and maintained the long-distance horses (which seem to be put through the ringer in such races). The sheikh was a humble and chatty fellow. He even singled out one of the horses and jokingly told the trainers, "I'm betting on this one to be at the top of the boards at the end of the day."

The sheikh's knack for small talk was not what amazed me. What amazed me was that he was a few feet away from me and everyone else, and I didn't see any bodyguards. I had heard, but didn't believe, that the Emirati leadership was this way. I didn't believe it until I saw it.

Something else was pretty clear, based on what I saw that day, and on ensuing ones. From the foreign equestrian workers, to the expats, to the Emiratis, almost everyone sincerely liked these two fellows, the prince and his father.

Omar provided some of the backstory on how the Emirates had come to be. Essentially, sheikhs at the helms of seven families got together and made an agreement to make a great country, which, to a certain extent, they have. People in Dubai seem to live well. And they appear happy. My impression was that there was a hopeful quality to the way things got done in Dubai.

And yet the Dubai vision, as sparkling as it is, has limits.

Free speech is fine; it just can't be disrespectful. Apparently, such is the dictate of the sheikh. Later, I read up on him. Although I disagree with his policy regarding free speech (that it should be free until he decides it shouldn't), other parts of his worldview do jibe with my own feelings, and those of most folks. In his opinion, ISIS and AQ exist because evil people take advantage of those who are not embedded in a good culture where they have an opportunity to work and contribute. So ISIS and AQ teach those people to blow themselves up, which appears to be the only honorable option for making one's family proud. The sheikh believes in trying to inoculate against that disease by creating the good cultures, where there is opportunity.

OK, but opportunity for whom? That's a fair question, especially in an absolute monarchy. The racetrack life is not a viable option for most Arabs, and it's really only a touchstone of commonality with a small part of the West's elite, the horse set. Also, for my part, the emirate's cult of Bigger and Better (when it comes to buildings, artificial islands, and malls) leaves me a little cold. I wouldn't trade the U.S., with all of its flaws, for even the racetrack version of that life.

But I can't shake the sense of hopefulness I felt while there. And I've tried to identify its source.

Maybe it has to do with the family that touched my life by sharing their happy and peaceful existence in a part of the world I'd written off as lost, at least to me.

THROWING A FRIEND UNDER THE BUS
(WHICH, IT TURNS OUT, IS A GREAT PLACE TO BE)

As raw as recovery is, and as blunt as we need to be when we're being honest, there are still some protocols of healing. There is still a certain decorum to parts of the process. Despite my attempts to hammer home the most important of these rules to the Fly Fisherman, he refused to internalize them.

A few days before one of my speeches, I called him and said, "Hey, I don't know what you're up to, but I've been asked to speak to an F-18 squadron at Naval Air Station Oceana. You want to come?" He said, "Sure." So I picked him up that Friday. It was a rainy day.

He had one condition for attending: "In your speech, I don't want you to acknowledge who I am." He is very humble, and he has an extreme aversion to the spotlight. A lot of us are that way, but he is even more so. In his career, it probably cost him. Had he promoted himself, or the things he did, he would have advanced through the ranks more rapidly and been rewarded with this and that, including pay bumps and position. But that is not his way. He's done serious work for a long time on a lot of different levels. He's formidable. Because of his abilities, he's been called in to complement other units and groups in extraordinary ways. And that, to me, creates a funny dichotomy. On the one hand, you have guys who've written books, even though they've never been in a gunfight. Then, on the other hand, you have the Fly Fisherman, who is telling me he'll be angry if I mention him by name in a private speech to F-18 crews.

It was odd to me that we were friends, because we're very different. In fact, I represent some characteristics that the Fly Fisherman would never want to demonstrate. He's a sniper. Extremely meticulous. Very detailed. Makes rational decisions. Highly organized. His cage at work was laid out perfectly, everything in its proper place. He's a tall, lanky guy from out west. Quietly Christian. Before he joined the military, he was pre-med, and he also took people on chartered fly-fishing expeditions, because the peace of fly-fishing appeals to him.

I admire him for these qualities, and I wish I had more of them. I'm a kick-the-door-in, be-an-idiot, scream-and-shout, write-books kind of guy. And yet, somehow, we were always friends, from the moment he joined our crew and we started doing deployments together.

One set of traits we shared: extreme laser-like focus when things were intense, and a matter-of-fact approach to suppressing stupid, silly nonsense that was affecting things it shouldn't. When it came to serious matters, we were oddly in tune. Even now, he understood what I was trying to do with these speeches—elevate the conversation and make people more comfortable sharing their struggles. In fact, he'd recently told me that I'd changed things at our unit, and that, because of what I'd gone through, it was now no big deal for a guy sitting in a team room to say, "Hey, I've got an appointment with someone to help me work through some things."

Which is why I knew he was the perfect guy to bring to my speech. Because it was serious stuff. And he'd respect that. Truth is, in addition to being pleased that he was coming, I was also pretty worried that I'd be emotional with him there, and I knew it would be especially difficult during those parts of the speech where I'd be talking about him, in his presence.

I also knew that, for the aviators, it was going to be one of those events on a Friday where afterward everyone gets released for Christmas leave, so there is a heightened expectation: you either deliver the goods in your presentation, or the audience dozes off and waits for you to shut the fuck up.

The event was held in an old Navy theater, which was windowless, with two doors, one in front and one in the back. It had theater seating and, at the bottom, a stage that was lifted about three feet. I had my laptop and a little remote to click through the slides, which would be visible on a huge, old projector screen.

First, the CO, who was younger than I, got up and addressed the whole squadron. He was a badass Hornet pilot himself. He pointed out that this can be a hard time of year, because the holidays bring out difficult emotions, which can contribute to maybe drinking too much or other bad decisions. "If you get into trouble," he said, "if you need a ride, during leave or after, before you do something stupid, call me . . . and here is my personal cell phone number," which he then provided. And the senior enlisted guy did the same thing. It was clear these two were invested in taking care of their people.

The CO then went on to introduce me, and I took the stage. I started my speech by saying that during my twenty-five years in the Navy, I don't know if I'd ever seen a CO offer his phone number to everyone, and that they were therefore quite fortunate.

The next thing I did was privately realize that I'd guessed right about how worried I'd feel with my guest there. Standing on the stage, and seeing the Fly Fisherman in the front row, I thought, *He's here, and I'm always emotional anyway, but now I'm going to discuss all of these things while looking at the guy who played a big part in my being not just here at this speech, but alive on the planet.* I love smashing Stigma, and being wide open, but with him there, I was being tested: I really didn't want to be emotional in front of my friend.

Making an effort to put that to the side, I started in with the slides. I discussed how I joined the Navy. Tried to become an action man. Quit. Went back. Got in. And started taking hits to my soul from things that happened while deployed, without realizing it at the time.

I talked about getting hurt, introduced the characters of the Fly Fisherman and the Mechanic, and discussed what happened in my last little gunfight. Then I chatted about how I descended into pathetic-human status, which led to the Fly Fisherman taking me to the mental hospital and the Mechanic coming to check on me while I was there.

I finished the slides and explained the things I've learned and the tools I've been given and the obligation I feel to talk about it, because I was fortunate and because those guys saved my life, and I need to make it worth their while.

I then kicked it into the Q&A phase, and in order to prime the crowd, I started by sharing a couple of questions I'm often asked. I said it's pretty normal for folks to inquire about how it felt to get shot. And the answer is that you need to imagine you're walking down the shoulder of a freeway, and Dale Earnhardt Jr. is driving his machine at top speed, and in his passenger seat, riding shotgun, is Albert Pujols wringing the neck of his Louisville Slugger, and as they drive by at 160 mph, Albert hits a home run into your femur.

People chuckled at that; they generally do. I then told the group that the second question I'm most often asked by military audiences has to do with worry. They're worried that if they tell people they have a problem, or admit they're struggling emotionally, they'll lose their security clearance. I reply, "That may or may not be true, but I can promise you this: If you are acting self-destructively, if you are showing up late to work, drinking yourself to sleep, not doing your job, then you're just a time bomb, and at some point you're going to get into trouble, and when you do, you will *certainly* lose your clearance."

The next thing I did was lay down the ground rules for the Q&A. There are only two. "First, I'd request that you not ask about classified things that could endanger my former crew or their families. And last, don't ask how many people I've killed, because it's a stupid question." I used the opportunity to editorialize a bit, and talk about the comic fallacy of the confirmed kill count. I said, "Imagine that we are in a fight, in this room, half of you against the other half, with guns. Now, which one of you will volunteer to wear a stethoscope and check the bodies on the floor, during the fight, in this mayhem, to see if they are actually dead and then, if they are, assign responsibility by quickly confirming with the shooter, 'Hey, you killed this one, right?' so that you can write it down in your notebook." And then I used my standby, which I'm rather fond of: "Can any of you tell me where the office in the Pentagon is that's called the Center for the Confirmation of Kills?" There was laughter, as there often is, but also a bemused look on some of the faces, as if they were thinking, *Hmm, I hadn't thought about it like that.*

Finishing my Q&A preamble, I remarked, "Now, having said all that, you can ask me anything else. Seriously. I'm not going to hide anything."

I scanned the room, and I saw a hand in the front row shoot up right away, before anyone else's. It was the Fly Fisherman. I nodded at him, wondering where this might lead, and said, "Yeah?"

Very loudly, he asked, "How many people have you killed?"

He was deadpan.

I.

Started.

Laughing.

I threw my head back, and I just shook and flexed with deep-body laughs. The poor audience was at a total loss. They didn't know who this guy in civilian clothes in the front row was, and they didn't know why I was laughing. This went on for a few seconds. Then the Fly Fisherman piped up, even louder this time: "How many people did you kill, really?"

What a bastard. What a gift.

Immediately, I was transported back to the dynamic in my unit, the place I missed so much. I was there. With him. And in the unit, of course, you can't just take a kick to the crotch without giving one back, so I promptly employed that precious trait I had in common with the Fly Fisherman—laser-like focus—to discern the appropriate counterattack. Of course. It was clear. I knew he didn't want me to out him and reveal his identity, but, to be fair, he'd also known that I didn't want to be asked about kills. So I determined that the only appropriate response was to quickly and expeditiously throw him under the bus.

I pointed to the disrespectful inquirer in the front row and said to the whole room, "Just so you know, this is the Fly Fisherman."

There was a beat. And then everyone jumped up out of their seats and started yelling and clapping. They were giving the Fly Fisherman a standing ovation. He just sat there. No comeback. All he did was nod once, while everyone kept on clapping around him in one of those spontaneous semicircles of humanity that form when someone worthy in our midst gets suddenly singled out.

I smiled at him. *I got you, motherfucker.*

But very quickly, I realized it was way more than that. I'd meant it as a playful jab, as payback. But as I looked at him, I could see a change. He's a pro, and so he did his best to just sit there stoically, and let them finish. No arm raised in acknowledgment. No nothing. But what was happening was moving, and it was affecting him. I could see the emotion well up in him. It became clear that I could not have designed a better way for this to happen—outing him as a hero. And I thought to myself, *You know what? Hell yes, I do want them to know that the reason I'm alive is because of that guy sitting there, and the Mechanic. I want them to see him and know who he is.*

It was beautiful.

And in that moment, I realized I didn't want to be helped by the Fly Fisherman anymore. I wanted to be the Fly Fisherman.

You should, too.

A NOTE ON THE TYPE

This book was set in Adobe Garamond. Designed for the Adobe Corporation by Robert Slimbach, the fonts are based on types first cut by Claude Garamond (ca. 1480–1561). Garamond was a pupil of Geoffroy Tory and is believed to have followed the Venetian models, although he introduced a number of important differences, and it is to him that we owe the letter we now know as "old style." He gave to his letters a certain elegance and feeling of movement that won their creator an immediate reputation and the patronage of Francis I of France.

Composed by North Market Street Graphics,
Lancaster, Pennsylvania

Printed and bound by Berryville Graphics,
Berryville, Virginia

Designed by Cassandra J. Pappas